Nature Walks in Northwest Vermont and the Champlain Valley

Nature Walks in Northwest Vermont and the Champlain Valley

REVISED AND UPDATED

Elizabeth Bassett

Photographs by Elizabeth Bassett and Sheri Larsen

Nature Walks in Northwest Vermont and the Champlain Valley
Revised and Updated

Elizabeth Bassett

Published September 2009 by Full Circle Press LLC

Photographs by Elizabeth Bassett and Sheri Larsen

All maps with permission of the Appalachian Mountain Club except for the map on page 148 which is courtesy of J.C. Davis

Mount Philo Press
1989 Mount Philo Road
Charlotte, Vermont 05445

PRINTING HISTORY
Appalachian Mountain Club, first edition paperback published in 1998 as Nature Walks in Northern Vermont and the Champlain Valley.

Library of Congress Cataloging-in-Publication Data

Bassett, Elizabeth, 1950-
  Nature walks in Northwest Vermont and the Champlain Valley / Elizabeth Bassett. -- Rev. and updated.
     p. cm.
  Includes bibliographical references.
  ISBN 978-0-9838582-0-1 (pbk. : alk. paper)
  1. Nature trails--Vermont--Guidebooks. 2. Nature trails--Champlain Valley--Guidebooks. 3. Family recreation--Vermont--Guidebooks. 4. Family recreation--Champlain Valley--Guidebooks. I. Title.
  QH105.V7B37 2009
  508.743'1--dc22
                              2009029718

Contents

Please note: All the walks listed here are ideal for family excursions.

• NORTHERN LAKE CHAMPLAIN AND THE ISLANDS •

   LOCATION: Swanton
   PETS: Allowed on leash
   DIFFICULTY: Easy
   WHAT TO ENJOY: Wetlands

   LOCATION: St. Albans Bay
   PETS: Not allowed
   DIFFICULTY: Easy to moderate
   WHAT TO ENJOY: Water with views, island

   LOCATION: North Hero
   PETS: Not allowed
   DIFFICULTY: Easy
   WHAT TO ENJOY: Water with views

   LOCATION: North Hero
   PETS: Not allowed
   DIFFICULTY: Easy
   WHAT TO ENJOY: Water, riparian forest, views

● **BURLINGTON AND CENTRAL LAKE CHAMPLAIN** ●

• MONTPELIER AREA •

● WATERBURY/STOWE AREA ●

MAP OF WALK LOCATIONS

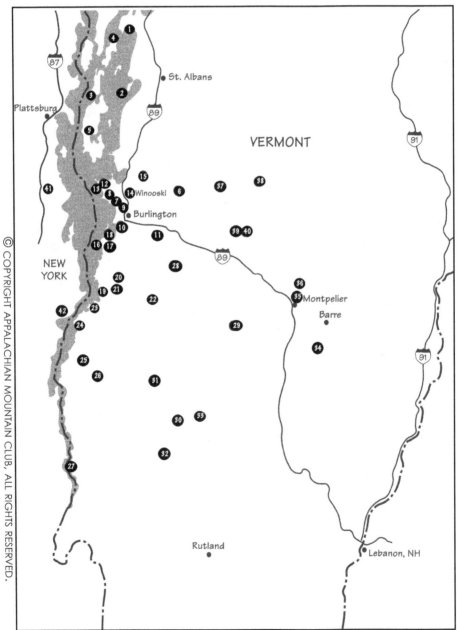

KEY TO WALK LOCATIONS

1. Missisquoi National Wildlife Refuge
2. Burton Island State Park
3. Knight Point State Park
4. North Hero State Park
5. Ed Weed Fish Culture Station
6. Old Mill Park
7. Intervale
8. Ethan Allen Homestead
9. Cassavant Nature Trail, Salmon Hole, and Winooski One
10. East Woods Natural Area
11. Mud Pond Conservation Land
12. Colchester Bog Natural Area
13. Delta Park
14. Sunny Hollow Nature Park
15. Colchester Pond
16. Shelburne Farms
17. LaPlatte River Marsh Natural Area
18. Allen Hill
19. Williams Woods Natural Area
20. Pease Mountain Natural Area
21. Mt. Philo State Park
22. Copp-Welch Loop
23. Kingsland Bay State Park
24. Button Bay State Park
25. Dead Creek Wildlife Management Area
26. Snake Mountain Wildlife Management Area
27. Mt. Independence State Historic Site
28. Green Mountain Audubon Nature Center
29. Mad River Greenway
30. Robert Frost Interpretive Trail
31. Abbey Pond
32. Leicester Hollow and Chandler Ridge
33. Texas Falls
34. Rock of Ages Granite Quarry
35. Hubbard Park
36. North Branch River Park/North Branch Nature Center
37. Tundra Trail, Mt. Mansfield
38. Sterling Falls Gorge
39. History Hike, Little River State Park
40. Stevenson Brook Nature Trail, Little River State Park
41. Ausable Chasm
42. Coon Mountain Preserve

To John, Putnam, Victoria, and Mom
With Love

Acknowledgments

I LOVED REVISING and updating this volume. I worked with wonderful collaborators and revisited dozens of beautiful places. Naturalists, conservationists, rangers, managers, caretakers, and volunteers all contributed wisdom, knowledge, passion, and advice.

For their generosity I would like to thank Ann Powers Brush, Rosalyn Graham, Gar Anderson, Chip Darmstadt, Chuck Woessner, Holly Knox, Laura Brines, Tim Bresett, Rick Paradis, Tim Larned, Todd Patton, Kevin Kelsey, Liz Thompson, Cathy Neary, Emily Boedecker, and Andrea Boggs Tursini.

The original book would not have been possible without the contributions of many of these same people. In addition I am indebted to Norman Pellett, Walter Poleman, Maryke Gillis, Everett Marshall, Jennifer Ely, and Geoff Beyer.

I am grateful for the encouragement and advice of Elizabeth and Josie, owners of the Flying Pig Bookstore in Shelburne- a treasure just down the road.

Several special people contributed photographs: Sheri Larsen, John Pane, and Susan Rittenhouse. To Lillie Bleau, my red-headed, cyber-Superwoman, I am deeply indebted. I cannot thank you enough.

The Appalachian Mountain Club, my original publisher, has discontinued its Nature Walks series. I appreciate that the AMC allowed me to purchase rights to re-use its maps in this revision.

I am grateful to my editor, Sonja Hakala, for her upbeat manner, knowledge, and professionalism. Bill Schubart, thanks for your generous support and encouragement.

Most of all, I thank my husband John who cheerfully fielded computer questions, took lovely photos, and roasted the bounty of asparagus that rolled in from our garden during deadline days of May.

Introduction

IN A REGION SO RICHLY ENDOWED, how did I select 42 walks? This book aims to showcase the astounding richness and variety in and around the Champlain Valley: bogs, granite quarry, sand plain, gorge, chasm, Arctic tundra, sandy beach, rivers, streams, lakes, ponds, wetlands, floodplain forest, Revolutionary War site, Gilded Age Estate turned environmental education center, fossils, microphotographs of snowflakes, fish elevator, and fish hatchery. Consider the walks as templates, setting the stage for further exploration.

These outings focus on the journey rather than the destination. They are about discovery. Nearly every walk is suitable for families, from young to old. Armed with your curiosity, venture out.

Many children today grow up spending little time in the outdoors. Adults who grew up exploring the natural world are more inclined to value and protect it. The sounds of the natural world are soothing. A walk is free or an inexpensive pleasure- and it's good for you!

I included two walks in New York's Champlain Valley. A ferry trip across Lake Champlain feels like an adventure. Coon Mountain is a splendid summer hike to blueberries and great views. Ausable Chasm is a national treasure. It's a thrill to raft or tube through it.

Nature is on the move- storms, floods, repairs. I've included many websites. Keep an eye on my website, www.NatureWalksVermont.com, for current information and updates on natural and man-made changes.

Sturdy shoes are adequate for most walks. Where hiking boots or waterproof boots are more appropriate, I have recommended them. For longer outings carry an emergency kit: compass; windbreaker or rain jacket; plastic bag containing waterproof matches, a candle, first aid kit, and toilet paper; seasonally, a hat and gloves or insect repellent and sunscreen; whistle; high-energy snacks; water; and binoculars. I pack a set of chemical hand warmers and a two-ounce emergency blanket the size of a deck of cards. Even in July, Vermont and northern New York can be cold places. Always bring appropriate maps.

Dress in layers for warmth and flexibility. Remember, cotton stays damp from sweat or rain. Long pants and sleeves are good protection against sun, poison ivy, brambles, or ticks.

Rabid wildlife is rare but rabies has appeared in raccoons, foxes, and skunks. If you see an animal acting strangely, give it wide berth and report it to the nearest game warden. Make sure your pet has a current rabies vaccination.

While Vermont is one of the safest states in the nation, it pays to be sensible. Remoteness has costs as well as benefits. If you walk alone make sure someone knows where you are and when you expect to return. Anyone can fall and get hurt. Cells phones do not work in all locations- don't count on them in an emergency.

Please note that pets are not welcome at some locations and must be leashed at others. (Service dogs are welcome.) These walks are on publicly accessible land much of which has been set aside because of its natural features. Please respect these special places and the rules designed to protect them. Dog policy is noted in the Contents and at the beginning of each chapter.

How to Use this Book

DO BRING THE CHILDREN. With their slower pace, curiosity, and proximity to the ground they often see things that adults miss. My children walked many of these trails when they were quite young.

The ratings are for walks, not hikes. A difficult walk might include steep hills or sections of rocky footing, neither of which would challenge an experienced hiker. If a walk is rated easy, it is manageable by young children or an older walker. The time allowances are generous to encourage exploration.

The bibliography does not include an obvious category, common guidebooks to wildflowers, birds, and trees. There are several popular series and each has its advocates. I urge you to spend time in a bookstore looking carefully at these volumes. They use different systems, focus on different information, and assume different knowledge in the user. The choice is a personal one.

The Table of Contents highlights a special feature or two on each walk in addition to pet policy. Nearly all walks are well-suited for children. The designation, "history," refers to noteworthy human history as every walk has a natural history.

Distances to the trailhead were measured in one or both of our family cars, with and without snow tires. Not surprisingly, results varied slightly. You will not get lost with these directions but, please, slow down before the intersections.

Nearly all of the walks are on public land and most of them have no admission fee. Vermont State Parks charge a modest fee. The Tundra Trail, atop Mt. Mansfield, is free but both the Toll Road and the gondola are privately maintained and charge users. It is certainly possible, but outside the parameters of this book, to hike up Mt. Mansfield. Both Ausable Chasm and the Rock of Ages granite quarry charge admission. To omit them would have been a shame as they are both fascinating places. An abandoned quarry at the Rock of Ages Visitor Center can be viewed without charge.

VERMONT STATE PARKS

Vermont State Parks open for the season in late May. Kingsland Bay, Knight Point, and North Hero close after Labor Day and Mt. Philo, Little River, and Button Bay close after Columbus Day weekend. Ferry service between Burton Island and Kill Kare State Park runs from Memorial Day weekend through Labor Day weekend. For exact dates check with the Vermont Department of Forests, Parks, and Recreation or the park itself: http://www.vtfpr.org/parks/index.cfm. (See Organizations in the appendix.)

Day use parks are open from 10:00 a.m. until sunset. Restrooms and phones are available. No dogs are allowed in day use areas. Park amenities include swimming, boating, picnic tables and shelters, camping, play areas for children, and, at Burton Island, a full range of marine services.

Daily admission is $3.00 for adults, age 14 and over. Children ages 4-13 are charged $2.00. Vermont resident seniors presenting the Green Mountain passport are admitted free. A 10-punch, transferable pass represents a 35% discount and can be used over several seasons. Frequent park users may buy an $80.00 Vehicle Season Pass for unlimited admissions by all passengers in the vehicle.

Campers registered at any Vermont State Park may use day facilities at any other park in the system (except Sand Bar) for the duration of their stay.

Vermont State Parks receive no General Fund tax money for operations and maintenance. Thus park fees and leases of seven ski areas on state land must cover all expenses. Parks are closed and facilities unavailable off-season. Gates are locked but the land may be accessed on foot. Please do not block the park gates.

WINOOSKI VALLEY PARK DISTRICT

The District manages eleven properties on 1,722 acres, including more than twelve miles of shoreline, in seven towns of the lower Winooski River Valley. The properties are open, free of charge, from dawn until dusk daily. All pets must be leashed. The district properties offer nature trails for walking, snowshoeing, and cross-country skiing; picnic facilities; public garden plots; and canoe and kayak access.

THE LAST WORD

The final selection of walks was difficult. In a region where northern hardwood forests dominate and Lake Champlain sits boldly astride the map, variety and balance were considerations. Off-season access was another. Don't put this book on the shelf in November. Many of these outings are accessible in winter boots or on cross-country skis or snowshoes. Snow is the perfect canvas for animal tracks. Identifying trees without leaves is easier than I'd imagined and, best of all, there are no bugs!

How, my friends asked, could I encourage people to visit some of our favorite places? My hope is that the beauty and bounty of the landscape and an understanding of it will inspire each of us to become more active in efforts to conserve and preserve these precious resources. Individuals can make a difference. The foresight, generosity, and determination of many have given us the privilege of enjoying these special places.

—Elizabeth Bassett

Northern Lake Champlain and the Islands

Black Creek & Maquam Creek Trails
Missisquoi National Wildlife Refuge

Wildlife and bird watching along two old channels of the Missisquoi River. Wear waterproof boots in spring and bug repellent in summer. Bring binoculars.

SWANTON, VT
1.5 MILES
1.5 HOURS
EASY
DOGS MUST BE LEASHED.

ESTABLISHED IN 1943, Missisquoi is a 6,338-acre refuge on the eastern shore of Lake Champlain which includes most of the Missisquoi River delta. One of more than 540 such refuges in the United States, Missisquoi is managed for the protection of wildlife and its habitat. Quiet waters and wetlands attract flocks of migrating waterfowl while upland areas are home to songbirds and mammals. Peak waterfowl viewing is during the fall migration when thousands of ring-necked ducks feed and rest in the company of hundreds of green-winged teal, mallards, and black ducks.

The wetland trails, which are very wet in spring, follow the banks of Maquam and Black Creeks, long-abandoned channels of the Missisquoi River. The swamp is rich in plant diversity and attracts a wide range of animals. The refuge is actively managed: water level in impoundment areas is manipulated and fields are hayed, mowed, or burned to keep them from reverting to woodland.

Portions of the refuge are open to hunting and fishing, boats and canoes may be launched from two landings, and cross-country skiing is permitted. Brochures are available at Refuge Headquarter and there are interpretive signs along the trail.

In recent years a new, "green" headquarters for the Refuge has opened on Tabor Road. Built with local materials including old beams from a local barn, this "smart" building makes use of geothermal cooling and energy-saving fixtures and appliances. A wind turbine and photovoltaic solar panels on the roof enable the facility to meter excess electricity back to the grid. Exhibits focus on wildlife and habitat and archeology of the earliest settlers, Paleoindians who settled in the region 12,000 to 9,500 years ago. In the past decade the trail network in the refuge has expanded, making it possible to spend much of a day walking through various

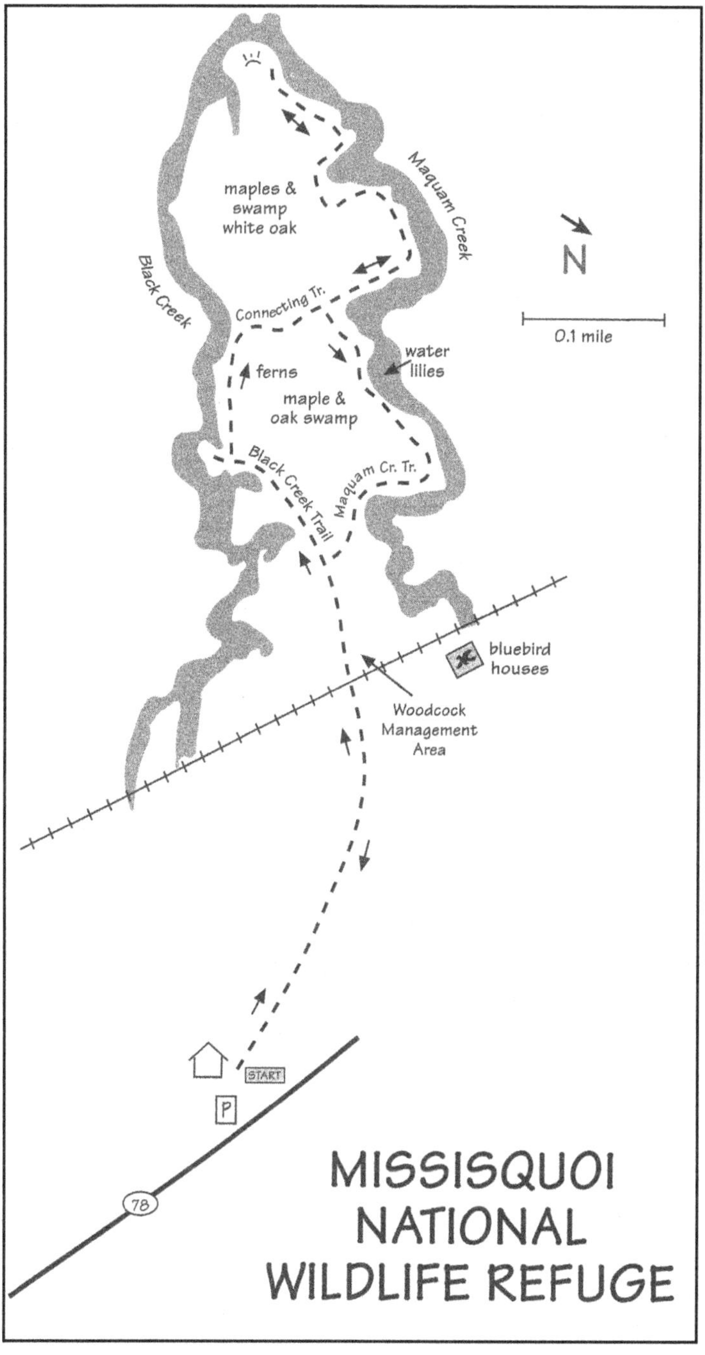

maples &
swamp
white oak

Maquam Creek

N

0.1 mile

Black Creek

Connecting Tr.

water
lilies

ferns

maple &
oak swamp

Black Creek Trail

Maquam Cr. Tr.

bluebird
houses

Woodcock
Management
Area

START

P

78

MISSISQUOI
NATIONAL
WILDLIFE REFUGE

ecosystems and habitats along the Missisquoi River and Bay. We will focus on the Black Creek and Maquam Creek trails.

• • • • • •

The walk begins as a mowed path across a hayfield, nesting habitat for field sparrow, bobolink and red-winged blackbird. Along the edge of the field is a row of bluebird boxes, although tree swallows often use them. (See bluebirds, page 28.) Look for red-tailed hawks soaring overhead in search of mice and voles.

The trail rises over the railroad track and enters young woods. In some years frogs are so prolific that they bound away at every footfall. Eastern garter snakes slither through the grass.

The woods are a mix of shrubs and young trees: speckled alder, buttonbush, elm, pin and chokecherry, willow, gray birch, and sumac. Moisture-loving sensitive fern is the dominant ground cover. In spring the fronds have a reddish cast and they wither at first frost- hence the name. In August or September beaded fertile stalks appear.

In about five minutes we pass a woodcock management area on the right. Woodcock, who thrive in scrubby young growth of alder and aspen, do not find food or camouflage in mature woods. As Vermont becomes increasing forested, woodcock are threatened. (See North Hero on page 44.)

Where the Maquam Creek Trail goes right, walk left on the Black Creek Trail. Swamp white oak, willow, and silver and red maple dominate the swamp and bright green duckweed coats the open water. Look for eastern spiny soft-shelled turtles sunning themselves on warm days.

The trail reaches the creek and turns right. Beware of poison ivy. Ferns are prolific and robust. The size of a fern is more dependent on the ecology of its home than that of a flowering plant. The four ferns in this damp soil, royal, sensitive, cinnamon, and interrupted, are clearly happy.

Royal fern, with oblong leaflets, looks like a locust tree. It grows to six feet in bogs, swamps, and near bodies of water. By contrast the sensitive fern grows to a maximum of two feet. Its wavy-edged, once cut leaflets often look as if they were not fully cut to the frond.

Interrupted fern gets its name from the absence of greenery in the middle of the fertile fronds. The dark brown spore cases interrupt the bright green leaflets along the frond. Interrupted fern, not particular about habitat, resembles cinnamon fern that prefers damp locations. Rusty wool covers the spring stem of cinnamon fern and its separate fertile fronds also turn to a cinnamon color.

The trail bends right away from the creek and an elevated boardwalk crosses swampy ground. A bridge passes over an inlet and wood duck boxes dot the creek.

Silver maple and swamp white oak, the latter ringed with chicken wire for protection against beavers, tower over sensitive and royal ferns. Across the creek a red maple can be identified in spring by the pendulous red seed keys already dangling before the tree leafs out.

At the end of the boardwalk turn right to connect to the Maquam Creek Trail. This connector may not be passable in spring.

At the T-intersection go left on Maquam Creek Trail. Winterberry, dogwood, northern wild raisin, and high-bush cranberry are abundant, their fruit and twigs eaten by grouse, pheasants, songbirds, deer and rabbits.

Royal ferns grow to great size along the perenially moist Black Creek.

Along both creeks you may see beaver runs that look like worn footpaths. Beaver uses these when they leave the safety of the water to seek food and building materials. Beavers also build scent mounds, spraying piles of mud in order to establish their territory.

The creek is on the right and the tree swamp on the left, still dominated by silver maple and swamp white oak. A swamp or red maple on the left has a characteristic birds-eye pattern on its bark. Red maple leaves have three shallow lobes, toothed edges, and red stems. Silver maple leaves are more deeply cut, longer and lighter green, with silver-white undersides. They generally have five lobes. Both trees, when mature, can have shaggy or peeling bark, and often have many trunks in a swampy setting.

The trail bends to left and passes over very wet ground. You may need waterproof boots to continue to Lookout Point, a spectacular wildlife observation spot at the end of the trail. Colorful songbirds flit through the canopy. Wood duck, hooded merganser, osprey, and great blue heron are commonly seen in the marsh or creek. Deer, muskrat, beaver, and rabbit leave their marks.

Return toward the parking area by retracing your steps. At the trail junction, continue straight or left on the mowed grass of the Maquam Creek Trail. Buttonbush grows along the creek and by late summer a carpet of white pond lilies float on the water. The trail leaves the creek behind and returns toward the railroad crossing and parking area.

BLUEBIRDS

Bluebirds are not blue, nor are many other blue birds. They owe their appearance to Tyndall scattering. Their feather structure bends light waves so that we see predominantly blue light. Grind up a bluebird's feather and the result is not blue. Bluebirds appear bluer on a sunny day when there is more light.

Bluebirds, like woodcock, are victims of lost habitat and competition. Their traditional homes, farms with open fields, fences for perching, and old tree cavities for nests, are fast disappearing. Bluebirds Across Vermont was established in 1986 to encourage the placement of bluebird boxes as homes to the small population returning each spring to nest. Audubon Vermont has assimilated Bluebirds Across Vermont. A walk at the Audubon Center in Huntington is on page 182.

LIFE CYCLE OF FERNS

Ferns are ancient non-flowering plants that lack true leaves, stems, and roots. Ferns have two generations, the gametophyte and the sporophyte, which look very different from each other. The sporophyte is the stage that we recognize as a fern.

The cycle begins with a spore, a dust-like speck containing chlorophyll and moisture, which germinates on damp ground. The resulting gametophyte, a tiny plant which most of us would never see or recognize, eventually produces egg and sperm cells. A drop of rain or dew allows the sperm to swim to the egg and fertilize it. (This is a link to primitive plants that required water for reproduction. More evolved flowering plants do not need water.)

The fertilized egg drops to the ground and takes root, sending up a green shoot that becomes a frond. As the fern develops it produces spores within a spore case, usually found on the underside of the frond. When the spores are ripe, these one-celled particles of life spill to the earth and begin the cycle anew.

Fern spores scatter by the millions and can remain viable for many years, quite impervious to climatic conditions. Ferns enjoy great mobility as spores can travel much farther on the wind than seeds of the higher order plants. Ferns also propagate from their rootstocks, creating an underground branching network. Some cinnamon fern rootstocks are a century old, standing like islands on swampy ground.

HOURS, FEES, FACILITIES
Dogs must be leashed. A waterless toilet is available year-round at the parking area.

GETTING THERE
Take Exit 21 from I-89. Go west into Swanton where Rte. 78 turns right. The parking and trailhead for the nature trails are on the left 2.3 miles from the turn in Swanton. To reach the Refuge Headquarters continue about 3.6 miles on Rte. 78. Just beyond West Swanton Apple Orchard on your right, look for Tabor Road on the left. There is a sign for the headquarters which is a short distance on Tabor Road on the left side.

FOR MORE INFORMATION
Missisquoi National Wildlife Refuge
P. O. Box 163
Swanton, VT 05488
802-868-4781
missisquoi@fws.gov
http://missisquoi.fws.gov

Burton Island State Park
St. Albans Bay

Circumnavigate an island in Lake
Champlain with ever-changing lake
and mountain views. A great walk
for kids.

ST. ALBANS BAY
3 MILES
2-3 HOURS
EASY
NO PETS IN DAY USE AREAS.

BURTON ISLAND IS A UNIQUE state park. Accessible by boat, the park is a 253-acre island in St. Albans Bay. Its many campsites are clustered along the northern shore leaving most of the land open to exploration.

As recently as 8,000 years ago, Burton Island was the tip of a peninsula. The land, compressed by mile-thick glaciers during the Ice Age, rebounded after the ice melted and the island was born. Until the 1950s, the land was farmed. Trees are now reclaiming the island. If left alone, Burton Island will be forested within a generation.

Two short nature trails are easily incorporated into a circuit of the island. The views alone justify the journey. The southwestern point of land, its shoreline wild and exposed, has several large shade trees, benches, and a mowed swath for lingering—the perfect destination for an afternoon picnic.

• • • • • •

When you disembark from the ferry, stop at the park office for maps and trail guides. Then take the gravel path along the marina to the left. Within a few minutes it reaches an intersection of several gravel roads. Follow a sign, left to the Nature Center. When the paths fork, do not go toward the water but right, toward the ranger's house. You will pass the small brown house and then see another just a few hundred yards distant.

The Nature Center is home to an informal collection of animals, rusty farm implements, and small educational exhibits. I particularly liked a meticulously labeled collection of rock samples from across the state.

The Island Farm Nature Trail begins at the water's edge overlooking St. Albans Bay. This was an important eighteenth century port for both lumber and potash, a byproduct of the clearing and burning of forested land. Glacial erratics litter the

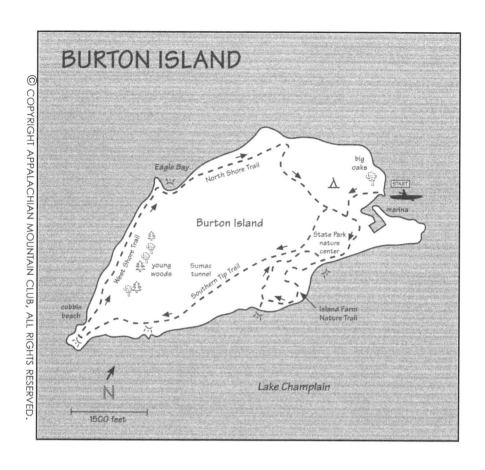

BURTON ISLAND

Eagle Bay

North Shore Trail

big oaks

START

marina

Burton Island

West Shore Trail

young woods

Sumac tunnel

Southern Tip Trail

State Park nature center

cobble beach

Island Farm Nature Trail

N

1500 feet

Lake Champlain

beach that is composed of cobbles of shale smoothed by years of water action. Silverweed, a creeping plant named for silvery hairs on the underside of its leaves, thrives on the rocky beach. A single yellow flower blooms in mid-summer on this hardy plant that grows as far north as the edge of the Arctic.

Back on the trail, look for monarch butterflies in the milkweed. They lay their eggs on only the healthiest plants assuring their offspring an optimal food supply. Goldenrod and hog peanut are abundant in the tangle of grasses and flowering plants. Ash, basswood, silver maple, cottonwood, and black locust trees grow along the shore at the edge of the meadow. The trail crosses a swampy area, a thicket of jewelweed, cattail, red raspberry, cow vetch, and thimbleberry. A rusty plow on the left is a reminder of the not-so-distant farm days. In one generation brush and saplings have overtaken the fields, a process we will witness again and again on Burton Island.

Within ten minutes the trail turns right to go inland, rising slightly through a grove of sumacs. We continue left, past the barn foundations barely visible through the thicket of raspberry canes. The trail continues downhill, bearing right to a splendid view of lake.

We pass through a young forest of quaking aspen, a fast-growing, sun-loving tree. These will eventually be replaced by more shade-tolerant trees: maple, oak, hickory, and elm.

The trail rises past some large shagbark hickories and into mature woods of northern white cedar, sugar maple, and hickory before turning right toward the middle of the island.

We cross a marsh on a boardwalk. Farm stock watered at this pond now filling with wetland plants: cattail, red-osier dogwood, wild bergamot, and smartweed, its spike of tiny pink flowers encased in a sheath of leaves around the stem. Wild bergamot has a pale lilac flower and looks like domestic bee balm, to which it is related. The August-flowering plant stands about three feet, has opposite, lance-shaped leaves that are serrated. If you have bee balm in the garden you will recognize it immediately. Spotted touch-me-not or jewelweed grows next to stinging nettle. Jewelweed's leaves and stems are thought to be a remedy for stinging nettles and poison ivy.

Still on marshy ground there are several spiky hawthorn trees. Its simple, alternate leaves are toothless and their shape varies even on the same tree. Hawthorns produce a red apple-like fruit and frequently hybridize, making it difficult to identify a species.

This trail will take about a half hour of leisurely walking. Just before it returns to the Nature Center, look for a passageway on the left to a dirt road. Turn left on the dirt road and, at the sign for Southern Tip Trail, walk left.

The grassy path, leading generally west, passes through a nearly continuous tunnel of impressively large sumac. Red raspberries -enough to snack on, ragweed, thistle, thimbleberry, and saplings attract choirs of songbirds. Occasional lake views open on the left.

Within twenty minutes the trail reaches the spectacular Southern Tip. Several specimen trees, wide-spreading red oak, sugar maple, and ash, shade benches on the mowed grass. To the south lies Ball Island. Peaks of the Adirondacks stretch to the southwest and the Green Mountains lie to the east.

A shoreline of black shale wraps around the promontory exposing the thin and brittle layers that, with erosion, become the beach cobbles. The sedimentary layers were metamorphosed under the pressure of deep layers of earth and ice, subsequently removed by passing glaciers.

When you are ready to leave this view, turn to the right, continuing clockwise

Look for oprey as well as green and great blue herons at Eagle Bay.

around the island. The trail goes along the beach edged with gnarled white cedars and red maples. In about five minutes, look for a large paper birch with multiple trunks and contorted roots at the edge of the woods. The narrow track begins here and meanders into young woods of red oak, white birch, green ash, elm, basswood, cottonwood, dogwood, quaking aspen, cherry, hickory, and maple.

After about ten minutes the trail comes to another cobble beach littered with glacial erratics. The shale bedrock has wavy stripes of black and orange. Notice the view to the west and how abruptly New York flattens north of the Adirondacks.

The trail continues along the beach until it reaches a tiny peninsula that forms the western edge of Eagle Bay, a picturesque cove bordered by white cedars. While you probably won't see an eagle here, look for green and great blue heron and os-prey. At a large rock outcropping a path leads inland and joins the North Shore Trail. (We walk the trail in reverse order of the numbered signs.)

The trail heads east, never far from the shore, through young forest predom-inantly of paper birch, green ash, cottonwood, and northern white cedar. The canopy then thickens and evergreens become dominant, white pines and hem-locks mixing with the cedars. Hemlock is one of the longest-lived trees in our area and many of these trees are 200 years old. This is one of the few parts of the island that was not cleared for farming.

A marshy area on the right, once a pond, is now filling with plants and sediment and the immediate area is drying up. The poor, thin soil is home to red and white cedars as well as poplars and birch. The shrubs and saplings offer food and protection to wildlife. Pencil-point stumps are evidence of beavers. Other mammals that have swum or crossed the ice to Burton Island include deer, red fox, muskrat, and raccoon.

The final stretch of trail passes through more sun-loving actors in the drama of early succession. Red raspberry, staghorn sumac, goldenrod, and willows dominate these abandoned fields. The North Shore Trail takes less than a half hour at a leisurely pace.

At the end of the Nature Trail the campground stretches to the left. Take the mowed path to the right through a swampy area. When the path joins a gravel road, follow the road to the right until it reaches an intersection with other gravel roads. Turn left to return to the marina.

Near the marina at the edge of the woods, look for several large bur oaks, one with a diameter of more than 3½ feet.

SUCCESSION

When farm fields are abandoned, sun-loving shrubs and saplings move in. These pioneers may include sumac, poplar, white pine, gray and white birch. They, in turn, are eventually replaced. Much of the sumac on Burton Island is poised to be replaced as the shady conditions created by the parent trees make it unlikely that a new generation will be as successful. Pioneer trees succumb to shade tolerant species including maples, shagbark hickory, ash, and oaks.

Grasses and herbs also diminish with decreasing sunlight. As young trees thicken and little sunlight reaches the forest floor, mosses and ferns return. Only in a mature climax forest, where the leafy canopy is at great height, do prolific spring wildflowers find enough sunlight to flourish.

SUMAC

The fuzzy branches of staghorn sumac resemble the antlers of a deer in velvet, hence the name. Its leaves are long with up to thirty-one toothed leaflets. The shrub grows to thirty feet, often in thickets. Native Americans made a lemonade-like drink from the red fruits and its tannin-rich bark and foliage were used to tan leather.

The rare poison sumac causes a severe rash. With care, it can be easily distinguished from staghorn sumac. Poison sumac is generally found in swamps and bogs and its twigs are hairless. It has fewer leaflets, a maximum of 13, and they are not toothed.

HOURS, FEES, FACILITIES

The ferry runs from Friday before Memorial Day through Labor Day, subject to weather conditions and lake levels. Six departures from Kill Kare State Park run from 9:00 AM to 6:30 PM, with service from Burton island six times daily, 8:30 AM to 6:00 PM. The trip takes ten minutes. The fare is $4 per person, round trip, for passengers over four.

GETTING THERE

Take I-89 Exit 19. At the stop sign turn right, following signs to Vt. 36. At stop sign, 0.6 mile, turn left onto Vt. 36 west. Continue to the Green in St. Albans at 0.8 mile. Turn right at the light and jog immediately left, staying on Vt. 36 west. In 3.0 miles go right when the road come to the lake, still on Vt. 36. After 0.9 mile you will turn left onto Hathaway Point. This access road meanders 2.7 miles to the entrance of Kill Kare State Park. The ferry for Burton Island is on the left.

FOR MORE INFORMATION

Department of Forests, Park, and Recreation
Burton Island State Park
802-524-6353
http://www.vtstateparks.com/htm/burton.cfm

Knight Point State Park

A quiet stretch of Lake Champlain shoreline. Extensive cobble beach. Some grand old sugar maples and shagbark hickories shade the grassy trail.	NORTH HERO, VT 0.7 MILE 45 MINUTES EASY NO PETS

AT FIRST BLUSH Knight Point looks an unlikely place for a nature walk. Yet beyond the stately brick Knight Point House, rolling lawns, and picnic tables, a narrow stretch of lakeside forest sits on a bluff above the lake. Cries of gulls mix with songs of woodland birds and the trail has several benches at scenic spots.

The islands of North and South Hero commemorate Vermonters who fought in the Revolutionary War. Knight Point is named for its first resident, John Knight, who began ferry service between the islands in 1785. His family ran this service until the first bridge was built in 1892.

The wooden wing of the Knight Point House is a replica of Knight Tavern, an inn for ferry passengers built in 1790. Its two-story porch was an unusual architectural feature in its time. The historic building now accommodates park staff.

The nature trail meanders above the shore to the northern border of the 54-acre park. The trail makes a loop and several spurs lead back to the meadow and picnic shelter.

• • • • • •

Start your walk on the south shore, west of the swimming beach. The mowed trail goes immediately into a thicket. The trees along the water's edge are those that don't mind wet feet: ash, cottonwood, and red maple. The shrubs, on slightly drier ground, include red cedar, red-osier dogwood, and young shade-tolerant saplings like sugar maple and the hickories.

Choking these trees, or trying to, are Virginia creeper and wild grape vines. Both opportunists twine their way upward to reach the sunlight and in so doing block the sun's rays to the trees that support them. While these vines provide food for birds and small mammals, they exact their price. Scouring rush or horsetail, looking like its namesakes, grows on damp soil. (See Horsetails, page 39.)

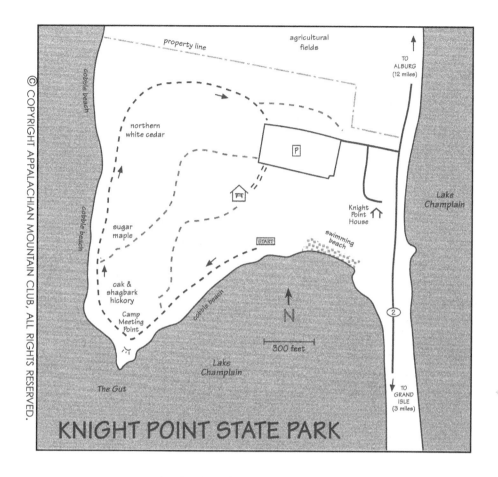

KNIGHT POINT STATE PARK

Mature sugar maple, shagbark hickory, and red and white oaks are scattered along the shore, some thought to be over 200 years old. One spreading sugar maple has a diameter of over four feet. Shagbarks, found only in warm microclimates near the lake, are at the northern extreme of their range here. Red oak, recognizable by the pointed lobes of their leaves, sometimes grow to seventy or eighty feet. The red is the northernmost of our oaks growing in well-drained soil, rich or poor. Its acorns do not ripen until the second autumn and in northern Vermont it is found at elevations of less than 1,400 feet.

About 10 minutes into the walk, a sidetrail branches to the right. The main trail stays left and soon arrives at Camp Meeting Point. With mowed grass, benches, and a picnic table, this is a lovely spot to savor views of the lake and Adirondacks. Great blue heron frequent the shallows off the point. To the south is the "Gut," a nautical term for a narrow passage like this one between the two islands.

For nearly a half mile along the shore, a cobble beach stretches below the bluff. This beach is the most extensive of its type in Vermont. The cobbles, the result of lake action on black shale, are small and smooth and harbor little vegetation. The beach is maintained by wave action, ice scouring, and seasonal flooding.

Spotted sandpipers, with long spindly legs, are thought to nest on this beach, in grassy or moss-lined depressions. While most of our familiar shorebirds breed farther north in Canada, this one nests in the area.

As the trail heads north the understory thickens. Some big, old field trees, oaks, shagbarks, and maples, dot the woods thick with saplings: hickory, maple, poplar, ash, elm, oak, and red osier dogwood. Staghorn sumac, a pioneer that prefers full sun, is on the decline, being replaced by more shade-tolerant trees.

Jack-in-the-pulpit thrive in rich soil in the shade of deciduous trees.

Several small trails fork right while the main path continues left. Northern white cedar, a tree that thrives on lakeside bluffs, becomes thick and hop hornbeam appear for the first time. I was enchanted, on a May day, when a scarlet tanager flitted from maple to maple with bright flashes of red.

The footing can be damp as the trail turns away from lake, a perfect place to look for animal tracks in the mud. Deer, red fox, and raccoon frequent these woods. Basswood, an indicator of fertile soil, grows among abundant spring wildflowers: yellow and purple violets, Canada violets, wood nettles, white trillium, jack-in-the-pulpit, and hepatica.

The trees thin out and a cedar-rail fence borders agricultural fields on the left. The trail passes through a grove of saplings- poplar, ash, quaking aspen, and sumac, before returning to the meadow.

NATURE'S WEAVERS

On a late summer morning the woods and meadows are a sticky tangle of spider webs. Spiders create these architectural and structural marvels to trap prey, provide transportation, and encase their eggs.

Webs come in several designs, the familiar orb or circular web (as in *Charlotte's Web*), sheet, and funnel. Spiders produce seven or eight specialized types of silk. It has great strength and elasticity; a one-inch-thick rope of silk would be stronger than a steel cable.

Late in the season, huge insects, entangled in sticky silk, destroy the webs, forcing the hungry spider to spin anew as often as once a day. A female spider's final act may be the weaving of an intricate egg sac, an effort that expends her silk-producing energy. Without silk a spider starves. The egg sac, tough on the outside and lined with the softest of silks, protects the eggs through winter and baby spiders hatch out in spring when food is readily available.

Humans have used spider silk for centuries, packing wounds and making fishing nets and thin hairline sights on telescopes. Ruby-throated hummingbirds also use spiders' webs, to glue together their nests.

HORSETAILS

Horsetails or scouring rushes are primitive fern allies. Their prehistoric relatives, the Calamitales, were large and abundant treelike plants that lived nearly 300 million years ago. The bounty of their spores produced great beds of coal that are still mined today!

Horsetails are found in wet places, often on sandy or gravely soil. When the stems branch they do so in regular whorls- picture a bottlebrush. Both stems and branches perform photosynthesis, a function usually reserved for leaves.

The most common horsetail is the field horsetail that has as many as seventeen different forms and grows like a weed. The fertile stem grows to only about six inches in height and generally has no branches or very stunted ones. The infertile stems, resembling a brush, grow to eighteen inches with regular whorls of branches along its length.

Like other fern relatives, horsetails have a two-stage life cycle. Spores are produced at the end of fertile stems and are carried by the wind. Horsetail spores, containing chlorophyll and moisture, live only a few days and must germinate quickly. When they do, they produce either male or female gametophytes that are dependent on moisture for fertilization. Once the sperm fertilizes the egg, a sporophyte is produced and the cycle begins anew.

KILLDEER DRAMA

In the meadows and parking area you may hear the plaintive cries of a killdeer circling overhead.

A brown and white shorebird the size of a robin with very long legs, the killdeer frequents open fields, golf courses, gravel lots, and rooftops (including schools and shopping centers!). In May, the male cries out as he stakes his territory. After a pair has made a nest, a depression scraped in the ground, the female feigns injury to distract from it, crying piteously and dragging her wings.

The fully feathered hatchlings are precocial, meaning they can walk and find food at birth, a necessary adaptation for ground nesters who cannot remain in the safety of a treetop nest.

GETTING THERE

Coming from the north on Rte. 2, the park is 3.4 miles south of the Town Hall in North Hero. From the south on Rte. 2 the park is immediately on your left after you cross the drawbridge from Grand Isle. It is approximately 17 miles from I-89 at Exit 17.

FOR MORE INFORMATION

Vermont Department of Forests, Parks, and Recreation
http://www.vtstateparks.com/htm/

North Hero State Park

An unusual floodplain forest on the shore of Lake Champlain. Beautiful lake and mountain views. Bring bug repellent, a bird book, and, in spring, waterproof boots.	NORTH HERO, VT 1.3 MILES 1-1.5 HOURS EASY NO PETS

IN ANTICIPATION OF a bounty of campers attracted by the Montreal Olympics, the state acquired North Hero State Park in 1963. To the chagrin of environmentalists, portions of a rare floodplain forest were filled to create roads, tent sites, and services. Nearly one third of the park's 400 acres sits below the 100-foot elevation mark (The unregulated water level of Lake Champlain fluctuates seasonally between 95 and 101 feet.) and each spring the lake rises over the camping area leaving low-lying areas water-logged and buggy. In 2009 the Vermont Department of Forests, Parks, and Recreation closed the park to campers. It remains open for day use.

This type of lakeside floodplain forest is found in Vermont only around Lake Champlain and this is one of the largest. The Nature Conservancy has recently preserved a stretch of riverfront riparian forest in Richmond. Details follow at the end of this chapter.

Annual spring flooding ordains the vegetation and animal life of a floodplain forest. While it lacks plant diversity, it is an interesting habitat, a spawning area for northern pike and pickerel. Signs of beaver and muskrat are commonly found.

Deer frequently browse in adjacent fields and the shore is a good place to observe waterfowl.

With no overnight visitors to the park the mowed loop of the nature trail will be only minimally maintained. The twenty to thirty minutes walk is pleasant but not as noteworthy as the riparian forest. I will describe it only briefly.

• • • • • •

The trail was intended to connect all three camping loops. I would recommend parking near or on Loop 3 as it is closer to the lakeshore if you choose to walk there and back. Once you reach the trail you can circle in either direction.

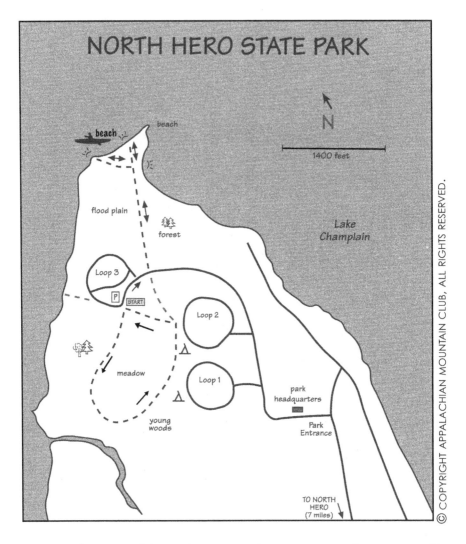

NORTH HERO STATE PARK

beach

beach

N

1400 feet

flood plain

forest

Lake
Champlain

Loop 3

P

START

Loop 2

meadow

Loop 1

park
headquarters

young
woods

Park
Entrance

TO NORTH
HERO
(7 miles)

Just stay to the inside of the circle ignoring the connectors to Loops 1 & 2. You will eventually circle back to Loop 3.

Occasional mowing of this meadow keeps it from succeeding to woodland, allowing grasses, flowering herbs, berries, and saplings to flourish. The rich mix of food, shelter, and camouflage attracts insects, snakes, small mammals, and birds. Breeding birds that prefer this habitat include the veery, blue-gray gnatcatcher, warbling vireo, yellow-throated vireo and Baltimore oriole. The vulnerable woodcock (see Woodcock, page 44) can be spotted and heard here, usually near dawn or dusk, with its comical round body, spindly legs, and long beak.

Several large swamp white oak, ash, and shagbark hickory tower over the

The aquatic arrowhead blooms in the wetlands along the shore. Ducks and muskrats enjoy the tubers, called duck potatoes.

meadow, shade or wolf trees left when this land was farmed. Saplings in the young woods that surround the meadow include willow, basswood, quaking aspen, gray birch, bitternut and shagbark hickory, red and silver maple, and a hybrid of the two maples.

In summer the meadow is a tangle of milkweed, grasses, goldenrod, grape vines, and Queen Anne's lace.

From the camping loops return to the main road and turn left toward the beach and boat launch. If the ground is dry walk beneath the trees but beware of poison ivy.

Unlike a swamp, where hummocks and pools provide a variety of growing surfaces, the floodplain forest lies on flat ground. This forest, at or below lake level, has less diversity than most plant communities in Vermont. The trees, green ash, swamp white oak and maple hybrid, are tall with few side limbs. Many maples have multiple trunks, the result of extensive firewood cutting several decades ago. There is almost no shrub layer and the ground vegetation is primarily sensitive fern and wood nettles. Along the road a few winterberry shrubs grow. Natural debris from spring high water covers the ground: stumps, leaf litter, broken branches, mud, and sand.

A ten-minute walk leads to the lake. To the right is a marshy area. In the summer it's possible to venture amidst cattail, arrowroot, purple loosestrife, and rushes. At the end of the road is a cobble beach facing due north. In the distance cars cross between Swanton and Alburg on the Rte. 78 bridge.

Map turtles lay their eggs on the east side of this beach in June and July. The area is roped off but you might catch a glimpse of the mothers scooping out their nests or laying eggs in the morning hours.

A detour to the left leads to the boat launch area. A few footpaths meander away, one to the woods and another to a tiny picturesque bay, its shore littered with mollusk shells. Shorebirds skittle along the water's edge and great blue herons fish in the shallows. This is a good place to observe waterfowl unnoticed.

WOODCOCK

The woodcock is long-legged shorebird with an unusually long, three-inch bill. It has moved to upland scrub from shoreline mud flats. Its feathers, resembling dead leaves, are camouflage against the overhead menace of hawks and owls as well as weasels and other ground predators. It lives on worms and insects in moist, fertile soil. Being a ground nester adds to the woodcock's vulnerabilities.

As shrubs grow into trees the habitat no longer protects and provides for the woodcock. Historically fires and the abandonment of farmland provided a continual supply of scrubby habitat. The woodcock is now dependent on human intervention for land management or logging.

PONDER THE INSECT

Between swats at black flies or mosquitoes, consider the insect. Without them we would have few flowers or fruits and no silk or honey. What would frogs eat and how would swallows, swifts, and bats fuel their flights? There are over a million known species of insects.

Unlike mammals, reptiles, birds, and fish, with internal bony skeletons, insects have an exoskeleton. This tough, protective layer covers the entire body including legs, feet, eyes, and antennae. This layer allows for little growth so insects must molt in order to grow. Many times in their lives insects shed a replica of themselves, right down to the claws of their feet.

Insects have six jointed legs and wings that allow them to escape danger and search for food. Unlike warm-blooded mammals, insects are cold-blooded. When the temperature drops, their metabolism slows. Very dependent on the sun's warmth, they spring to life on the first spring day.

Insects begin life as eggs. They hatch into a larva, usually a grub or caterpillar, which undergoes a metamorphosis, or change. The larvae feed and molt repeatedly, eventually becoming an adult quite different from the larval stage. The winged adult, like familiar bees, butterflies, dragonflies, and grasshoppers, have the mobility to lay eggs in spots favorable to the next generation. The Monarch butterfly, for example, lays her eggs on the larva's favorite food, a milkweed plant.

GETTING THERE

From the north on Rte. 2, cross the bridge onto North Hero and take an immediate left on Bridge Road. After 0.5 mile the road turns right and continues to a T-intersection at 1.8 miles. Turn left onto Lakeview Drive. The park gate is 1.6 miles on the left.

From the south on Rte 2, pass through the town of North Hero. From the Town Hall drive north 3.5 miles to a fork. Bear right on Lakeview Drive. Continue 3.7 miles to the park entrance on your left.

Inside the park, drive 0.7 mile on the main road to Loop No. 3. Follow the loop counter-clockwise 0.3 mile to the water spigot where there is parking.

• ALSO IN THE AREA •

ALBURG DUNES STATE PARK

A new acquisition on the southern coast of the Alburg peninsula, this park has a half-mile, white sand beach strewn with sea grass and mollusk shells. Sand dunes have been destroyed by foot traffic and are fenced in the hope that they will rebuild over time. At the end of a long stretch of open lake with prevailing south winds, the beach is the recipient of wind and water carried sand.

Hidden in the acreage is an inaccessible black spruce swamp and bog, a very northerly feature in one of the most moderate of Vermont's climates, a demonstration of the extraordinary insulating ability of peat.

The park is south of Rte. 129 on the western side of the peninsula. From the junction at Rte. 2, take Rte. 129 west to a left turn at 1.2 miles. Follow this road until it ends at the park, 1.6 miles.

RICHMOND RIPARIAN CORRIDOR

The Nature Conservancy has protected floodplain forest acreage along the Winooski. In summer ostrich ferns tower over the heads of children.

From the Round Church at the south end of the bridge in Richmond, drive east on Cochran's Road. In 0.5 mile park at the cemetery on the right side of the road. Across the road from the western boundary of the cemetery a path leads down a ramp toward the floodplain. A yellow sign for The Nature Conservancy marks the property. A worn trail leads toward the water and continues eastward along the riverbank.

5　Ed Weed Fish Culture Station

Vermont's largest fish hatchery produces 260,000 pounds and more than a half million fish each year for the state's lakes and rivers. A lakeside exploration through the process of fish rearing. An on-site wind turbine contributes electrical power. Children's activities in the Visitor's Center.

GRAND ISLE, VT
0.8 MILE
1-1.5 HOURS (INCLUDING TIME AT THE VISITOR'S CENTER)
EASY
SERVICE ANIMALS ONLY INSIDE BUILDINGS. OUTDOORS, PETS MUST BE LEASHED.

VERMONT'S FIVE HATCHERIES rear over a million fish each year. They stock 400 locations for recreation and to support populations threatened by overfishing, pollution, erosion, dams, and loss of habitat.

The Ed Weed Fish Culture Station is the newest and largest of the state hatcheries, raising landlocked Atlantic salmon and brook, brown, rainbow, steelhead rainbow, and lake trout. More than a quarter million of these fish go directly into Lake Champlain each year.

In addition to the hatchery, an "upstream path" has been constructed for adult salmon and trout returning to spawn. Each year returning fish jump and swim upstream in an environment designed to mimic their native habitat. The best viewing is in April and May and again in October through December.

The fish hatchery is part of a 100-acre parcel of state land that provides excellent bird watching. Bring your binoculars in spring and fall.

. . . . . .

Be sure to pick up a brochure for the self-guided tour just inside the door.

Take some time in the Visitor's Center where the hatchery is fully explained. A fish census lists the number and types of fish delivered across the state each spring from all of the state hatcheries. (In 2008 Ed Weed stocked more than 310,500 fish to Lake Champlain and close to a half million to inland waters across the state.) Historic exhibits begin with the paleo-Indians and end with Colonial history of Vermont. A film demonstrates the entire process of fish culture. There are also several activities for young children.

You will exit to the raceways where fish spend most of a year before being

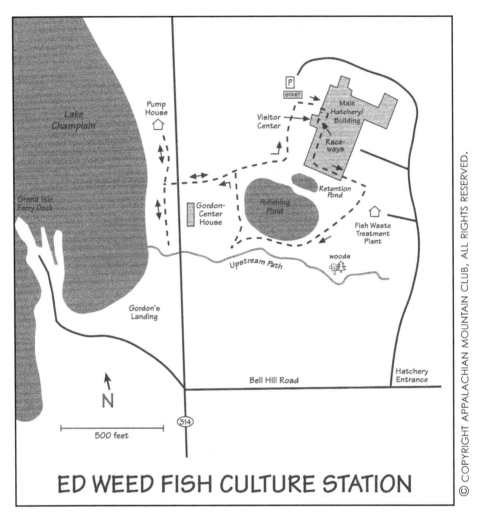

ED WEED FISH CULTURE STATION

stocked. They are moved here when they are about two inches long. The fish in the ten pairs of raceways are labeled by species. You will often see the fish being hand-fed. The raceways are enclosed to protect this tempting dining site from otters, minks, great blue herons, and kingfishers.

Follow the fish stenciled on the sidewalk. A gravel path leads to the fish waste treatment plant and a facility where all trucks used to transport fish are thoroughly cleaned. The trail skirts the polishing pond. On the left are trees typical of the warm Lake Champlain lowlands including white oak, basswood, hickory, maple, and ash.

A short spur on the left leads to the outfall where treated water returns to the lake. The channel is designed with strategically placed cobbles and boulders to prevent scour and erosion.

The trail continues to a driveway and turns left passing beneath several impressive ash and shagbark hickory trees. The Federal style Gordon-Center House on the left was built in 1824 of Isle La Motte limestone and is listed in the National Register of Historic Places. It houses the Lake Champlain Basin Program that focuses on the environmental, historic, economic, and cultural life of the lake.

Cross the road and turn left onto the gravel path leading to the man-made stream. The culvert that carries the hatchery outflow has been adapted for returning trout and salmon. Concrete baffles create resting pools enroute. The pool on the right of the culvert, at the top of an eighteen-inch jump, allows fish to rest before continuing the uphill journey. The metal rake-like projection prevents lampreys from spawning in the stream. (See Pests of the Lake, page 50.)

Retrace your steps and continue north on the gravel path toward the pump house. Ferries have operated here since 1796. During cold spells, water under pressure is circulated around the hulls to prevent overnight ice formation. Once the boats are moving they can break through a thin accumulation of ice, but if they freeze in the slip they cannot move.

About 4,400 years ago, eight to ten Indian families summered nearby. The site, to the north of the pump house, is protected from further development.

Three-quarters of the pump house is built into the bedrock below. Two intake pipes, at different levels, control the temperature of the eleven million gallons of water that pass through the hatchery each day. This enormous volume is required to maintain water quality where fish are raised in such crowded conditions.

In addition to pumps, the building houses an emergency diesel generator to produce electricity for the entire hatchery in the event of a power outage. This generator was used for several days after the ice storm of January 1998.

The trail returns to the gravel driveway and back to the Visitor's Center. A small depression on the right is the retention pond where any medication or disinfectants can biodegrade before the water is returned to the lake.

LIFE IN THE FISH LANE

Each fall over two million freshly spawned eggs are delivered to Ed Weed. Hunters and fishers hand strip the brood fish to collect eggs. At the hatchery additional fish are anaesthetized and stripped, their eggs and milk collected. The male milk remains viable for only thirty seconds.

The fertilized eggs are bathed in chilly water for four to eight weeks as embryos develop. Once the eggs hatch the fry are transferred to start tanks. In late spring, as two-inch fingerlings, they are transferred to the outdoor raceways where they will spend eight to ten months. The fish will be eight to ten inches long when they are stocked.

PESTS OF THE LAKE

Many non-native plants and animals have been introduced to Vermont over the centuries. An absence of natural controls- predators, weather, or disease allows uncontrolled reproduction of these pests.

The sea lamprey, Petromyzon marinus, has adjusted to life in fresh water by developing a taste for salmon, trout, and northern pike. Decades ago this eel-like vertebrate devastated commercial fishing in the Great Lakes. The lamprey has an appetite for a significant portion of the species in Lake Champlain.

The adult spawns in streams where up to 100,000 eggs hatch into ammocoetes. These burrow into the streambed where they thrive on plankton and decayed material for three to fourteen years. When the six-inch lampreys emerge, they swim to the lake where, with a disk-like mouth, they feed on the blood and flesh of host fish.

It takes only two days for a seven-ounce lamprey to kill a lake trout more than twice its size. Larger fish have a higher survival rate, but their size, health, and reproduction are ultimately at stake.

The Polishing Pond is part of the journey during which water is treated and cleaned en route back to the lake.

Use of lampricides in Lake Champlain tributaries each spring is keeping the lamprey population in check. Wounding rates are down and more fish are growing to a size appropriate to their species. For more information: http://www.vtfishandwildlife.com/fisheries_lamprey.cfm

Eurasian water milfoil (Myriophyllum spicatum L.) is a non-native aquatic plant that infests many Vermont lakes including large areas of Lake Champlain. Growing up to 20 feet a year from a fibrous root, it out-competes and eliminates beneficial native plants. Its dense growth discourages fish spawning and recreation while the plant is rarely used as a food source.

Eurasian water milfoil spreads whenever a broken fragment travels to a new location. Boat owners have unwittingly transported fragments from lake to lake across the state.

Currently the plant can only be controlled, not eliminated. Divers use suction hoses and hydro rakes or remove roots and shoots by hand. The grass carp, a natural predator native to China and partial to Eurasian water milfoil, is currently illegal in Vermont. Other biological controls, such as insects, bacteria, or fungi are being tested.

Zebra mussels, with striped clam-like shells, usually smaller than one inch, are making a similar assault on the lake. Discovered in Lake St. Clair in 1988, the zebra mussel entered Lake Champlain from the south in 1993. A female can produce a million eggs each season and, in the absence of predators, the tiny mollusks disrupt the ecosystem and clog water intakes, boat hulls, and cooling systems. Great care is taken to filter hatchery water in order not to infest other lakes.

The sheephead fish has been seen consuming zebra mussels. But how many zebra mussels can a fish eat? Unfortunately, not enough.

HOURS, FEES, FACILITIES

The Visitor Center is open every day of the year from 8:00 a.m. to 4:00 p.m. Admission is free and restrooms are available. Guided group tours may be scheduled.

GETTING THERE

From I-89, Exit 17, take Rte. 2 west for 10.2 miles. Turn left on Rte. 314 north and continue for 2.3 miles. Turn right on Bell Hill Road. The hatchery entrance is on your left at 0.2 mile. The gravel drive loops left around the building and brings you to the parking area in 0.3 mile.

FOR MORE INFORMATION
Ed Weed Fish Culture Station
802-372-3171
Department of Fish and Wildlife
http://www.vtfishandwildlife.com/fisheries_ed_weed.cfm

• ALSO IN THE AREA •

HYDE LOG CABIN, ROUTE 2, GRAND ISLE

Built in 1783 of logs hand-hewn by Jedediah Hyde, Jr., an engineer and Revolutionary War veteran, the cabin was one of the first buildings on the islands. It was home to the Hyde family for over 150 years.

Burlington and Central Lake Champlain

Old Mill Park

A river with potholes and striking bedrock erosion on a woodland walk. An exhibit of Snowflake Bentley's photographs.

JERICHO, VT
0.8 MILE
1 HOUR
EASY TO MODERATE
PETS MUST BE LEASHED.

SIX MILLS WERE ONCE LOCATED along this stretch of the Brown's River, the earliest built in the 1820s. In the 1880s the adjacent Chittenden Mill was one of the first in the country to convert from traditional grinding stones to the roller process for making flour. The mill was named for Thomas Chittenden, first governor of Vermont and ancestor of owners Lucius and Frank Howe. Early in this century, as competition from the midwestern states grew, the mill converted to making animal feed and in 1946 it was closed.

Both the river with its beautiful potholes and the woods are cool and welcoming. Several benches sit along the river at particularly scenic spots.

The Winooski Valley Park District manages this park. A coalition of seven towns in the lower Winooski valley, it preserves and maintains historic and natural areas. Several other walks in this book are on WVPD properties (www.wvpd.org).

• • • • • •

The walk begins behind the map. The wetland on the left once lay beneath the millpond behind the dam. Through the 1960s the pond was used for ice-skating. With the dam gone, cattails and other marsh vegetation took root. These plants create a mat of vegetation that in turn allows other plants to establish themselves on drier ground. The process continues as water-loving shrubs and trees invade. Willow, box elder, and speckled alder thrive here now. This land will become drier and eventually return to woods.

Across Clay Brook the trail enters the woods. Go straight rather than left at the sign for the Hilltop Loop. Tall meadow rue, alternate-leaved dogwood, and sensitive and interrupted ferns are lush here. Indian poke or false hellebore dies back in early July, its huge, conspicuously veined leaves yellowing until the entire plant

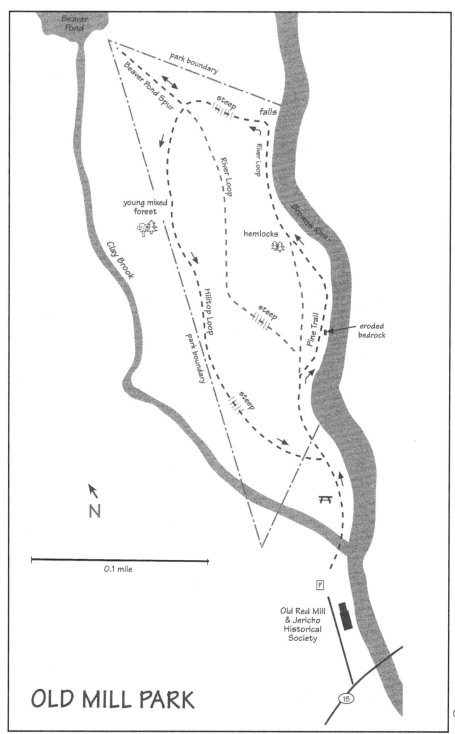

Beaver Pond

park boundary

Beaver Pond Spur

steep

falls

River Loop

River Loop

young mixed forest

hemlocks

Browns River

Clay Brook

steep

Pine Trail

eroded bedrock

Hilltop Loop

park boundary

steep

N

0.1 mile

P

Old Red Mill & Jericho Historical Society

15

OLD MILL PARK

Pink lady slippers are great beauties of the forest.

withers away. Native Americans once used the leaves to make cigars.

On the drier left side of trail, the twice-cut New York fern grows. Its fronds taper to both ends. It is unusual among ferns in not preferring wet sites.

Take the Pine Trail right toward the river. We pass through thick banks of jewelweed and cinnamon, sensitive, and bracken ferns before the trail rises under a thick canopy of hemlocks. The river, with beautifully sculpted bedrock, is on the right. One stretch looks like the inside of an abalone shell. Don't miss the water skaters or striders on the quiet pools trolling for dinner.

Water skaters (and water boatmen) are true bugs, a group of insects with feeding tubes adapted to piercing and sucking. They inject their prey with digestive juices and then suck out the resulting potion. Like all insects, water skaters have six legs: the front pair grasps prey, the middle set propels the skater, and the rear ones steer. They skate across the surface of quiet water patrolling for potential victims, dead or alive.

Skaters can walk on water because of surface tension, a phenomenon that allows some objects with a greater density than water to float. The bond between water molecules at the surface is greater than between those beneath it. Only if the insects do not break the water's surface can they stay on top of it. Legs covered with thick pads of water-repellent hair facilitate this feat.

Returning to the Pine Trail, we continue beneath thick hemlocks. Unlike white pines which need sun, hemlocks grow in shady ravines or beneath a leafy canopy. Once they are established, little can grow beneath them. The few ferns here are beneath small sunny openings.

The Pine Trail bends left and rejoins the other trails. We follow the River Loop to the right.

As the deciduous trees thicken, wildflowers bloom, especially those tolerant of acidic conditions. Pink lady's slippers, with a pair of heavily ribbed lance-shaped leaves, are one of the great beauties of the forest. Wood sorrel, partridgeberry, starflower, Indian cucumber, goldthread, bunchberry, trillium, Clintonia, and wild lily-of-the-valley are thick here. Goldthread has bright gold-colored roots and astringent properties. Once chewed for mouth sores, it is also called cankerroot. Its shiny, evergreen leaves resemble flat-leaf parsley, the three leaflets both toothed and scalloped.

Trailing arbutus, becoming less and less common, hugs the trail. It prefers

Delicate starflowers float above a whorl of leaves.

open edges to deep leaf litter, making it vulnerable to traffic. Also called Mayflower, trailing arbutus is the earliest bloom of spring with tiny, sweet-scented pink or white flowers.

The trail rises and falls over eroded sections of hillside as it continues along the river. Tree roots are exposed and the footing can be slippery. Several pools of clay have slumped out from beneath the mossy hillside creating light gray puddles.

Just below the falls, the trail turns left and climbs away from the river. Follow signs for both loop trails. The understory flourishes in inverse proportion to the hemlocks in the canopy as we rise through the woods.

A spur to a Beaver Pond goes right. At the end of the short trail a beaver dam and lodge are visible upstream, to the right. It's not possible to be sure from year to year where beavers will live but their operations are fascinating whenever we get the chance to observe them.

Return from the detour and go right onto the Hilltop Loop. The trail continues on higher ground where maples and white pines dominate old pastures. This is a common pattern of succession as sun-loving white pines quickly colonize open land. A photo in the Jericho Historical Society shows Jericho Village from this hill when fields rolled down to the village.

A large white pine on the right side of the trail is a wolf or field tree. Its strong side branches grew in an open field, something not possible in the confines of crowded woods. Like a wolf, such trees once stood alone in the field. Both names are commonly used.

At a fork in the trail, stay right on the Hilltop Loop. Red and sugar maples, beech, white oak, and yellow and paper birch dominate the woods. Several gray birches are dead or dying, perhaps for lack of sunlight. Beech saplings sprout from roots of parent trees. Striped maple or moosewood is plentiful and conspicuous with its pale green striped bark. Its leaves are huge to catch enough sunshine in the understory.

Several water bars cross the trail to keep it from eroding as we descend to the valley. At the base of the slope the trails merge near a picnic table and the spur returns to the parking area.

SNOW AND SNOWFLAKE BENTLEY

Jericho is the home of Snowflake Bentley. For nearly a half century, W. A. "Snowflake" Bentley (1865-1931), a farmer and self-taught photographer, shivered through the winters in an unheated shed, capturing snow crystals on film for science and posterity.

After catching a snowflake on a black board, Bentley hurried to shelter. With a magnifying glass he identified a promising specimen and then nudged it into position on a microscope slide using a small wing feather. His camera fitted with a microscope, Bentley pointed it to the sky to capture the snowflake with light coming through it. The average exposure time was 20 seconds!

Snow is crystallized water that forms on a particle of dust, its underlying structure too small for the naked eye to see. When we see snowflakes, in various six-sided forms, we are seeing a mass of individual crystals.

Many plants and animals depend on an insulating blanket of snow for winter survival. As snowflakes fall, landing every which way, air is trapped between them. Not only does the snowy layer retain warmth, it hides animals and their food caches from predators.

Snow can lift shorter animals up to branch tips and a snow crust may support white-tailed deer as they search for food. A deep dump of powder is a problem for deer with their thin legs and tiny, cloven hooves. Small animals, like mice and voles, are light enough to stay on the surface while larger predators, foxes, coyotes, and the cats may be hampered by deep accumulation.

A thick coating of snow on an ice-covered pond keeps the ice from thickening and gives beaver and muskrat more room to maneuver to their stored food. Snow protects plant roots from deep cold spells as well as from damaging freeze and thaw cycles.

A history of Snowflake Bentley and a selection of his photographs are on display in the Jericho Historical Society located in the Old Mill.

GETTING THERE

From the Five Corners in Essex, the intersection of Rte. 15 and Rte. 2A, take Rte. 15 east. Follow Rte. 15, 5.3 miles to the Old Mill on the left. Parking and the trailhead are to the rear.

FOR MORE INFORMATION

Winooski Valley Park District
www.wvpd.org

7 Rena Calkins Trail and Bike Trail Intervale

One sixth of all open land in Burlington is in the Intervale. Fertile farmland in the Winooski River floodplain is an incubator for sustainable agriculture projects.

BURLINGTON, VT
0.6 MILE ON RENA CALKINS TRAIL, PLUS ABOUT 1 MILE, ROUND-TRIP, ON DIRT FARM ROAD.
1-1.5 HOURS
EASY
(BIKE TRAIL TO ETHAN ALLEN HOMESTEAD, 2.1 MILES, ONE-WAY.)
PETS MUST BE LEASHED.

THE DICTIONARY DEFINES INTERVALE as low, flat land between hills or along a river. Near the Winooski River, in the towns of Burlington, Colchester, and Winooski, the Intervale is 3,900 acres of fertile agricultural and wetland. This floodplain was first inhabited at the end of the Ice Age, about 10,000 years ago.

Archeologists have dated a settlement near the Ethan Allen Homestead to 4,500 years ago. Six hundred years ago in the Intervale, Abenakis experimented with cold-resistant corn hybrids while growing the traditional three sisters, corn, bean, and squash.

In Colonial days, the Intervale became a breadbasket, producing grains, flax, meat, dairy products, and lumber for export. Later, with competition from western states, dairy farms became dominant, a situation which prevailed into this century.

In the last one hundred years, commerce and industry took advantage of the under-appreciated land. Paupers camped and dumps and a slaughterhouse dotted the landscape. Since 1950, a landfill, the Northern Connector (Route 127), an electrical generating plant, and several radio towers have been constructed.

Today, the Intervale is being renewed. In the 1970s the Winooski Valley Park District began acquiring land for public access and the City of Burlington established community gardens. In the early 1980s, Gardeners Supply, a catalog company committed to organic gardening, located in the Intervale, spearheading clean-up efforts and the restoration of the soil to organic certification. In 1988, the non-profit Intervale Foundation was established to continue these efforts and to

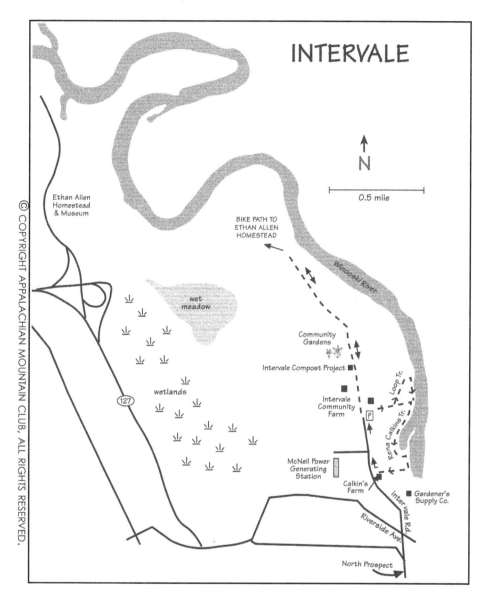

INTERVALE

N

0.5 mile

Ethan Allen
Homestead
& Museum

BIKE PATH TO
ETHAN ALLEN
HOMESTEAD

Winooski River

wet
meadow

Community
Gardens

Intervale Compost Project ■▶

Loop Tr.

wetlands

127

Intervale
Community
Farm

P

Rena Calkins Tr.

McNeil Power
Generating
Station

Calkin's
Farm

Gardener's
Supply Co.

Intervale Rd.

Riverside Ave.

North Prospect

revitalize the area as a social, economic, and natural resource. The foundation, now called Intervale Center, serves as a laboratory for sustainable, community-based agriculture and has a goal of supplying ten percent of Burlington's food needs.

To fully appreciate the Intervale, I recommend a walk along the river, past the businesses, and through the farmlands. A series of pedestrian-friendly dirt trails and farm roads follow the river two miles to the Ethan Allen Homestead. (See page 65.) An exciting addition in 2008 was the grooming of cross-country ski trails.

The Local Motion Trail finder is the best source for up-to-date conditions: www.localmotion.org/trails/

• • • • • •

Begin on the Rena Calkins Trail. Walk through the split rail fence and look for white blazes with the interlinked letters, RC. A strong musty smell is a reminder that the compost project is not far away.

Water-loving trees dominate the woods on this fertile river bottom soil. Cottonwood, green ash, crack willow, American elm, silver and red maple, and box elder are the dominant trees, the cottonwood growing to greatest height. Box elder usually does not grow beyond forty feet and often has multiple trunks at odd angles. Jewelweed and wood nettles join sensitive and ostrich ferns to create a tall, lush understory. Remember, wood nettles have alternate leaves and stinging nettles opposite leaves.

River flooding is a regular spring occurrence, coating everything in mud and littering the floodplain with leaves and branches. For thousands of years the Winooski has carried topsoil downstream, dropping it in the delta.

The Loop Trail, blazed LT, makes a detour to the left. The trail turns right and then bears right again continuing along the riverbank through the floodplain forest. A tangle of vines adds to the feeling of a forest primeval. Hog peanut, with three leaflets, usually creeps near the ground while wild cucumber and Virginia

Hogs like to eat the underground seed pods of the hog peanut.

creeper climb high in the trees. Virginia creeper leaves, with five, toothed leaflets, turn a deep red in fall and it produces blue berries eaten by birds, mice, chipmunks, and skunks. Deer browse its foliage and twigs. Wild cucumber, also called balsam apple, has maple-like leaves and produces a spiny fruit containing four flat seeds.

In the shallows along the river, you may see shorebirds: great blue heron, green heron, black crown night heron, Virginia rail, and sandpiper. Migratory waterfowl may include Canada and snow geese and mallard, American green-winged teal, ring neck, and wood ducks.

Beavers have gnawed a number of trees as the trail continues on the sandy river bank. Shaggy-barked silver maple and crack willow have roots seasonally in the water. This is an opportunity to compare the distinctive barks of two hydrophilic trees. Cottonwood bark is deeply and regularly ridged while silver maple bark shreds vertically.

The river appears to be barely flowing. Water striders skim over the flat pools and falling insects dapple the surface like raindrops. Turn right, away from the river toward the Gardener's Supply building. Walk across the fields and through the well-tended gardens. Return to the road and turn right.

The McNeil Electric plant lies across the road from Gardener's Supply. This innovative facility burns wood chips, a forest byproduct. The wood depot, adjacent to the McNeil plant, diverts scrap wood, brush, and Christmas trees from the landfill into the hoppers at McNeil.

The Calkins Farm, the last dairy farm in the Intervale, is on the right. The 1860 farmhouse is registered with the State of Vermont Division for Historic Preservation. Continue on the dirt road past the Rena Calkins Trailhead.

You will pass the Intervale Compost Project on the right. ICP is a cooperative partnership between the Intervale Center and Chittenden Solid Waste District. The ICP received Vermont's first permit for commercial-scale food composting. Fletcher Allen Health Care adds the hospital's (pre-patient) kitchen waste to a soup of leaves, yard waste, food, and horse manure. The compost is used by Intervale farmers and sold to the public.

The Intervale Center's Farms Program incubates new farms, giving access to affordable land, shared equipment, greenhouse space, and irrigation for small-scale organic farmers. You will pass a number of these farms along the dirt road.

The Intervale Community Farm (ICF) is also on the left, a venture in Community Supported Agriculture. ICF is a share-based organic garden providing members with weekly allotments of produce throughout the growing season. Members' shares pay for labor, equipment, and seed. On your right, you will pass fields that stretch to the river. Some are worked by ICF, others by Arethusa Farm.

On the left, beyond ICF are community gardens. One of many such locations in Burlington, these community gardens provide an important bit of earth and continuity to Burlington's growing population of immigrants, many of whom arrive bearing seeds from the old country.

Although the road is closed to vehicles by a metal gate, the walking and bike paths continue. Corn, hay, and alfalfa fields stretch toward the river on the right. An algae-covered, tire-filled pond is a reminder the Intervale's past. The farm road turns to gravel and winds through agricultural land, some of which is fallow, arriving eventually at the Ethan Allen Homestead.

Turn around where you wish and retrace your steps.

LOOK BEFORE YOU TOUCH

Stinging and wood nettles look similar and it's best to recognize them without doing a touch test because stinging nettles leave raised welts which sting and itch.

Both plants have coarsely toothed oval leaves. Leaves of the stinging nettle are opposite each other along the stem while wood nettle leaves come off the stem alternately. Stinging nettle leaves have heart-shaped bases. Very young shoots and leaves of stinging nettle can be made into soup!

GETTING THERE

From Main Street and South Prospect Streets at the University of Vermont. Take Prospect Street north. It jogs slightly to the left at 0.3 mile as it crosses Colchester Avenue (becoming North Prospect Street). Continue to a traffic light at Riverside Avenue, 0.6 mile. Go straight, although you are now on Intervale Road which crosses the railroad at 0.1 mile. The road turns to dirt in 0.3 mile. The parking area is another 0.1 mile on the right.

FOR MORE INFORMATION

Intervale Center
128 Intervale Road
Burlington, VT 05401
802-660-3508
www.intervale.org

8 Ethan Allen Homestead

Wetlands and fertile farmland share the floodplain of the Winooski River, land that attracted Native Americans thousands of years ago. The homestead of Ethan Allen and historical exhibits in an education center are open to visitors.

BURLINGTON, VT
HOMESTEAD AND PENINSULA LOOPS TO
WETLANDS WALKS NORTH AND SOUTH
2.8 MILES
1.5 TO 2 HOURS
EASY
PETS MUST BE LEASHED.

THE WINOOSKI VALLEY PARK DISTRICT (WVPD) manages one of the largest urban natural areas in Vermont. Seven towns in the lower Winooski watershed, Burlington, Colchester, Essex, Jericho, Williston, Winooski and South Burlington, share the cost of conservation of these properties.

The final few miles of the Winooski River, as it meanders to Lake Champlain, are a broad fertile plain. The wetlands and fertile soils attracted Native Americans as early as 3,000 BC. Later, the Abenakis relied on the Winooski as a transportation route for canoes in summer and as an icy pathway in winter.

Early European settlers lost no time in exploring the valley for its fish, wildlife, timber, farmland, and waterpower. Samuel de Champlain first paddled the lake in 1609. By 1790 a settlement was growing at the falls a few miles upstream.

In 1787 Ethan and Fanny Allen built their home in the Intervale. The Park District preserved the homestead in 1981. Exhibits at the Hill-Brownell Education Center elaborate on early Vermont history and the life of Ethan Allen.

The Homestead and Peninsula Loops, each less than a mile, give the flavor of the lazy meanders of the Winooski. Two wetlands walks occupy long-abandoned river channels now evolving into drier land. The seasonal River Loop lies at the edge of meadow, young woods, and river. A pedestrian-friendly bike trail links the Homestead with the Intervale (see page 60) two miles distant. A paved recreation path connects with the extensive network of area bike routes. We will walk around the peninsula and through the wetlands.

Pick up a map and wetlands walk brochure at the outdoor information kiosk near at the parking area.

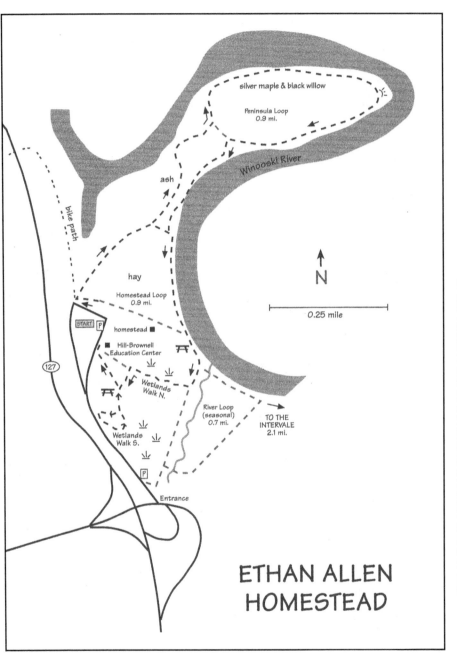

silver maple & black willow

Peninsula Loop
0.9 mi.

Winooski River

ash

bike path

N

0.25 mile

hay

Homestead Loop
0.9 mi.

START P

homestead ■

■ Hill-Brownell
Education Center

Wetlands
Walk N.

River Loop
(seasonal)
0.7 mi.

TO THE
INTERVALE
2.1 mi.

Wetlands
Walk S.

127

P

Entrance

ETHAN ALLEN
HOMESTEAD

• • • • • •

Begin by taking the Homestead Loop, which crosses a grassy hayfield. Go left and then right across the fields toward the end of the peninsula. After about ten minutes, the Homestead Loop circles right and the connector to the Peninsula Loop goes straight ahead. Go straight, passing through low, oft-flooded woodlands. These willows, green ash, cottonwood, and silver maple trees spend part of each spring with their roots submerged. After about five minutes the trail reemerges into another field. This is the Peninsula Loop that follows a meander of the Winooski. Walk this loop clockwise looking for blue herons in the shallows.

Along the perimeter of the peninsula are black ash trees. Their blossoms attract mourning cloaks, dark brown butterflies with a band of yellow and white trim along the edge of their wings. Mourning cloaks overwinter as adults and warm up with the spring sunshine. They can be found looking for sparse nourishment in early flowers or tree sap.

Cottonwood and black willow grow to great size in this moist environment, their huge trunks rooted near the water's edge. Several red or swamp maples, with shaggy bark, have multiple trunks. The river is slow and tranquil and the scene of cows, grassy fields, and picturesque silos across the river could be an English landscape painting.

Look for animal and bird tracks in the mud at river's edge. The trail bends right at the end of the peninsula after about ten minutes. The riverbanks are steeply cut and sediment has been dropped on the inside of the turn. Sun-loving sumac grows on the left as the trail returns toward the Homestead.

After another five to ten minutes the Pond Trail goes left, passing through the low wooded stretch again. Beavers are sometimes in evidence here. Poplar trees are among their favorite foods. River flooding has deposited sandy soil. In another five minutes the trail rejoins the Homestead Loop. Bear left and be wary of crumbling banks along the river. The soft soil is eroded every year by high water. After another five minutes the trail arrives at a canoe launch and a picnic table in a shady grove.

Turn your back to the river and follow signs to the River Loop Trail. Then look for signs to the Wetlands Walk North.

The Wetlands Walk North trail soon branches to the right. It passes briefly through young woods before arriving at a boardwalk. This old channel of the Winooski River is returning to dry ground. Slow your pace to a crawl as the wetland is teeming with life.

Smartweed, milkweed, joe-pye weed, ragweed, box elder, elm, bur cucumber, sensitive fern, and orange spotted jewelweed tangle in a marsh and field on the left.

As the ground becomes more waterlogged wetland plants dominate, silver maple, box elder, willow, speckled alder, turtlehead, and cattails. Duckweed coats the open water. Arrowhead (Sagittaria latifolia) is a wetland beauty. Its leaves are shaped like arrowheads and in late summer a leafless stalk bears small, three-petaled white flowers. Ducks and muskrats eat its underwater tubers or rhizomes. Another stunning denizen of the wetland is water arum or wild calla (Calla palustris). Related to jack-in-the-pulpit and philodendron, which it resembles, water arum produces a broad white bloom similar to the calla lily. It looks surprisingly tropical for Vermont.

A boardwalk crosses very wet ground and frogs scatter at our approach. Grasshoppers, green frogs, raccoons, and muskrat co-exist in the marsh. Red-tailed and marsh hawks may soar overhead and red-winged blackbirds nest in cattails. Aggressive males fight for territory in the spring and are very protective through the nesting season.

At the end of the boardwalk take the steps up the bank. Follow signs left towards Wetlands Walk South. This seasonal trail is only available in summer and fall. Walk past the New Discovery Garden and picnic shelter, across a grassy meadow to the trail. If you plan to follow the self-guided tour with numbered stops, follow the gravel road left 0.1 mile to a second sign on the left for Wetlands Walk South. The trail begins at the bottom of the steps.

On the bank several musclewood trees present quite a sight. As many as twenty young trunks spring from the roots of each tree.

Skunk cabbage (Symplocarpus foetidus) is abundant in the drier reaches of this wetland, emerging in early spring. When the plant is bruised an odor resembling decaying flesh attracts insects to pollinate it. Skunk cabbage sprouts so early in the spring that respiration resulting from its rapid growth can melt surrounding snow.

Its flower is a remarkable sight. A deep red-colored cup, the spathe that resembles a leaf, opens to reveal a golf-ball sized knob, called the spadix that is covered with tiny yellow flowers. The leaves are bright green and resemble a loose head of cabbage. Skunk cabbage, near the northern limit of its range, is only found in the Champlain Valley of northern Vermont.

To the right is a remnant of open pond, filling rapidly with non-woody or herbaceous plants like cattails, jewelweed, and arrowhead. This first stage of wetland succession produces a marsh. Insects and amphibians breed in the open water.

Water-loving ferns flourish. Cinnamon, sensitive, and royal fern are robust. By late summer sensitive fern sends up its beady fertile frond and royal fern sports feathery tips on its fertile fronds.

Skunk cabbage in early spring.

The second stage of wetland succession is a swamp, which includes woody trees and shrubs: speckled alder, witch hazel, red-osier dogwood, red or swamp maple- with many trunks, and willow. Black or swamp willow (Salix nigra) can tolerate several feet of standing water as its roots resist rot. It often resembles a giant shrub with multiple trunks. Black willow branchlets are very brittle at their base and, when broken off by the wind, readily take root. Willows provide drier islands where less water-tolerant plants can grow.

The middle section of the wetland is very wet indeed. Cattails tower overhead and water-loving plants create a luxuriant tangle. Among the ferns, arrowhead, jewelweed, skunk cabbage, and cattails, turtlehead (Chelone glabra) bloom extravagantly in late summer. A wetland plant, its white, pink, or lavender flowers resemble turtle's heads. They bloom at the end of a stalk that can range from one to four feet.

Steps climb out of the wetland. At the top, next to a picnic table, notice a red maple, with a diagonal design around its trunk, which grew with a vine entwining it.

WETLANDS

Wetlands may be marshes, swamps, swamp forests, fens, or bogs, all of which occur in Vermont. They occur where upland and aquatic environments meet, either beside bodies of water or in isolation. Wetlands exist where soil is waterlogged for any part of the growing season, from one week to year-round. Once the soil becomes waterlogged, its oxygen is quickly depleted. Even after the water has receded the oxygen is slow to return to the soil.

A marsh develops when non-woody plants take root in the shallows of open water. A swamp follows as woody shrubs and trees invade, eventually becoming a swamp forest when the trees thicken to form a canopy of leaves. A bog (see Colchester Bog, page 88) is an acidic wetland with little or no flow of fresh water. Sphagnum peatlands and heaths dominate bogs. Fens host similar plants but a flow of groundwater supports a wider range of vegetation.

Upland plants die in wetlands while plants adapted to a waterlogged environment thrive. Adaptations of wetland plants include shallow root systems with significant aboveground sections to maximize contact with the air, multiple trunks for the same purpose, and a biochemical ability to thrive in anaerobic (without oxygen) conditions. Carnivorous plants also live in bogs and fens.

Surface water is filtered and absorbed in wetlands making them important to flood control. Wetlands provide food, camouflage, and shelter to birds and animals not available in other habitats.

HOURS, FACILITIES

Open from dawn to dusk. A waterless outhouse near the picnic shelter is open year-round. Restrooms in the foyer are open seven months of the year. The Ethan Allen Homestead has separate hours and an admission charge.

GETTING THERE

From Burlington take the Northern Connector, Rte. 127, north for 0.9 mile to the first exit, North Avenue and Beaches. While still on the exit ramp you will see a sign to the Ethan Allen Homestead at 0.4 mile. Turn right and follow the entrance road past the first small parking area to the welcome center and main parking areas at 0.5 mile.

FOR MORE INFORMATION

Winooski Valley Park District
www.wvpd.org
Ethan Allen Homestead
Ethan Allen Homestead
Burlington, VT 05408
802-865-4556
www.EthanAllenHomestead.org

9 Cassavant Nature Trail, Winooski One, and Salmon Hole

The Cassavant Nature Trail is a scenic walk along the Winooski River including some dramatic cliffs. A half mile away, Winooski One is a modern 7.4 megawatt hydroelectric dam that incorporates a fish lift. It was the first in Vermont to receive Low Impact Certification. Across the river, in Burlington, the Salmon Hole is traditional fishing spot that was once at the base of the natural falls. The river has carved potholes and other formations in the limestone. Salmon Hole is connected by a 0.7 mile walking path, the River Walk Foot Path, to Intervale Road, just a short distance from the Intervale. (See page 60.)

WINOOSKI AND BURLINGTON, VT
CASSAVANT NATURE TRAIL
1.4 MILES
1 HOUR
MODERATE
PETS MUST BE LEASHED.
WALK TO WINOOSKI ONE, **0.5** MILE, EASY
WALK TO SALMON HOLE, **0.2** MILE, EASY

AS EARLY AS 3,000 BC, the Great Falls on the Winooski River were a focus for human settlement. Winooski means wild onion in the Abenaki language. Until about 1,000 AD, hunter-gatherers spent time in the area.

Winooski Falls was attractive to early European settlers because of its proximity to farmland in the Intervale, pine woodlands, and water to power mills. In 1772, Ira Allen, youngest brother of Ethan Allen, built a log cabin here with Remember Baker. By 1790 a community, including an iron foundry, had grown up around the falls. At the Salmon Hole, deeper than it is today, small ships were built and barges loaded with logs for Quebec. The only way to cross the river was on the ice or Ira Allen's ferry.

Over the years mills clustered around the upper and lower falls: flour, grist, paper, saw, textile, and mills that turned flaxseed into linseed oil. In 1870, a gristmill produced 500 barrels of flour each twenty-four hours.

CASSAVANT NATURE TRAIL

Salmon Hole Park
and Winooski One

Central Vermont R.R.

West Canal St.

2 & 7

CITY OF WINOOSKI

Main St.

E. Allen St.

SALMON HOLE PARK

to River Walk

START

15

Riverside Ave.

Winooski One and fish lift

CITY OF BURLINGTON

park boundary

Exit 15

89

Cassavant Nature Trail

oats

cliffs

Winooski River

N

0.25 mile

Villages grew up on both sides of the river but fire and successive floods on the Burlington side eventually spelled an end to industry there.

Woolen mills prospered intermittently. During the Merino sheep boom in the 1830s, Vermont's woolen mills exploded from thirty-three to 334. In 1837, the Burlington Woolen Mill had nine buildings, among them the largest in Vermont. It was powered by a water mill thirty-six feet in diameter.

Living in mill-owned tenements, unskilled immigrants worked long hours in poor conditions. Business ebbed and flowed over a century, booming as wool was used for Civil War uniforms, railroad and police uniforms, and again during both World Wars. In 1954 the last mills closed.

In the late 1970s, civic and business groups joined forces to renew the area.

The Champlain Mill was transformed into commercial space, the Colchester Merino Mill became the Woolen Mill Apartments, and Winooski One produces renewable energy. More recently mixed-use buildings have brought new life to the area. Vermont Student Assistance Corporation (VSAC) has its headquarters here and there are hundreds of new housing units. The River Walk, a public park, stretches along the river.

• • • • • •

The Cassavant Nature Trail starts behind the wooden barrier, plunging from a busy street into the woods. A distant urban cacophony lingers: airplanes, helicopters, the peel of midday church bells, and car and truck traffic. At certain times of day a symphony of railroad horns, whistles, diesel engines, screeching wheels, and crossing bells fills the air. Young, sun-loving trees grow in the damp soil: box elder, big-toothed aspen, green elm, dogwood, and sumac. An open cattail marsh and tree swamp are visible to the right as the trail descends and traffic noise disappears.

Boardwalks cross a few wet sections and false Solomon's seal grows to large dimensions, producing cascades of rosy berries. A stream bursts from a culvert at the top of a hillside and rushes toward the swamp. Cattails, orange spotted jewelweed, hog peanut, and ragweed form a wetland thicket.

The trail crosses a bridge, rises slightly, and passes a huge red oak with a double trunk. Swamp maple, shagbark and bitternut hickory, red oak, hop hornbeam, paper birch, ash, cherry, and blue beech or ironwood fill the woods. The marsh towers with enormous phragmites, invasive reeds topped with showy tufts of seeds. Duckweed flourishes on open water and speckled alder thrives in the wet soil.

The path arrives at the edge of the Winooski River. A right turn takes us along the river and to the River Walk in the center of Winooski. For the moment, however, we will turn left. The river is wide and lazy with sandy patches of shoreline. The trail passes beneath a gargantuan Interstate bridge. It then regains the bank with lovely views upriver to the falls and railroad trestle. Sheer limestone cliffs dotted with northern white cedar form the opposite bank.

The trail rises through young woods dominated by multi-trunked red oak, hop hornbeam, and alternate-leaved dogwood. A detour to the right ends at the sandy riverbank. The main trail continues uphill to the top of the cliffs through woods of northern white cedar, white pine, and red and white oak. Bracken fern dominates the understory. Beware of poison ivy.

Hang on to young children here. The trail, which ends just before the railroad track, affords magnificent views of the falls and limestone cliffs of the Winooski Gorge. Linger for a moment on this sunny perch listening to the water crashing over the falls.

Retrace your steps. At the trail intersection by the river turn right to return to the parking area or continue on foot to Winooski One and the Salmon Hole.

At Winooski One a fish trap combined with a truck program enable migra-

Limestone cliffs along the Winooski River.

tory salmon to return to their upriver spawning grounds. The fish lift is a cooperative program involving federal and state fish and wildlife agencies along with Green Mountain Power and the Winooski One Partnership. Installation and operation of the fish passage facility is a requirement of Winooski One's license. If you are lucky, you may see fish being measured and tagged before trucking. (Call ahead for information.)

Until the early 1800s, salmon was abundant in Lake Champlain. Adult salmon swim up the tributaries of their birth to spawn each fall. Heavy logging in the colonial era caused erosion and silt buildups. Silt suffocated incubating eggs and the loss of forest cover allowed the sun to heat streams to temperatures threatening to young salmon. Dams prevented salmon from returning to spawn and the huge population of salmon blocked below the dams made for easy harvests.

Restoration programs began in 1973. These many faceted programs include stocking, sea lamprey control, monitoring of land-use practices, pollution reduction, and fish transport. The stocked fish are raised at the Ed Weed Fish Hatchery in Grand Isle. (See page 47.) Trucked fish are placed upstream of Winooski One and two other dams where they have access to twenty miles of the Winooski and more than eight miles of tributaries.

Playing with nature is tricky business. Over the years the Department of Fish and Wildlife has introduced young fish to multiple locations at various ages to find the most successful combination of age, location, and flow patterns. If the fish are not introduced to the tributaries at a time of high flow, they will not smolt, or leave the mouth of the river to live in the open lake. Experimentation continues in the hope of maintaining a stable population of migratory fish in Lake Champlain.

Salmon Hole, a favorite fishing spot, is just across the Winooski River in Burlington. Many of the game fish of Lake Champlain spawn here. Walleye, pike, steelhead trout, and landlocked salmon are among the species caught here. The river has carved potholes and other interesting formations in the 500 million-year-old limestone.

GETTING THERE

From I-89, take northbound Exit 15. Turn left on Rte. 15 and continue west for 0.3 mile. Parking area for Cassavant Nature Trail is on left.

To reach Winooski One by car, continue west 0.4 mile on Rte. 15 (East Allen). Go around the rotary and take a right on West Canal Street just before the bridge. Parking is at meters on the street.

From Winooski One to the Salmon Hole, cross the Winooski River on Rte.

7 and go immediately right at the light. Parking is on the right, 0.2 mile from West Canal Street. A path leads down to the Salmon Hole.

FOR MORE INFORMATION

Steelhead, an introduced sport fish native to the Pacific, spawn in the spring and migrate upstream from April through June. Salmon return to spawn in October or November. You may call for information on the migrating fish at the Winooski One lift.

Department of Fish and Wildlife
111 West Street
Essex Junction, VT 05452
802-878-1564 or 800-640-3714.
http://www.vtfishandwildlife.com/
City of Winooski
Department of Recreation
655-6410
www.onioncity.com

10 East Woods Natural Area

Old woods and a brook saved from suburban sprawl. A nice winter destination and good for children.	SOUTH BURLINGTON, VT **0.6** MILE **45** MINUTES MODERATE PETS MUST BE LEASHED.

EAST WOODS NATURAL AREA is testimony to a committed community. In 1930, neighbors raised $4,000 to protect the woods from being cut for saw timber. At the urging of Botany professor Dr. H. E. Perkins, the University of Vermont (UVM) contributed the additional $7,500 needed to buy the land. The original preserve was more than twice its current size. In the 1960s the interstate connector bisected the land and the parcel north of the highway was sold.

This isle of natural beauty, surrounded by highways and sprawl, is one of UVM's Natural Areas and is used as an outdoor laboratory by students. East Woods has been said to support as many as 56 species of woody plants on approximately 50 acres. The area contains some of the largest hemlocks and red and white pines in the Burlington area and has the richest flora of any known area of comparable size in northern Vermont. A mixture of forest types nestles in its contours and Potash Brook flows between sandy banks.

• • • • • •

The trail begins just beyond an interpretive sign of the Lake Champlain Byways. In late summer sprays of elderberries cluster in the understory. Several uncharacteristic white pines are scattered through this stretch, with multiple tortured trunks that begin five or six feet above ground. White pines have bundles of five (w-h-i-t-e) long needles and healthy specimens have one trunk. When these white pines were young an insect, the white pine weevil, attacked the terminal shoot. Side branches, usually small and horizontal, compensated to produce these unusual trees. White pine, like northern white cedar, contains vitamin C in its bark. Before the availability of year-round fruit, those who suffered from scurvy, a deficit of vitamin C, consumed these barks.

Spring wildflowers that tolerate acidic conditions grow beneath the canopy of

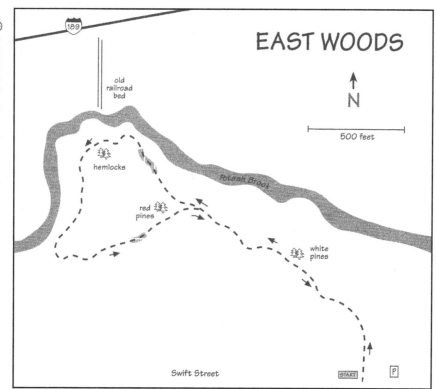

EAST WOODS

N

500 feet

old
railroad
bed

hemlocks

red
pines

Potash Brook

white
pines

Swift Street

START

P

189

pines: star flower, partridgeberry, and wild lily-of-the-valley. Conifers block sun-light year-round and the understory is dwindling with increasing shade.

The trail descends a gully, testimony to the power erosion in sandy soils. East-ern hemlocks are thick on these banks of sand. (See Eastern Hemlocks, page 81.) Potash Brook gurgles below to the right. Potash was one of the first exports of the United States. As farmers cleared the forests and burned the trees, tons of wood ash resulted. This ash was boiled and the resulting potash was sold to Europeans to make fertilizer and soap.

Here and across the brook we see a prepared railroad bed. In 1898, a small commuter railway was being constructed until funding was cut.

Hemlocks are thick overhead and there is very little understory. Rotting trunks of paper birches and conifers crisscross the thick carpet of needles underfoot. The birches, deprived of sunlight, failed to thrive and died. East Woods is littered with fallen trees, or blow downs, due at least in part to the sandy soil. Even the giant hemlocks have shallow root systems. Somehow they cling to these hillsides for many years before windstorms or the weight of a falling neighbor ends their life.

Another denizen of these woods is wintergreen (Gaultheria procumbens). The small evergreen heath hugs the ground with alternate, dark green leaves. It bears a white bell-like flower and eventually a red berry. Wintergreen prefers cool, damp woods and is often found beneath oaks and pines. Its glossy leaves are aromatic with wintergreen oil.

The trail continues downhill to the banks of Potash Brook. Hemlocks now share the sunlight with beech, red oak, and ash. The sandy path follows the stream for several minutes. Hobblebush, a member of the viburnum family, likes cool, damp woods and is usually found at elevation. Perhaps cool air slumping down the ridge across the brook makes these shrubs think they are in the mountains. Their heart-shaped leaves lie nearly horizontal along the stem and their white blossoms can be six inches in diameter.

The sand underfoot is the remnant of an old beach. At the end of the Ice Age, about 10,000 years ago, with the land still compressed from the weight of glacial ice, salt water flowed south from the St. Lawrence River to create the Champlain

White trillium thrive in the lowlands of the Champlain Valley.

Sea. (See Button Bay, page 158.) This sea covered an area greater than that of Lake Champlain. East Woods would have been on its shore.

The trail leaves the brook and curves left. As the path climbs trillium, trout lilies, and jack-in-the-pulpit thrive here. In a few minutes we arrive at a plateau. Mature hemlocks and red and white pines, many of them giants, mix in these woods. It's interesting to compare the barks of the three in close proximity. You can distinguish the hemlock by its short needles and the red pine by the reddish patches of bark on its trunk.

Striped maple, with its green and white candy stripes, shades a large patch of partridgeberry on the right. This evergreen ground cover has tiny dark green, heart-shaped leaves with a white central vein. Its red berries are a favorite of the partridge.

With the exception of one or two arrows the trail is almost never marked. Yet the worn track is easy to follow.

A white pine on the left has been excavated by a pileated woodpecker. Their excavations are rectangular in shape and often large. This begs the question of whether these woodpeckers are beneficial or destructive to living trees. While they remove harmful insects from beneath the bark they also expose the pulp of the tree to destructive fungus and bacteria. Both theories have supporters.

When you arrive back at the main trail turn right to return to the trailhead.

EASTERN HEMLOCKS

Hemlocks often grow in pure stands as they shade out competitors. Their needles are flat, about a half inch long, and are soft to the touch. One of our longest-lived trees, hemlocks can live six centuries and grow to eighty feet (in the Appalachians they have reached 160 feet). They favor cool, shady ravines and will grow in a wide range of soils. Hemlocks can germinate in any moist locale and are often found growing on boulders or rotting stumps.

There is concern for the health of hemlocks as a devastating insect defoliator, the woolly adelgid, moves north through New England. No hemlock has been known to survive its attack.

GETTING THERE

From Interstate 89, take Exit 13 to I-189. Follow the connector to the end. Turn left onto Rte. 7 south. At 0.1 mile, turn left at the light onto Swift Street. Park at a turnout on the left side of the road in 0.6 mile. There is space for a number of cars.

FOR MORE INFORMATION
University of Vermont
Environmental Program
http://www.uvm.edu/~envprog/

• ALSO IN THE AREA •

Another UVM Natural Area, Redstone Quarry, is nearby. Reddish-brown Monkton quartzite was quarried here for over 100 years. A rock cliff exposes colorful striations, showing the layering of the sandstone, which, under conditions of heat and pressure, metamorphosed into quartzite. The small wetland at its base attracts birds, frogs and other wildlife. It's a nice place for a picnic.

From the light at I-189 and Rte. 7, take Rte. 7 north for 0.9 mile to Hoover Street. Turn right and continue 0.2 mile to a small parking area.

11 Mud Pond Conservation Land

Hemlock woods give way to alder swamp, marsh and bog at the edge of the pond.

WILLISTON, VT
1 MILE
45 MINUTES
EASY
DOGS PERMITTED.
NO HORSES OR BICYCLES.

NOT FAR FROM WILLISTON'S TAFTS CORNERS, Vermont's often-maligned symbol of sprawl, lays an island of tranquility. Deep hemlock woods muffle the hum of the interstate and the roar of departing jets. Mud Pond, headwater of Allen Brook, is surrounded by wetlands and a 141-acre oasis in one of Vermont's fastest growing towns.

Six-acre Mud Pond fills a kettle hole left by receding glaciers of the Ice Age. The shallow water covers up to forty feet of decomposed of organic debris. Mud Pond has characteristics of both a bog and a fen, and is one of only two examples of this type of pond in the state of Vermont. A perimeter peat mat and bog vegetation encircle the open water. Pollen from core samples of this peat indicates it is more than 6,000 years old. In more recent times the land has been used for logging, agriculture, gravel mining, peat extraction, and ice harvesting. Stands of white pine have grown up on the old pastureland.

Horses, carts, cars, and kids have all gotten stuck in the legendary mire that gives Mud Pond its name. In an effort to preserve the peat mat and bog plants the shoreline is no longer accessible. A small set of bleachers near the pond affords great viewing.

• • • • • •

Take the trail from the parking area. White pine needles cushion your footfall. The trail is easy to follow although rarely marked. Follow the black arrows and you will not get lost.

White pines give way to woods of hemlocks, black cherry, hop hornbeam, yellow and paper birch, oak, and maple. Canada Mayflower, partridgeberry, starflower, Indian cucumber-root, goldthread, wood sorrel, and trillium are among the wildflowers tolerant of acidic conditions. The vegetation reflects the underly-

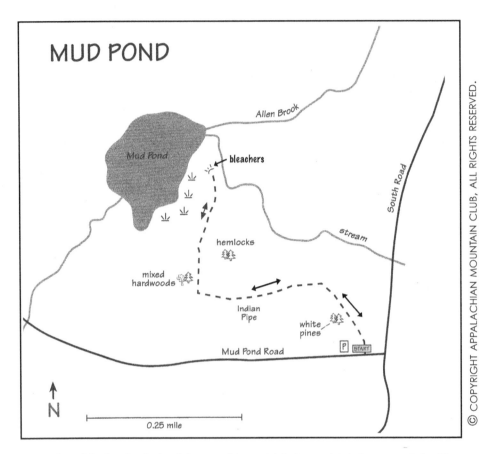

ing soil and bedrock, derived from schist, which is not high in natural fertility. There is no bloodroot or basswood in these woods.

Within five minutes the trail goes downhill briefly before coming to an intersection. Turn left toward the pond as indicated by an arrow.

Clumps of club moss or Lycopodium dot the forest floor. Common names include princess pine, fir club moss, ground cedar, ground pine, and running cedar, sometimes the same name given to two or more species. (See lycopodium, page 87.) Indian pipe (Monotropa uniflora) is prolific in mid- to late summer, its nearly translucent pink or white stems rising from beneath the leaf litter. The plants have no chlorophyll and derive their nourishment from decayed organic matter. The clustered stems turn black as they die.

Boardwalks pass over several wet sections where hummocks of moisture-loving sensitive and cinnamon fern abound. Cinnamon fern can be distinguished from interrupted fern by a woolly tuft at the base of its leaflets. Look carefully at the underside of the frond.

When the trail comes to an intersection with a wider path, follow the arrow right toward the pond. (A left turn at this point will lead to a year-round trail to Oak Hill Road. Fellowship of the Wheel maintains these bicycle trails.) The track descends through woods of birch, beech, red maple, and hemlock. Striped maple, saplings, and herbs are lush in the understory and the occasional red trillium nods its head. Partridgeberry is also abundant, its orange-red berries poking from a thicket of tiny green and white leaves.

The trail levels out at a mucky section that explodes in summer with jewelweed or touch-me-nots. Several sections of boardwalk cross the sodden stretches.

*Indian pipes have no chlorophyll and derive their nourishment
from decayed organic matter.*

One of several evergreen clubmosses, Lycopodium.

On drier ground woodland plants return, wild lily-of-the-valley, partridge-berry, wood sorrel, bunchberry, Indian cucumber-root, and goldthread, its glossy parsley-like leaves shimmering in the sunshine.

A set of wooden bleachers sits beside the pond, a great place for a picnic or bird watching. Hummocks of sphagnum moss support black spruce, tamarack, and northern white cedar. Other bog plants include Labrador tea, bog rosemary, leather leaf, and pitcher plant.

Some wetland vegetation is visible from dry land. Cattails fill the marsh and speckled alder, meadowsweet, and red maple dominate the swamp. One swamp maple has sixteen boles or trunks. Swamp or red maples show red in every season: buds in winter, flowers in spring, leaf stems in summer, and leaves in fall. Some swamp maples begin to color in August.

You will return along the same path. Between the string of boardwalks and the left turn you may see a nurse log (a stump, actually) that is home to moss, wintergreen, goldthread and two beech saplings. The trees are likely to be short-lived but the ground vegetation could cover this rotting stump for years to come. You may also see blue-bead lily or Clintonia, a cluster of yellow lily-like flowers on a single stem in spring and deep blue berries in late summer. The plant has a pair of shiny oblong leaves and prefers moist, acid soils.

FRIENDS DON'T LET FRIENDS PICK LYCOPODIUM

Creeping underfoot, usually in the shade of their namesakes, are tiny evergreen plants with names like running pine, ground cedar, and running moss. These members of the fern family are club mosses, Lycopodium.

Fossils of club mosses date to the Paleozoic Era, more than 300 million years ago. Their ancestors were a part of vast fern jungles that ultimately produced, largely by their spores, coal still mined today.

Club mosses prefer cool, damp, shady sites with acidic soil. Several species inhabit the sphagnum bog, the ultimate wet acidic environment.

Club mosses grow very slowly and a sustainable colony may take seventy-five years to develop. They propagate most efficiently by runners since the reproductive cycle of two generations takes nearly twenty years. The unknowing who pick these diminutive greens for holiday decorations can destroy a century's growth in minutes.

The spores of club mosses are so minute and uniform in size that they were once used for microscopic measurements. Water-repellent and dust like, spores coated pills. They were also used for fireworks and photographic flashes as they give off an explosive flash when lit. The leaves and stems have been used in dying woolens and as emetics and poisons!

GETTING THERE

From the intersection of Rtes. 2 and 2A at Tafts Corner in Williston, take Rte. 2 east. In the village of Williston, 2.3 miles, turn right on West Hill Road. Turn left, just past the interstate, onto South Road at 0.3 mile. After 1.9 miles turn right on Mud Hill Road. Parking is on the right.

FOR MORE INFORMATION

Public Works Department
Town of Williston
722 Williston Road
Williston, VT 05495
802-878-1239

12   Colchester Bog Natural Area

A boardwalk to the suspended world of the bog and its extraordinary vegetation.

COLCHESTER, VT
0.5 MILE
1 HOUR
VERY EASY
DOGS MUST BE LEASHED. THE BOARDWALK IS NOT AN APPROPRIATE PLACE FOR PETS.

COLCHESTER BOG IS ONE of two large peat bogs adjacent to Lake Champlain. The larger 800-acre Maquam Bog is part of the Missisquoi National Wildlife Refuge. (See page 24.) Colchester Bog, at 184 acres, is a University of Vermont Natural Area. A 400-foot floating boardwalk allows visitors to see the unusual and very fragile vegetation without harming it. A nearby recreational path also passes through a section of the bog (see In the Area).

Colchester Bog began forming about 9,000 years ago in an old channel of the Winooski River. When the river shifted a sand bar developed along the shoreline cutting off the flow of lake water.

There are no streams entering the bog. A bog evolves when there is no fresh supply of water. (See About Bogs, page 91.) Over the millennia a thick carpet of sphagnum moss or peat has grown, twenty feet deep in places. Almost none of Colchester Bog is open peatland as trees and shrubs have grown up over the years.

As the sand barriers are porous, the water table fluctuates with the lake level. The annual spring flooding pours water over the sandbars providing a yearly surge of oxygen and nutrients.

• • • • • •

Walk to the right of the children's playground toward a wooden barricade of posts at the edge of the trees. This stockade protects an endangered plant, downy hudsonia (Hudsonia tomentosa). Colchester Point was once mostly dunes and this sandy site is one of only four in Vermont where this low shrub survives. Its long, delicate root fibers enable it to thrive despite shifting sands.

To the left of the barrier locate a small path which passes between an oak on the left and a small cherry tree on the right then into a tunnel of white pines.

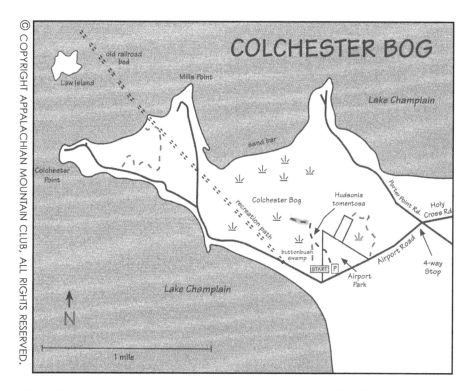

Emerging from the trees you intersect a worn path. Turn left. After about fifty feet, turn right around a medium-sized red oak into an allée of gray birch. The narrow path is sandy and worn. Notice the reindeer moss, tufts of gray-green lichen, along the trail. Lichen thrive in inhospitable environments, like this nutrient-poor, sandy soil.

The path slopes downhill through young deciduous woods to the edge of the bog that looks like a wet depression. Turn right, still on a sandy path, and walk a few hundred feet to the wooden boardwalk on the left.

Slow your pace to a crawl on the boardwalk. The bog is exploding with life, much of it quite unfamiliar.

At the edge of the bog, runoff from higher ground neutralizes the acidic water somewhat. Royal ferns, meadowsweet, and jewelweed live in these first few yards along the edge.

Trees on the bog are scrubby: swamp maple, tamarack or larch with its soft, bright green needles, gray birch, black spruce, and pitch pine, this last an anomaly as it usually prefers well-drained, sandy soils.

The shrub layer is at eye-level since the boardwalk is elevated. High-bush blueberries, eight or ten-feet tall, are laden with an astonishing crop of berries. In mid-summer speckled alder still cling to some of last year's tiny wooden cones. Black alder, or winterberry, is also here. A member of the holly family, it is not related to speckled alder. Clusters of two or three tiny star-like white blossoms ripen to scarlet berries in the axils of the shrub's oval, serrated leaves.

Near the boardwalk several acid-loving bog plants grow to a height of two or three feet. Rhodora is a member of the heath family and the rhododendron genus, which may help you recognize it. Early purple-pink flowers precede the leaves. The inch-long, gray-green leaves are oblong and roll under at the edges.

Also easy to recognize because of their domestic cousins are the laurels, sheep and bog laurel, both of which have pink flowers and thrive in northern bogs. Sheep laurel, sometimes called lambkill, is poisonous to livestock. Its flowers are in the middle of the stem. Bog laurel leaves are thinner, more like rosemary leaves, and its flowers are at the end of the branch.

One of the dominant shrubs is leather leaf, an evergreen plant two- to four-feet high. Its leathery, toothless leaves are oblong and between one and two inches long. White bell-shaped flowers may appear as early as March on this bog pioneer. Leather leaf can advance bog development by forming floating mats around the edges of open water.

Many bog plants are northern species adapted to stressful conditions. Despite the abundance of water, acidic conditions make it difficult for plants to absorb it. Thick, leathery leaves preserve moisture and protect the plants from transpiration.

At the bottom of all this is the deep, underlying mat of sphagnum moss. Over the thousands of years since the shift of the Winooski River channel, the moss has been thriving in this acidic, oxygen poor environment. Tufts of sphagnum form the floor of this bog and support its specialized vegetation.

In the herb layer you may recognize huckleberry and bog cranberry. The cranberry is similar to cultivated fruit but the leaves are tiny, about a half inch long. Arrowhead, with leaves shaped like arrows, is also called duck potato as ducks and muskrats eat its rhizomes. A rhizome is an underground stem, not a root, which often has enlarged nodes for food storage.

Wild calla, or water arum, is a vine with a showy, tropical looking flower. Its leaves are heart-shaped and the flower a bold white spathe (not a petal although it looks like one) around a spadix, a spiky growth covered with tiny yellow flowers.

Last but not least, the most spectacular of the bog plants is the carnivorous pitcher plant whose leaves resemble red and green organ pipes. There are quite a number at the far end of the boardwalk, lying low against the sphagnum mat. A single, spectacular purple-red flower on a leafless stem rises a foot or more over the equally extravagant curved leaves. The leaves form tubes that fill with rainwater for trapping insects. Stiff downward-pointing hairs prevent the prey from escaping. The plant's digestive juices eventually break down the captives and the plant absorbs the nutrients. The insects provide nitrogen not otherwise available in this suspended, soilless world.

BOGS AND SPHAGNUM MOSS

While most bogs in Vermont are kettle bogs, formed when retreating glacial ice left depressions in the bedrock, the state's two largest bogs are the result of shifting river courses.

With leaves like organ pipes, pitcher plants grace the bog.

Bogs occur in an environment of stagnant water. As plants grow, die and decay, the dissolved oxygen in the water is depleted and bacteria can no longer live. Decay ceases and the water becomes sterile. Most plants cannot live in this highly acidic, nutrient- and oxygen- poor environment.

Over thousands of years, special bog vegetation has evolved. Sphagnum moss is one of the most successful of these plants and generally provides the surface on which other plants grow. It can absorb up to one hundred times its weight in water and floats on the surface of the bog. As the moss dies it does not decay but accumulates as peat. Nearly ten thousand years of sphagnum have filled Colchester Bog to a depth of twenty feet.

The surface of the bog is sponge-like and jiggles underfoot. Mats of sphagnum are sometimes called quaking mats. The peat can be dried and used in gardens and as fuel for fires. Because of the absence of decay, peat bogs preserve historic records. Bodies, tools, artifacts, and pollen found in bogs can reveal remarkable information.

GETTING THERE

Coming from Burlington, take the Northern Connector, Rte. 127 north. The road crosses the Winooski River into Colchester and is no longer a limited access highway. Turn left at the first traffic light onto Porter's Point Road. When the road forks, stay left and continue 1.4 miles to Colchester Point Road. Turn left and drive 0.6 mile to Airport Park on the right.

FOR MORE INFORMATION

University of Vermont
Environmental Program
http://www.uvm.edu/~envprog/

• ALSO IN THE AREA •

The Recreation Path/Causeway Park begins 0.3 mile farther along Airport Road. This path cuts across a corner of the bog before extending several miles into Lake Champlain on an old railroad bed.

After crossing a tree-dominated swamp, the narrow marble-banked trail reaches across open water nearly to South Hero. It's a great place to walk when mud or hunting seasons limit choices. Terrific for viewing waterfowl as well as the Green Mountains and Adirondacks.

13 Delta Park

River delta and a glimpse of sandy shore and dunes once common along Lake Champlain. Expansive lake views and sunsets. Good walk for even the youngest children.

COLCHESTER, VT
.75 MILES , NO ELEVATION GAIN
30 MINUTES
VERY EASY
DOGS MUST BE LEASHED.

FROM ITS VAST DRAINAGE BASIN to the east, the Winooski River carries a huge volume of water and sediment to Lake Champlain. As the riverbed widens and the water slows down, the smallest of these suspended particles settle out and a river delta is created. At the mouth of the Winooski, deposited silt has created extensive marshes and swamps on both sides of the river.

Delta Park preserves 55 acres of marsh, silver maple swamps, and sandy shoreline. Over thousands of years wind-whipped waves have deposited sand here at the widest section of open lake. The southern shore of Colchester Point was once covered by sand dunes. At Delta Park, vestigial sand dunes and several rare plants give us a chance to imagine that landscape.

The elevated 12-foot-wide boardwalk provides a good vantage point into the adjacent swamp and delta. Fencing keeps bikers and young children from falling off the edge. At busy times when bikers are speeding to distant points, it could be dangerous for young children. Find a quiet time for a family outing.

• • • • • •

The boardwalk begins at the park gate. On the right you will see a sandy berm, a tangle of prickles and vines, among them rosa rugosa, raspberries, blackberries, grape vines, and Virginia creeper. The Winooski River is to the left across a swamp. Cottonwoods, willows, silver maples, and red osier dogwood grow near the water's edge, all at home with wet feet. Box elder thrive here, too. A member of the maple family with opposite, compound leaves, this sturdy tree grows to 30 or 40 feet. Its seeds and leaves recall the ash family, but its leaflets can be irregular and multi-lobed, unlike the ash.

Throughout Delta Park there are many pencil-pointed stumps indicating beaver activity. Many of the poplars have resprouted.

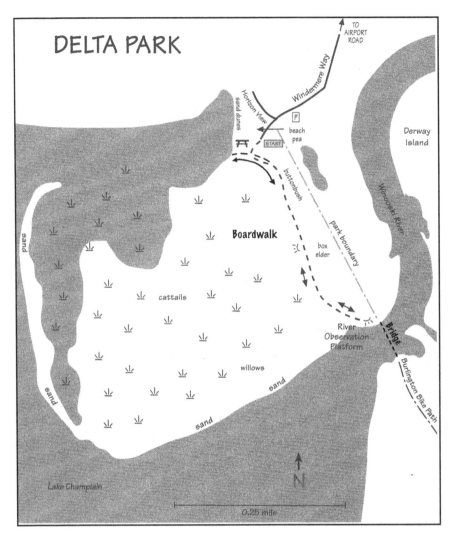

DELTA PARK

TO
AIRPORT
ROAD

Windermere Way

Horizon View

sand dunes

P

beach
pea

START

buttonbush

Derway
Island

Winooski River

Park boundary

Boardwalk

box
elder

cattails

River
Observation
Platform

Bridge

willows

sand

sand

sand

sand

Burlington Bike Path

N

Lake Champlain

0.25 mile

Be sure to look for buttonbush in the swamp on the left (beside the river). Its white flowers resemble tiny pincushions and its fruit is a pale brown spherical ball. This water-loving shrub, often found near rivers and lakes, can grow to about twenty feet. Irregular branches may lean every which way giving the plant an odd shape. Shiny, poisonous foliage remains untouched while its seeds are a delicacy for ducks, water birds and shorebirds.

By mid-summer vines entangle every vertical and horizontal surface. Hog peanut, with its three (h-o-g) yellow-green leaflets, twines along the ground. Honeysuckle, groundnut, Virginia creeper, wild grape, Queen Anne's lace, red raspberries and milkweed all contribute to the chaotic thicket.

A leisurely ten or fifteen-minute walk leads to the river observation point at the bridge. The Burlington Bike path crosses the Winooski River connecting the towns of Colchester and Burlington.

Gaze out at the lake and upriver. Look for fish and turtles near the shore. Snapping turtles are said to lay their eggs in the sand along the river channel.

The elevated bike path limits access to this fragile ecosystem. At the same time it is easier, especially in summer when heat and ample water turn this swamp to a near-jungle, to see across the delta to the lake. Willows here spend at least part of the year submerged. You can recognize their long, brittle twigs even in winter. Jewelweed, a lover of wet places, grows to over four feet and looks limp in the midday heat.

Return along the boardwalk. Just before the end of the park, turn left when you see a fenced path toward the water. This passageway threads between fencing that protects vestigial sand dunes from foot traffic. The endangered beach pea grows here. It's vines look similar to those of a garden pea, likewise its purple flowers and leguminous pods. The beach pea will look familiar to visitors to Cape Cod where the beach pea thrives on the dunes.

The white pompoms of buttonbush dot the swamp in late summer

Imagine that miles of sand like this once stretched along the shores of Lake Champlain. The shore is buried in driftwood. High water has washed stumps and dead tree trunks onto the beach and a few tenacious trees cling to life. Several red maples and willows, more dead than alive, have clumps of leaves. Red maple saplings have sprouted just above the high water mark. At a safer distance from the water, some silver maples thrive, with multiple trunks and deeply lobed, silvery leaves. Red-osier dogwood is robust as well.

GETTING THERE

From Burlington, take the Northern Connector, Rte. 127 north. The road crosses the Winooski River into Colchester and is no longer a limited access highway. Turn left at the first light, Porter's Point Road, 4.4 miles from the beginning of Rte. 127. When the road forks, stay left and continue 1.4 miles to a stop sign at Colchester Point Road. Turn left and drive 0.5 mile to Windermere Way on the left. The park is 0.7 mile at the end of Windermere.

FOR MORE INFORMATION

Winooski Valley Park District
www.wvpd.org

• ALSO IN THE AREA •

HALF MOON COVE

One of the few lakeshore wetlands on the northern shores of Lake Champlain, Half Moon Cove is an important fish spawning and waterfowl-breeding habitat. As a result, it's also a great place to watch hungry muskrats, turtles, and great blue herons. Once a meander of the Winooski River, the cove is now isolated except in spring floods. There are several short paths to the edge of the cove.

On Rte. 127, after crossing the Winooski River bridge into Colchester, take the second left, 0.6-mile, into Holbrook Court. Walk down the path at the end of the residential cul-de-sac.

Sunny Hollow Nature Park

A Cape Cod walk in Vermont: pitch pines, oaks, and heaths on glacially deposited sand. Can be buggy.	COLCHESTER, VT 1 MILE, OR LESS 1 HOUR, OR LESS EASY, OR MODERATE DOGS MUST BE UNDER VOICE CONTROL AT ALL TIMES.

DON'T BE PUT OFF by the neighborhood -light industry and megastores, or the ten-minute walk through a natural gas pipeline right-of-way. This walk is an outlier in Chittenden County and worth at least a peek, if not a long visit.

The unusual feature, for Vermont in any case, is a remnant of pitch pine-black oak-heath woodland like that which once covered the sand plains of Colchester. Deposited by the receding glacier, this sand has the same Ice Age pedigree as many of the sand and gravel pits in Colchester and neighboring towns. The sand plain forest contrasts sharply with the adjacent ravines leading to Sunderland Brook where moisture and nutrient run-off support a greater diversity of trees, shrubs, and herbs.

The pitch pine-black oak-heath woodland is within the trails of the Blueberry Loop. The Fellowship of the Wheel, a mountain bike advocacy organization in Chittenden County, creates and maintains trails at Sunny Hollow in cooperation with the Town of Colchester. Their signs, FOTW inside the gear of a bicycle, mark the trails.

All of the other FOTW trails eventually lead downhill into the moister, more fertile ravines. We'll consider these trails in passing but the main natural attraction at Sunny Hollow is the remnant of the pitch pine-black oak-heath woodland on high ground.

If you lose the trail and go astray you will not get lost. Several spur trails leave the property but you are immediately put on notice by red signs: Leaving Sunny Hollow Natural Area Property. The natural area is small and bounded by industry, highways, Camp Johnson, and Sunderland Brook.

• • • • • •

Take the gravel road behind the gate. An industrial building sprawls on the left and

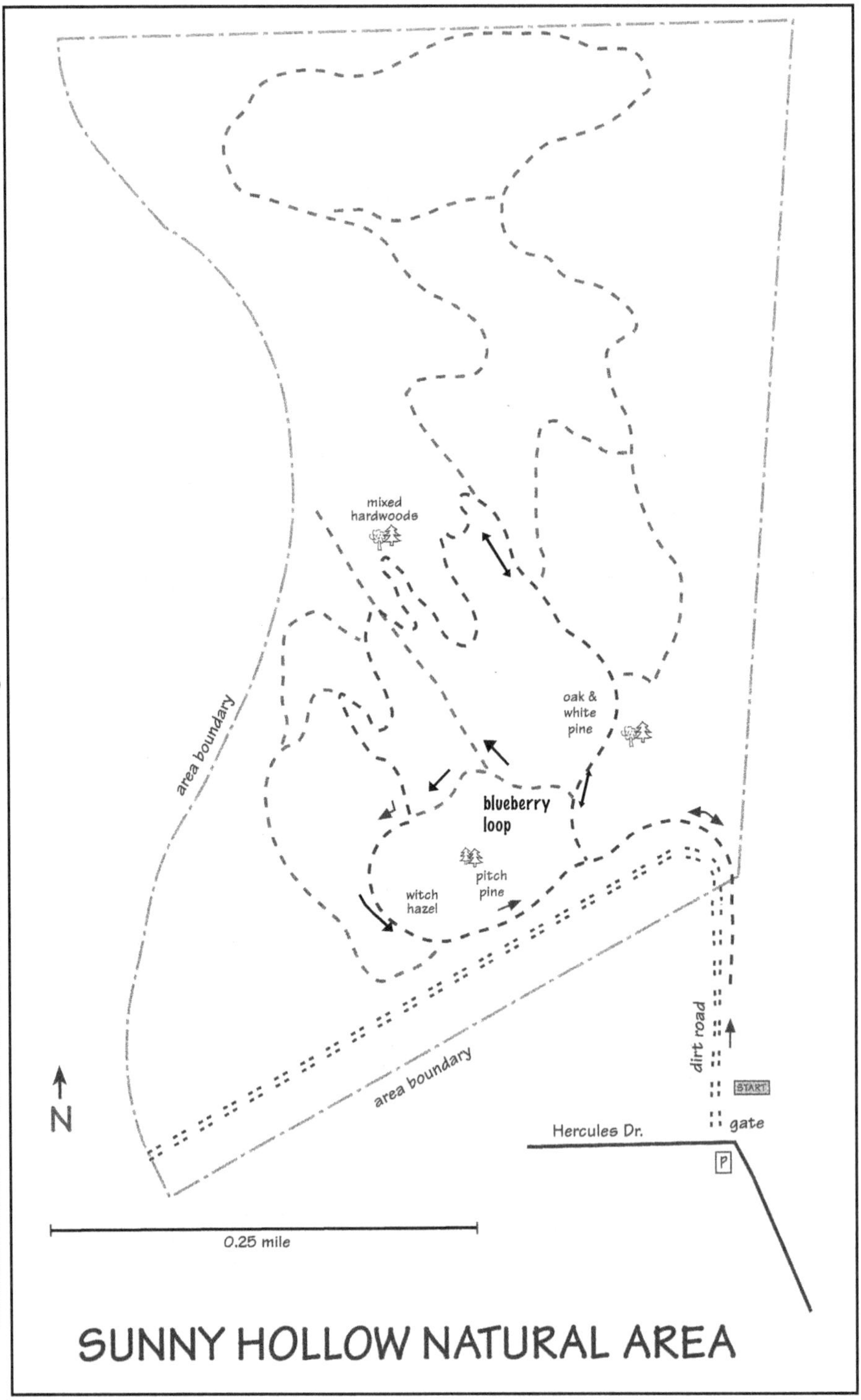

SUNNY HOLLOW NATURAL AREA

mixed
hardwoods

oak &
white
pine

blueberry
loop

pitch
pine

witch
hazel

area boundary

area boundary

dirt road

Hercules Dr.

START

gate

P

N

0.25 mile

a scruffy thicket of poplar, gray birch, and willow is on the right. The land is maintained for access to a buried natural gas pipeline. Common wildflowers bloom along this stretch including black-eyed Susan, Queen Anne's lace, cow vetch, and birdsfoot trefoil. The latter has a cheerful yellow pea-like flower on stems with three leaves, hence its name. The plant is low, usually less than one foot, and is found in sunny fields and roadsides.

A Fellowship of the Wheel information sign welcomes visitors with a map and trail guidelines. From the sign, follow the worn trail that leads left. Shortly a less-worn trail forks to the left. Stay on the main trail, the right fork. Soon you will arrive at an intersection where the Middle Finger Trail goes right. You will go left onto the trails of the Blueberry Loop.

The Blueberry Loop is actually a series of loops. We will make a counter-clock-

Pitch pine trees can sprout from the trunk, enabling them to recover after a fire.

wise circuit of the plateau. Bear left at each intersection, trying to stay in the heart of the dry sand plain.

Trees are scrubby and the canopy open. Red and white oaks share the canopy with white pine and the occasional gray birch or maple. None of the trees is very large because of the dry, sandy soil. Oak leaves, slow to decompose, litter the ground. The dry, sandy soil supports only vegetation that doesn't require rich soils. Acid-tolerant plants grow well in this soil, among them several heaths, the rare trailing arbutus, sheep laurel, a small shrub with pink flowers similar to its cultivated cousin, wintergreen, with glossy, dark-green leaves, and low bush blueberry. Bracken fern, its three-part fronds lying nearly horizontal, shuns the limy soils usually favored by ferns and is abundant here as are wild sarsaparilla, sweetfern, and partridgeberry.

Fires, if they occur here, are suppressed. As a result few pitch pines remain. Small trees with bunches of three needles two to five inches long, pitch pines grow to a maximum of sixty feet. Their hard, nearly round cones have prickles and may remain on the tree for up to a dozen years. Pitch pine grows more slowly than many of its competitors, especially white pine, and depends on fire to survive. After a fire, pitch pines sprout from the stump and from tufts of needles along the trunk. No other pine can do this. Fire also releases nutrients as it burns fallen needles, providing clear ground for seed germination. Blueberries benefit from periodic burning as well. Old wood is destroyed and the plant puts forth new, prolific branches.

Black oak, at the northern extreme of its range in the Champlain Valley, also grows here. With pointed rather than round lobes, its leaves resemble red oaks. Like the red oak, it produces acorns in two years not one. Black oak, sometimes confusingly called yellow oak because of its yellow or orange inner bark, thrives on dry, upland, sandy soils. It was once used as a source of tannin, medicine, and yellow dye.

The heaths, early and late low-bush blueberries, sheep laurel, and black huckleberry, are abundant as are bracken fern and sweetfern (Comptonia peregrina). Despite fern-like foliage, sweetfern is a flowering plant. Grouse and white-tailed-deer feed on its aromatic twigs and leaves. Witch hazel joins the understory in several spots.

On a visit in 2009 I spotted only two pitch pines, one of modest size with many cones in its healthy branches. The other, with four trunks, looked more vulnerable but had many tufts of needles on its trunk. These pitch pines need a fire to destroy their fast-growing competitors!

If you wish to linger at Sunny Hollow, consider descending one of several trails into the ravine. If the trails are busy with mountain bikers, consider visiting at another time for the trails are narrow with many switchbacks.

As the trails descend into the ravine the vegetation changes before our eyes. This is a landscape more familiar in Vermont. The soil collects moisture and nutrient run-off from the sandy plain where sand particles are too big to retain water well. Trees are suddenly taller and maple and paper birch join the oaks and gray birch. Hemlocks grow in the shade. Red, mountain, and striped maple saplings grow in the understory along with starflower, wild lily-of-the-valley, goldthread, and Clintonia. Clintonia is acid-tolerant but prefers damp soil. You will also see hobblebush and cinnamon fern in the damp soil.

At any point retrace your steps to the sand plain and follow the dirt road to the entry gate.

FIRE IN NATURE

Lightning has always caused fires in nature. Only in recent years have humans intervened, usually to protect human habitation. Without fire, nature's balance is jeopardized in communities like Sunny Hollow.

Some types of forests are more vulnerable to fire than others. Where pine needles and oak leaf litter accumulate, few herbaceous plants can grow. The combination of flammable debris and the absence of a damp, green ground cover, makes oak-pine communities especially fire prone.

Fire has long been an effective forest management tool. In *Reading the Forested Landscape*, author Tom Wessels maintains that Native Americans in the northeast used fire to help control insects, maintain berry production, make the forest floor quiet for stalking and hunting, and encourage the growth of nut-bearing trees. Several of the region's most prolific nut producers have the most fire-resistant bark: white oak, shagbark hickory, and the nearly extinct American chestnut.

GETTING THERE

Take I-89 Exit 16, Rtes. 2 & 7. Turn right and follow the combined routes north for 0.4 mile. Turn right onto Hercules Drive. At the bend in the road, 0.3 miles, park on the left at the turnout near the gate. Walk down the gated road about ten minutes to the trailhead.

FOR MORE INFORMATION

Town of Colchester
Recreation Department
Blakeley Road
Colchester, VT 05446
802-655-0811

• ANOTHER EXAMPLE •

CLINTONVILLE PINE BARRENS, AUSABLE FORKS, NEW YORK.

To see an excellent example of this ecosystem, consider a day trip across Lake Champlain. (Combine it with a visit to Ausable Chasm or a hike up Coon Mountain.) The Adirondack Nature Conservancy and Adirondack Land Trust actively manage a 900-acre pitch pine-heath barrens in Clintonville.

Contact the Adirondack Nature Conservancy for further information. (See Organizations at the end of this book.)

Colchester Pond

Circle a large pond in the near-wilderness of Chittenden County.

COLCHESTER, VT
2.5 MILES
2 HOURS
MODERATE WITH STEEP, ROCKY SECTIONS
PETS MUST BE LEASHED.

COLCHESTER POND IS THE NEWEST acquisition of the Winooski Valley Park District. Surrounding a one-mile-long pond with 2.4 miles of shoreline, this park provides a greenway link to Indian Brook Reservoir, a scenic overlook of the Champlain Valley, and a wilderness home to deer, bobcat, fisher, and fox. The 693 acres were dedicated in 1997 after a nine-year effort to combine eight separate acquisitions.

• • • • • •

The trail leads down the grassy slope to the water's edge and turns left along the shoreline. Hayfields rise to the left and a hedgerow grows along the pond. Jewelweed abounds near the shore and milkweed spreads through the hayfield, attracting monarch butterflies. The trail tunnels through hedgerows where several spreading basswood and shagbark hickory trees tower over sumac, a few intimidating hawthorns with two-inch thorns, opposite-leaf dogwood, honeysuckle, and spirea.

In the shallow water bur reed, cattails, wild celery, stonewort, spike rush, and bulrush flourish. In the adjacent wetland, jewelweed, and spotted joe-pye weed are lush.

As the trail leaves the open fields sweetfern grows on left, an indicator of dry, acidic sites. A flowering plant with fern-like foliage, it has a woody stem. Sun-loving white pines give way to deciduous woods as the trail rises and falls following white blazes with WVPD logo in green. The blazes are clear until the trail reaches the ridge on the far side of the pond.

False Solomon's seal is abundant in the understory along with partridgeberry, meadow rue, and jack-in-the-pulpit. The woods are a mix of young red and white oak, paper birch, hop hornbeam, serviceberry, elm, big-toothed aspen, red and

False Solomon's seal grows in a wide range of soils.

sugar maple, and ash. The footing is rocky as the trail climbs gently.

The trail makes a right turn onto the Peninsula Trail, an out-and-back detour from the Loop Trail to the edge of the pond. It follows a damp course downhill. Bloodroot, an indicator plant, grows in what must be fertile soil. In these damp sections sensitive fern and jewelweed flourish.

Return to the Loop Trail that climbs a steep and rocky hillside. The vegetation changes as we climb. American beech, maple, paper birch, basswood, and hemlock grow among the rocky outcroppings. Many trees with multiple trunks and a few charred stumps are remnants of a fire that raged here about sixty years ago. While multiple trunks often indicate logging, it is unlikely that every species would have been harvested at the same time.

As the trail rises over rocky ledges, hemlock perch precariously on ledges. Three evergreen ferns grow, Christmas, polypody, and spinulose woodfern.

Blazes mark the path as striped maple, a favorite of deer, becomes abundant in the shrub layer. After a final steep section the trail goes right and picks up an old logging road along the quartzite ridge. Drier, less fertile soil supports fewer plants than the more moist and fertile lower slopes. Red and white oak and hop horn-

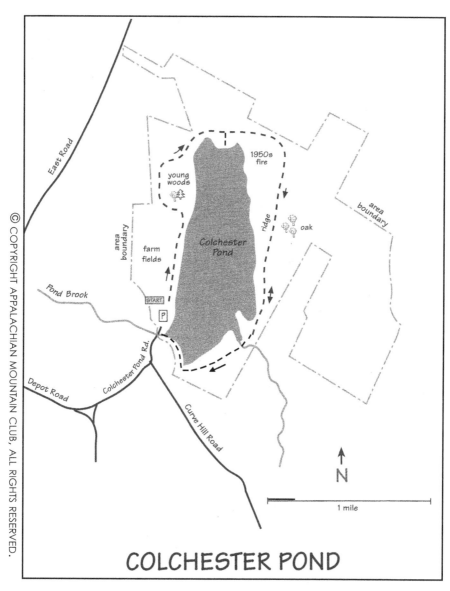

East Road

young woods

1950s fire

area boundary

area boundary

farm fields

Colchester Pond

ridge

oak

Pond Brook

START

P

Colchester Pond Rd.

Depot Road

Curve Hill Road

N

1 mile

COLCHESTER POND

beam dominate with the occasional hickory. There are no large diameter trees. We pass a red maple on the left with a birdseye pattern on the bark. Understory plants that tolerate either dry or acidic conditions predominate, including wintergreen, lowbush blueberry, starflower, bracken fern, Indian pipe, Indian cucumber-root, and partridgeberry. Masses of clubmoss grow and many asters flower in September.

Please stay on the trail as bobcat den among rocky ridges nearby where the undulating topography provides isolation and protection. These secretive predators are not tolerant of human interference.

The trail continues along the ridge until it reaches open fields near the south end of the pond. It crosses a sturdy wooden bridge and then continues as a mowed path across two more hay fields. The trail loops right along the shore and wetlands returning to the bridge on Colchester Pond Road. Cross the bridge and return to the parking lot.

AMPHIBIANS

Spring is announced by the mating call of frogs- the male's distinctive aria to females of the same species. Even while ice lingers on the ponds, the couple produces a jelly-like mass of bead-like, fertilized eggs. The dark yolk within the clear orb will divide and divide until, several weeks later, a tadpole swims free.

Amphibians live on land and in water and, like fish, reptiles, birds and mammals, are vertebrates. Unlike birds and mammals, they do not need to maintain their body temperature in winter. Cold-blooded animals merely decrease their activities as the temperature plunges.

In the Devonian period, 360 million years ago, close relatives of fish may have been attracted to land by ample food and fewer enemies. Lungs evolved for breathing and fins evolved into limbs. Most of these animals became extinct but a few evolved into modern amphibians.

Three groups of amphibians are frogs and toads; newts, salamanders, and sirens; and the little-known tropical wormlike caecilians. Tailed amphibians- newts, salamanders, and sirens include 360 species, most found in temperate, forested regions of the northern hemisphere. There are 3,500 species of frogs, a term often used to include both frogs and toads.

Frogs tend to be more active than toads, live in or near water, have smooth skin, long hind legs, and fully webbed feet. In contrast, less active toads prefer land, have dry, warty skin, short legs and little or no webbing.

Amphibians have naked skin, no hair, feathers or surface scales, and can breathe through their skin as well as their lungs. This distinguishes them from reptiles that have dry, scaly skin.

Water is essential to amphibians because porous skin allows for great loss of moisture. Most require water for reproduction as their eggs are laid in water and the larval stage is water-bound.

Among their adaptations, most amphibians are dark-colored above and light below, making them less visible to both overhead and underwater prey as they blend into their respective backgrounds. Their dark-colored backs also better absorb heat from the sun.

While the amphibian diet includes insects, spiders, snails, slugs, and earthworms, they represent dinner to turtles, otters, and snakes, among others.

GETTING THERE

Take I-89 Exit 16. Go right on Rte. 7 for 1.7 miles. Turn right on Severance Road. After 1.0 mile, turn left on Mill Pond Road. At a stop sign in 1.6 miles, go straight onto East Road. Turn right on Depot Road, 0.2 mile. You will cross the railroad and the road turns to dirt. Fork left on Colchester Pond Road at 1.1 miles. The parking area is on the right in 0.2 mile.

FOR MORE INFORMATION

Winooski Valley Park District
www.wvpd.org

Southern Chittenden County

16 Farm Trail, Shelburne Farms

On the shores of Lake Champlain, a Vanderbilt Webb agricultural estate now a non-profit educational foundation and working farm. A wonderful walk for children to the Farm Barn and Lone Tree Hill.

SHELBURNE, VT
4.25 MILES
3 HOURS
MODERATE
(LONE TREE HILL, ROUND TRIP, 2 MILES AND 1.5 HOURS, MODERATE)
PLEASE LEAVE YOUR PETS AT HOME.

DR. WILLIAM SEWARD WEBB and his wife Lila Vanderbilt Webb created Shelburne Farms during the gilded age. With the Champlain Valley on hard times after the collapse of the wool market, the Webbs bought failed sheep farms on Shelburne Point. By the turn of the century they had acquired thirty-two farms totaling 3,800 acres.

Shelburne Farms was more than a luxurious retreat for the wealthy; it was a model farm and an expression of the new conservation movement. Landscape architect Frederick Law Olmsted, designer of Central Park, created the visual landscape with winding roads, ponds, lawns, fields, and forests. No view was left to chance as 10,000 trees and shrubs were planted every year for ten years.

The first head of the US Forest Service, Gifford Pinchot, began his career at Shelburne Farms. Pinchot developed a plan to maximize yield and sustain productivity of the woodlots.

The years between 1895 and 1910 were the heyday of Shelburne Farms. The five-story farm barn with its two-acre courtyard, gaslights, steam conveyors, and elevators, was the hub from which two hundred and fifty workers and forty teams of horses and mules tended to herds and crops. A breeding barn was built for Dr. Webb's Hackney horse breeding project, at the time the largest barn in the country. Flowers filled steam-heated greenhouses and more than 100,000 trees and shrubs grew in the nursery.

Velvet lawns and gardens spilled down to the lake from the 110-room Queen Anne Revival "cottage," designed by Robert H. Robertson. The mansion was the Webb's family home, where they raised their four children and entertained a Who's Who of social and political luminaries of the day. A plan to build a grander man-

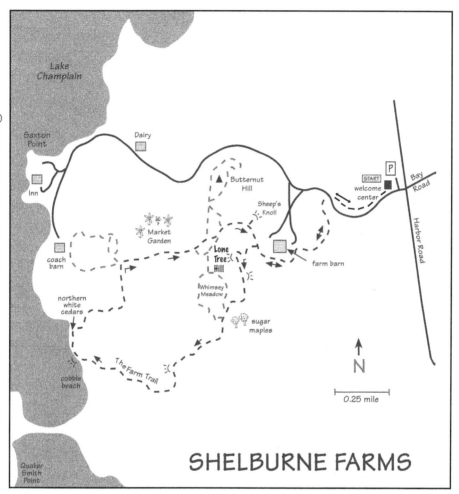

SHELBURNE FARMS

sion on Lone Tree hill was abandoned in favor of adding a north wing and third story to accommodate their many guests.

With the introduction of federal income taxes in 1913, it became more difficult to maintain the estate. In 1914, Dr. Webb gave a large portion of the property to his son James Watson Webb as a wedding present. The latter's wife, Electra Havemeyer Webb, founded the Shelburne Museum in 1947 on some of this land. (See In the Area.) With the death of Dr. Webb in 1926 and his wife Lila in 1936, the estate was further divided by inheritance.

In 1938, the Webb's grandson Derick began to re-energize the farm, experimenting with modern farming techniques, introducing Brown Swiss cattle, and building a modern pole barn and milking parlor, then a novel idea with its open design.

Architectural treasures punctuate the landscape at Shelburne Farms: the Farm Barn.

Farming did not provide adequate income to support the maintenance of the large property with its historic buildings. Derick Webb began to explore strategies for selling some of the land for development. However, his six children, imbued with the spirit of the 1960s, saw a greater vision for the future of Shelburne Farms. With their father's support they developed the new model for a non-profit corporation whose mission is to teach and demonstrate the conservation and stewardship of natural and agricultural resources.

Today Shelburne Farms is a 1,400-acre working farm and environmental education center. The Farm's stewardship and conservation ethic provide a model for sustainable development that is being replicated around the world.

The non-profit, membership organization is supported by the revenue from its cheddar cheese production and the Inn at Shelburne Farms. After major rehabilitation the lakeside mansion was opened as an inn and restaurant in 1987. Each year thousands of teachers and students of all ages participate in a wide range of educational programs; visitors from around the world tour the property; and the public enjoys festivals, concerts, and walking on the network of trails.

As you enjoy the woods, fields, and lakeside bluffs, take a moment to appreciate that this spectacular property is performing a vital mission and is not a subdivision of lakefront mansions. The entire property, both land and buildings, is on the National Register of Historic Places.

The loop from the Welcome Center to Lake Champlain via Lone Tree Hill is more than four miles long. While it may be too long for young children, they might happily stay behind (with an adult) at the Farm Barn where they can milk cows and goats, collect chicken eggs, comb an angora bunny, and watch piglets romp in their pen. Lone Tree Hill is a perfect destination for a family walk and picnic. The Farm Cart in the courtyard of the Farm Barn offers local specialties for lunch or snack.

Be sure to watch the 15-minute film about the Farm before or after your walk.

• • • • • •

The gravel walking trail begins at the Welcome Center and parallels the main farm road before crossing it within a few minutes. The trail then rises gently through a field and the massive Farm Barn looms on your right. You will cross another farm road as you approach the Farm Barn. The trail leads into the fenced farmyard where chickens in a rainbow of colors peck in the grass. Pass through the gate and into the Farm Barn where a magical world unfolds.

The daily schedule may include milking a cow, searching for eggs, or the chicken parade- an afternoon round up of all the fowl for the night. See if you know your animal droppings- play Name that Scat. If you can tear away the young-at-heart, enter the courtyard. Order a farm fresh lunch (Shelburne Farms grilled cheese, Shelburne Orchard cider and apples, farm-grown salad greens) and visit the cheese makers. Fine woodworkers craft furniture from Vermont lumber, and O'Bread Bakery fills the air with the fragrance of organic treats: bread, croissants, and cookies.

The trail continues uphill past the Farm Barn on a farm road. As you climb glance back at the Green Mountains stretching beyond the clock tower.

The Farm Trail is well marked and within minutes a sign points left across the grass toward the woods. In addition to signs, occasional white arrows on blue circles mark the route.

You will climb through woods that host maple, birch, ash, white pine, basswood, and hickory. Red elderberry is a frequent shrub. Its compound leaves, with five to seven elliptical leaflets, resemble the ashes. The leaves are opposite and the clustered flowers recall the viburnums to which they are related. Its scarlet berries color the woods as early as July.

A spur trail to the right opens to a vista of the Inn and the lake from a grassy knoll. Returning to the trail you will soon reach the stone bench atop Lone Tree Hill. Savor the view: farm fields, the Inn, Lake Champlain, the Green Mountains, and the Adirondacks.

Follow the Farm Trail sign. The mowed path slopes down across a grassy field toward the woods. Keep your nose alert for the warm fragrance of wild strawberries and red raspberries!

Just before you enter the woods, look left toward Camel's Hump. This is a signature tableau, one of many with which Frederick Law Olmsted punctuated Shelburne Farms. Your eyes are drawn across the meadow to the mountain framed between banks of trees.

The woods are primarily maples with little understory other than maple saplings. Deer graze these woods heavily. The trail is a farm road and easy to follow as it rises and falls through the woods. Stay on this road as the Whimsey Meadow Trails go right.

Within fifteen minutes of Lone Tree Hill, the trail leaves the woods and passes into a meadow. On the left is another of Olmsted's framed vistas of Camel's Hump. The trail passes between woods on the right and a clump of trees on the left. Other views unfold, to the south-southwest toward Charlotte's Pease Mountain and Mt. Philo beyond. The sheepback shape of Mt. Philo is particularly visible from here.

A cluster of trees atop a knoll is another Olmsted hallmark. The trail crosses a farm road and enters one such clump of trees. Huge bitternut hickories thrive here; the bigger ones have vertical fissures on their gray bark. Bitternuts are an indicator of fertile soil. At the far edge of the woods a bench on the left has a lovely view towards the lake and farm on Quaker Smith Point with the Adirondacks as backdrop.

From the bench a mowed path swings left and slopes downhill. The trail turns right and continues beside these woods rich with beech, maple, oak, elm, hop hornbeam, ash, and cherry. Elderberries flourish here.

The trail jogs right on a dirt farm road before a blue arrow indicates a left turn on mowed grass across the hayfields toward the lake. In a few minutes a spur leads to a lovely cobble beach. One May day I watched blue herons, ducks, loons, swallows, and geese from this spot. You might want to bring a bird book and lunch.

The trail continues along the shore through young woods. It jogs right then reemerges into fields, rising slightly as it leaves the lake. After about ten minutes signs point left onto a gravel farm road. This is a working farm and we pass fragrant mounds of hay and manure, old equipment, stacks of firewood, beehives, and compost piles.

The Farm Trail turns right while signs point left toward the Market Garden. The dirt road to the left visits the organic gardens that supply the Inn and a vista of the Inn and Coach Barn. We turn right, continuing on the Farm Trail, beneath arching hardwoods.

In a few minutes the Farm Trail goes straight at a four-way intersection of dirt roads. Signs indicate the route.

Basswood and bitternut hickory, indicators of rich soil, are scattered through the woods beside less particular trees: maple, beech, hop hornbeam, black and paper birch, black cherry and oak. The beech here are falling victim to the beech blister, a fungus. Flowering herbs include trillium, jack-in-the-pulpit, and false Solomon's seal. Stinging nettles are also abundant.

As the road rises through the woods plastic tubing runs between the sugar maples. Although the taps are removed after spring sugaring the network of tubes often remains. On the left two trails indicate a loop to Butternut Hill. Eventually we emerge from the woods to fields and vistas opening on the left. Stop to admire the view at Sheep's Knoll before descending to the Farm Barn.

From the Farm Barn follow the walking trail back to the Welcome Center.

HOURS, FEES, FACILITIES

In season, mid-May to mid-October, trails are open from 9:00 a.m. to 5:30 p.m. Admission is $9 adults, $8 seniors, $7 children 3 to 17. Free to children under three and members. Admission includes the walking path, a tractor-drawn wagon ride to the Farm Barn, children's farmyard, and the cheddar cheese operations.

Please leave your pets at home.

Off-season, trails are open without charge, weather permitting. Check-in at the Welcome Center (802-985-8442).

Water and restrooms are at the Welcome Center and Farm Barn.

GETTING THERE

From Shelburne drive north on Rte. 7. At the third light, 1.9 miles, turn left onto Bay Road. The road ends, in 1.5 miles, at the Welcome Center.

From the north, travel south on Rte. 7 from South Burlington. Bay Road is on the right, 3 miles from the I-189 interchange.

FOR MORE INFORMATION

Shelburne Farms
1611 Harbor Road
Shelburne, VT 05482
802-985-8686
www.shelburnefarms.org

• ALSO IN THE AREA •

SHELBURNE MUSEUM

America's premier collection of its arts, architecture and artifacts. A country store, round barn, side-wheel steamboat, slate jail, and a Shaker shed are among the 37 structures at this unique museum. The collection, spread over 45 acres, includes quilts, children's toys, a merry-go-round, blacksmith shop, and Monet's haystacks. Eclectic, fun, and fascinating. On Rte. 7 in Shelburne.

17 LaPlatte River Marsh Natural Area

Channels and wetlands of two rivers as they enter Lake Champlain. A great place to observe wildlife and to ski or snowshoe.

SHELBURNE, VT
1.75 MILES
1-1.5 HOURS
EASY
PLEASE LEAVE PETS AT HOME.
SERVICE ANIMALS ARE WELCOME.

ONE OF MANY PROTECTED PARCELS on Shelburne Point, the 245-acre preserve is at the confluence of McCabes Brook and the LaPlatte River. Shelburne Farms sold the LaPlatte River Marsh to the Nature Conservancy in 1975 which in turn transferred it to the town of Shelburne. The Vermont Chapter of the Nature Conservancy currently manages the property.

In 1985, Christopher Fastie, a student in the University of Vermont Field Naturalist Program, wrote a master's thesis on the LaPlatte River Marsh, an area larger than but including this preserve. Fastie estimated that 60 species of birds, 20 species of mammals, and 50 species of reptiles, amphibians, and fish breed in or near these wetlands. This meeting of swamp, marsh, forest, river, delta, and lake is rich territory indeed!

The Town of Shelburne owns adjacent Shelburne Bay Park (see Allen Hill, page 123) and Shelburne Farms has preserved over 1,400 acres to the west. In 2009 the Nature Conservancy protected an additional 143 acres that adjoin this preserve. The new parcel includes den sites for bobcat and floodplain acreage with 280-year-old trees. A few sizable private holdings adjoin these properties creating a large area of wildlife habitat stretching from lake to bay across the peninsula.

• • • • • • •

Begin your walk at the information kiosk and sign-in box. For a brief stretch you will parallel the Ticonderoga Road. In 1955, over frozen ground, workers laid temporary railroad tracks from Shelburne Bay to the Shelburne Museum. They then towed the huge, nineteenth-century sidewheel steamboat, the Ticonderoga, to its home at the Museum.

The trail turns left toward the water, through a thicket of red-osier dogwood, honeysuckle, staghorn sumac, and ash saplings. The only trees are fast-growing white pines.

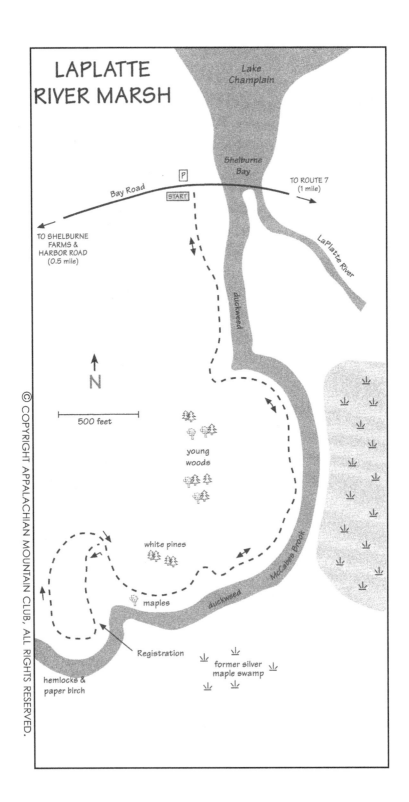

LAPLATTE RIVER MARSH

Lake Champlain

Shelburne Bay

P

START

Bay Road

TO ROUTE 7 (1 mile) →

← TO SHELBURNE FARMS & HARBOR ROAD (0.5 mile)

LaPlatte River

duckweed

N

500 feet

young woods

white pines

McCabee Brook

duckweed

maples

Registration

former silver maple swamp

hemlocks & paper birch

You are walking on the west bank of McCabes Brook. The channel is wide as the brook joins the LaPlatte River. Yellow-green duckweed flourishes from the earliest warm days of spring and soon covers the water. Air pockets keep duckweed leaves afloat and new plants are produced by shoots that break off and float away. The tiny fronds of this flowering plant provide food for snails and insect larvae.

Keep an eye out for cormorants drying their wings on dead branches. You may also see great blue herons, black-crowned night herons, and several kinds of ducks.

A young forest of sun-loving pioneers is growing on abandoned farmland: poplar, gray birch, white pine, maple, and ash. Young sassafras trees grow knee-high on the left. The untoothed leaves come in three patterns, one lobed or egg-shaped, two lobes like a thumb and mitten, and three-lobed, more like fingers. The leaves and bark are fragrant when crushed and tea can be made from the roots. Bark extract is used as an orange dye. Songbirds, bobwhite, wild turkey and black bear eat its fruits and marsh and cottontail rabbits and white-tailed deer browse its twigs.

After ten minutes we overlook the channel and an assortment of water-loving plants: cattails, purple loosestrife, arrowhead, white water lilies, and pink flowering rush. There's a lot going on here. Frogs jump, turtles sun themselves on rocks and logs, and, in spring, bullfrogs sound like the rhythmic sawing of logs. Ducks nest along the banks, great blue herons wade in shallow water, and a pileated woodpecker frequents the woods. Keep your eyes out for a towering white pine with squarish holes made by this giant woodpecker. The holes are about twelve feet above the ground.

Along the banks a hybrid maple grows, with characteristics of both silver and red maple. Both trees are swamp and river-edge dwellers. The leaves of the hybrid are deeply cut and five-lobed like the silver maple but without the characteristic silver underside. The stems are rosy like those of the red maple.

Increasingly white pines fill the woods while honeysuckle and buckthorn, both invasives, dominate the shrub layer. White pines grow quickly, especially when there is abundant water. Until the 1950s this was pastureland. The trail turns right to bypass an inlet and continues through piney woods.

Several turns in the trail are marked by green and yellow Nature Conservancy blazes, although the path is obvious. An arrow indicates a bridge to the loop trail around a peninsula. Hemlocks and paper birch mix with the pines. Several herbs characteristic of an acidic, evergreen forest grow here: partridgeberry, wild lily-of-the-valley, goldthread, and starflower. Fringed polygala provide a bright burst of pink in May.

There is a long view up McCabes Brook, a nice place to watch birds or wait for turtles to appear. Across the channel, in the midst of the cattail marsh is a for-

*Sharpened stumps tell us beavers once drowned this
silver maple swamp before moving on.*

est of dead stumps. While silver maples (Acer saccharinum) are adapted to a damp
environment, they cannot live under water. Why did these trees, once so large and
healthy, drown? The clues are scattered about in the sharpened stumps of trees. In
the 1980s a population of beavers (see beavers, page120), attracted by abundant
poplars and gray birch, drowned the silver maple swamp with their dams. The
beavers have since moved elsewhere.

As the trail bends away from the brook, look for the brilliant August-flowering cardinal flower. The bright scarlet flowers are fertilized primarily by hummingbirds since most insects cannot navigate the long, tubular blooms. These
beauties are threatened by overpicking. The path crosses a second bridge and rejoins the outbound trail.

As you return, look for animal tracks in this rich edge habitat. Edge is where
two or more plant communities meet. Each habitat attracts animals to its unique
mix of food, cover, and denning or nesting sites and materials. These assets mul-
tiply where communities meet attracting a variety of wildlife. The wetlands in this

preserve also provide access to water necessary for the courtship and reproduction of many species.

TRACKING

Tracks can be found in dust, mud, snow, and grass, but for the inexperienced, snow and mud are best. Tracking is a detective game as you look for prints, scat, nibbled or broken twigs, claw marks, fur, quills, feathers, blood, and bones.

Tracking books use a distinct vocabulary: print is the mark made by one foot, track is a series of prints, straddle is the width of the track, stride is the distance between prints of a walking animal, and leap is the distance between sets of four prints made by hopping or bounding animals.

The pattern of tracks reflects the animals' gaits. Deer, moose, canines- foxes, dogs, wolves, and coyotes, and felines- cats and bobcats, all have regular walks. Canines often leave toenail marks while cats usually keep their claws retracted.

Bounders include weasels, mink, marten, fisher, otter, and squirrels. Their

A pileated woodpecker left its calling card in this white pine.

tracks are clumped, leaving two or four prints, as they hop from place to place.

The prints of leapers and hoppers have hind feet positioned ahead of the front feet, the hind being the larger of the two. This happens as the animals propel themselves with strong rear quarters and land on their front feet. You will become familiar with this pattern because rabbits are so prolific and their tracks so abundant on a snowy morning. Hares, raccoons, chipmunks, and mice hop similarly.

By contrast waddlers are heavy and lumbering and include a range of animals. Generally awkward, they use means other than speed and agility to escape danger. We know the weapons of skunks and porcupines! Woodchucks escape to their burrows, beavers and muskrat into water, and raccoons, porcupines, and bears climb trees. These animals often leave drag marks, from dragging feet or tails.

Look for location clues. Are the tracks near water, in the protection of woods, or leading to a hole in the snow? Look for nibble or claw marks. Bears claw beech trees while porcupines will strip bark in neatly gnawed, irregular patches, some very high off the ground. Just inches off the ground, a cottontail will gnaw twigs or the bark of fruit trees.

Positive identification from tracks and signs is both an art and a science. Put a tracking chart in your pocket and enjoy!

GETTING THERE

From Shelburne drive north on Rte. 7. At the third light, 1.9 miles, turn left onto Bay Road. Just after crossing the LaPlatte River, turn right into the state fishing access at 1.1 miles. The trailhead is directly across Bay Road.

From the north, travel south on Rte. 7 from South Burlington. Bay Road is on the right, 3 miles from the I-189 interchange.

FOR MORE INFORMATION

The Nature Conservancy- Vermont Chapter
http://www.nature.org/wherewework/northamerica/states/vermont/
Keeping Track
P. O. Box 444
Huntington, VT 05462
802-434-7000
http://www.keepingtrack.org/
Keeping Track trains high school groups and community organizations involved in habitat monitoring. Some local conservation commissions offer tracking classes in cooperation with Keeping Track.

18 Allen Hill, Shelburne Bay Park

A lakeside hill with a rare stand of chestnut oaks, nice views of Lake Champlain, and early spring wildflowers. Wear sturdy walking shoes or hiking boots

SHELBURNE, VT
1.5 MILES, 180 FOOT ELEVATION GAIN
1–1.5 HOURS
MODERATE WITH A FEW STEEP SECTIONS
DOGS MUST BE LEASHED.

ALLEN HILL SITS on a small peninsula in Shelburne Bay, rising abruptly 180 feet over Lake Champlain. Its south-facing, lakeside slopes are unusually warm, even for the Champlain Valley. As a result, Allen Hill is one of the few places in northern Vermont where the chestnut oak grows. Spring wildflowers bloom early on the hill's dry summit and it is a good vantage point for watching the comings and goings of waterfowl at the mouth of the LaPlatte River.

The 93-acre Shelburne Bay Park adjoins other large holdings of preserved land on Shelburne Point: LaPlatte River Marsh, 1,400 acres at Shelburne Farms (of which this property was once a part), and several large private parcels.

Two trails lead to Allen Hill, the Clarke Trail and the Recreation Path. The Clarke Trail follows the shore and has many nice views. It can also be very muddy. The Recreation Path, to the west, is a smooth gravel trail that is less interesting to walk but is always passable.

I recommend the Clarke Trail except for muddy times. Allen Hill itself is very dry and won't be wet except during active rains.

• • • • • •

The Clarke Trail begins at the north end of the northernmost parking area, next to the lake. It enters mixed woods of white pine, hemlock and deciduous trees. Two large cottonwoods grow next to the lake. To the left of the trail polypody ferns grow on a white quartzite outcropping. This small evergreen fern with its leathery leaves prefers damp shallow soil, usually on rocks or cliffs.

The understory, all the vegetation beneath the canopy of tree leaves, is varied. Young maples, honeysuckle, and buckthorn are the dominant shrubs while marginal woodferns, hepatica, wild lily-of-the-valley, and ground pine are in the herb layer.

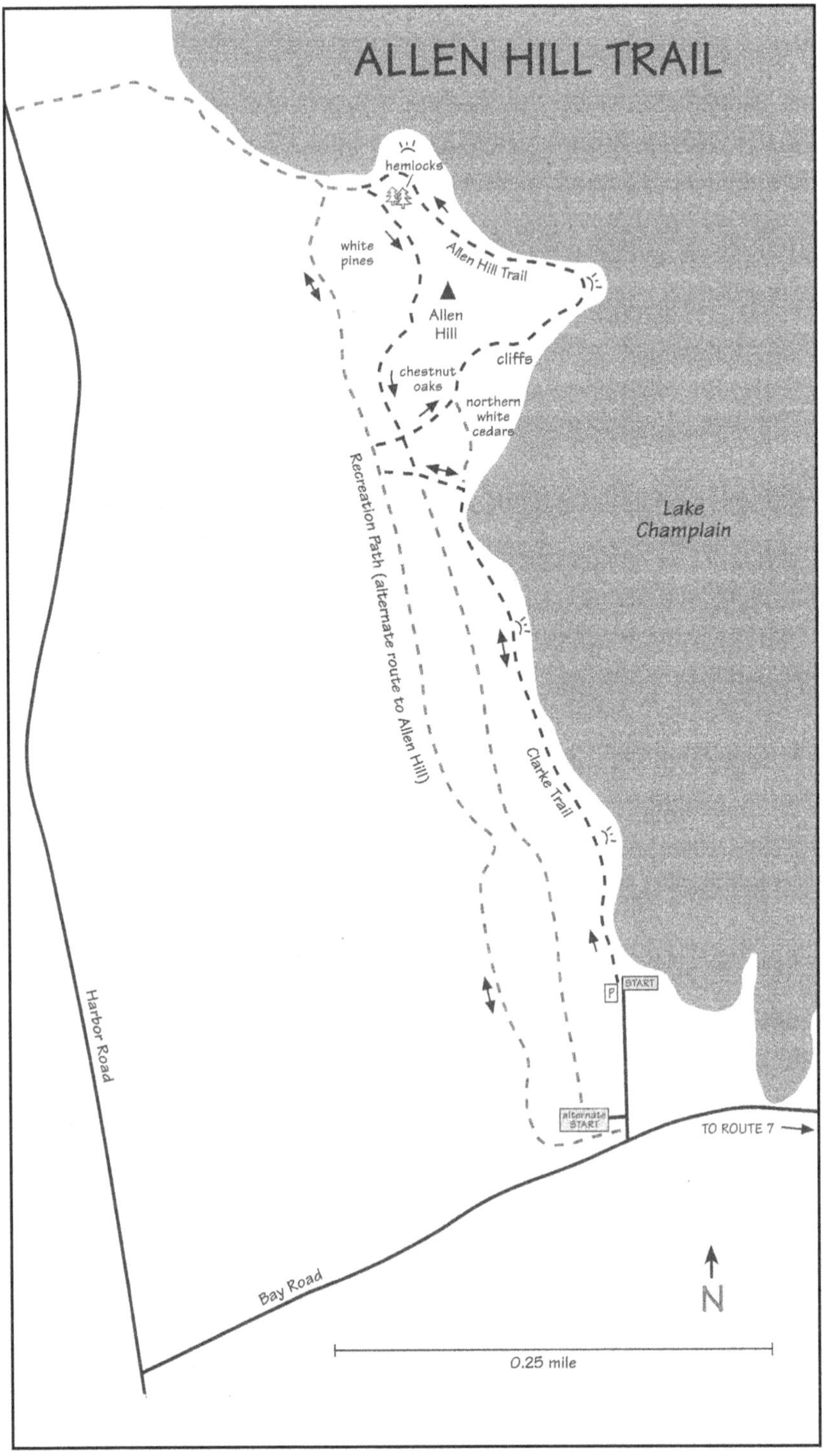

ALLEN HILL TRAIL

hemlocks

white pines

Allen Hill Trail

▲ Allen Hill

chestnut oaks

cliffs

northern white cedars

Lake Champlain

Recreation Path (alternate route to Allen Hill)

Clarke Trail

P START

alternate START

TO ROUTE 7 →

Harbor Road

Bay Road

N

0.25 mile

Several lichen-covered rock outcroppings border the lake. Lichens are pioneer plants needing nothing but occasional moisture to survive. They perform photosynthesis while clinging to nearly any surface, including bare rock. Lichen, in turn, provides a surface where moss spores can germinate. Several patches of moss grow on these rocks, the next actors in the drama of plant succession. As moss dies and decomposes it adds organic matter to the mat. Seeds that germinate in the damp moss now have a chance at survival. Someday, wildflowers and grasses will bloom on these rocks.

The trail crosses a small stream after about twenty minutes. Follow the path left and slightly uphill to the confluence of several trails.

Look for a huge red oak that has barbed wire embedded in its west side. In April or May a sea of trout lilies surrounds the oak. Take the trail that goes right, uphill of the tree, in the direction of the lake. It climbs gently before making a left turn and then climbing steeply.

The woods are now a mixture of beech, sugar maple, shagbark hickory, hemlock, hop hornbeam, and cherry as we continue a steep scramble over rocky shards. Red and white pines are still occasional.

We begin to see chestnut oak on both sides of the trail, many with multiple trunks. They seem to relish growing at odd angles to the hillside, often in defiance of gravity. These remarkable trees have deeply furrowed bark and their leaves are toothed, like the elm, rather than lobed like most oaks. Chestnut oaks are an indicator species, plants found almost exclusively in their preferred habitat, limy soil. (See calcareous communities, page 210.) They are rarely seen in this part of Vermont, the northeastern extreme of their range. Only in the warmest lakeside location with a southern exposure do we find chestnut oaks in the Burlington area.

The trail jogs right then left and continues its climb past many chestnut oak, hop hornbeam, shagbark hickory, red and white oak, and basswood trees. None of these is extremely tall because of the shallow, dry soil on the rocky summit. This hill was one of the many sheep farms bought by the Webbs for Shelburne Farms and it's likely that sheep had overgrazed this pastureland thus exposing the bedrock.

The limy soil supports a variety of wildflowers. Because this hilltop is dry, spring wildflowers bloom early, especially those sheltered from the cool spring winds off the lake. White trillium, hepatica, bloodroot, false Solomon's seal, and early meadow rue bloom in April or early May.

At the crest of the hill, look west, before the trees leaf out, for a view to the open lake. The trail continues along the ridge as white cedars and the occasional hemlock begin to mix in. Below the trail on the bay side, the rocky hillside is densely forested with mature northern white cedar, another tree that favors limy or alkaline soils.

Allen Hill is home to a beautiful patch of trout lilies.

The trail begins to descend, bearing slightly to the right, toward a rocky promontory. There are nice views to the south and east, often with good bird watching. I've seen and heard geese, cormorants, herons, and one day, at very close range, a turkey vulture. As I approached this spot it perched on the edge of the promontory, its back to me as it scanned the lake below. I was not prepared for its shrunken red head.

The trail turns to the left and the footing is rocky although not slippery. On a cool day, the north wind tells us we've changed exposure. Waves, from the more open water to the north, splash against the shore below. There is less sunlight on the north side of the hill and more hemlocks, moss, and ferns as a result. There are occasional large white oaks, perhaps left as shade trees when the land was farmed. There are lovely vistas, especially in summer, as sailboats crisscross the bay.

The trail follows the shoreline and soon reaches an intersection. The Allen Hill Trail goes left. (If you prefer the drier route continue about 100 yards before turning left on the Recreation Path.)

The Allen Hill Trail rises beneath a dense canopy of white pines and can be wet underfoot. A few scraggly cherries struggle to reach the light but there is very little understory.

As the trail approaches the drier hillside on the left, deciduous woods of maple, ash, shagbark hickory, and oak replace the dense white pines. The understory returns and within a few minutes we are back at the barbed-wire fence oak and the junction of the trails.

To return on the Recreation Path, turn right and then left when you reach the gravel trail. To return on the Clarke Trail bear left toward the lake. You will be back to the parking lot in twenty minutes.

LIMY SOILS AND INDICATOR SPECIES

Allen Hill is one of several in the area with a summit of calcareous or limy bedrock. It joins nearby Pease Mountain in Charlotte in supporting plants that thrive in these limy, alkaline conditions.

The underlying bedrock of much of the Champlain Valley is limestone and dolomite. These rocks were once sea-bottom sediments and are composed of calcium-rich layers contributed by the shells of marine creatures. Calcium is an important nutrient for plant growth. Magnesium, another critical nutrient, is also available to plants in limy soil.

Calcareous or limy soil usually produces a higher diversity of plants that in turn attract a greater number of animal species.

This, in a nutshell, is why the Champlain Valley supports a diversity of flora not seen in granite mountains. The sandy soil that erodes from granite cannot support this wide range of plants. It is not by accident that the Champlain Valley is the historic breadbasket of Vermont.

HOURS

The park is open from dawn to dusk. Dogs must be leashed.

GETTING THERE

From Shelburne travel north on Rte. 7. At the third light, 1.9 miles, turn left onto Bay Road. Just past the fishing access, turn right at 1.2 miles, Shelburne Bay Park. The parking area straight ahead is closest to the Clarke Trail. On the left is the beginning of the Recreation Path.

FOR MORE INFORMATION

Parks & Recreation Department
Town of Shelburne
Shelburne, VT 05482
802-985-9551
http://www.shelburnevt.org/departments/339.html

19 Williams Woods Natural Area

One of the best remaining examples of the lowland forests once common in the Champlain Valley. Wear boots in wet seasons. Ideal on snowshoes.

CHARLOTTE, VT
1.3 MILES
1 HOUR
EASY
PLEASE LEAVE PETS AT HOME.
SERVICE ANIMALS ARE WELCOME.

BOUNDED BY WORKING DAIRY FARMS, Thorp Brook, and the Vermont Railroad, Williams Woods is an island of old forest in the flat and fertile Champlain Valley, land which has been extensively farmed since pre-colonial times. It is the rare woodlot that has grown untouched by man for over a century.

In the late eighteenth and early nineteenth centuries when sawmills dotted the lake's tributaries, forests this close to Lake Champlain would have been among the first to be cleared for timber. Lewis Creek, just to the south, was home to a number of mills.

In deeds dating back to the 1850s, Williams Woods was refereed to as a "greenbush," a piece of land used for selective firewood cutting. Perhaps the wet soil and undulations of the terrain made the land undesirable for corn or hay fields. The woodlot was isolated from grazing cattle when the railroad was built in 1850. Arthur Williams, who owned the property until 1983, deliberately protected the trees for a least the previous forty years.

On June 27, 2007, a freak microburst with tremendously high winds swept into Williams Woods. In just ten seconds the woods near the trailhead were crisscrossed with toppled and snapped hemlocks and pines. Some blowdowns were estimated at between 200 and 300 years old.

The fertile, moisture-retentive clay soil and relatively long growing season combine to provide favorable growing conditions for these trees.

• • • • • •

The trail begins in the filtered light beneath a canopy of large hemlocks. Frequent green and yellow blazes featuring the oak leaf logo of the Nature Conservancy indicate the route. The understory is sparse.

You will notice immediately, perhaps by tripping, that tree roots grow along

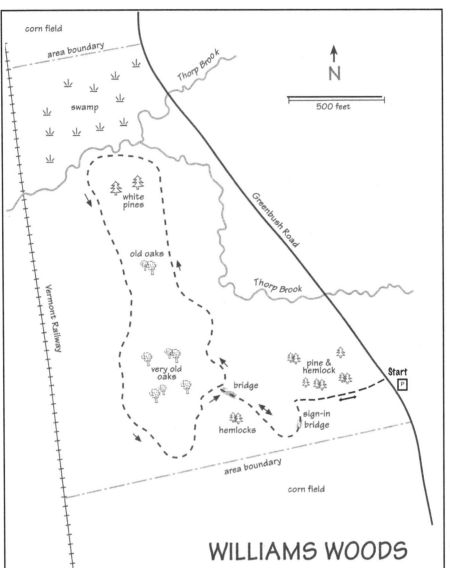

WILLIAMS WOODS

the surface. Yellow birch and hemlock roots often spread across a rocky hillside forest but in Williams Woods waterlogged soil is the cause. A high water table and clay soil make for very damp ground. The shallow root systems account for numerous blowdowns throughout the woods. You will even see giant oaks sprawled over the ground, their tiny root balls unable to sustain them.

When soil is waterlogged, even briefly, its oxygen is quickly depleted and it becomes anaerobic (without oxygen). Even after the water recedes oxygen is slow to return to the soil. Wetland trees, like willow, silver and swamp maple, and cot-

With shallow roots, even large trees have toppled in Williams Woods.

tonwood, have evolved shallow root systems with significant aboveground sections to maximize contact with the air. Multiple trunks can perform the same function.

Towering old hemlocks dominate the beginning of the trail with only spinulose wood fern growing in the sparse light. The many blowdowns have created sunny openings and pocket wetlands in the waterlogged soil. Young, fast growing white pines, have seized these opportunities and are overtaking the hemlocks.

You will walk on a narrow boardwalk over the most sodden ground and many of the surface roots. Sign in on the left.

The trail turns left and crosses the first bridge within five minutes of the trailhead. Hardwoods are more common and several ash trees with deeply furrowed bark grow near Thorp Brook on the right of the trail.

Cross Thorpe Brook again on a wooden bridge and turn right at a double blaze.

An increase in deciduous trees provides more sunlight to herbs. Bloodroot, jack-in-the-pulpit, and common elderberry, indicators of fertile soil, make appearances. The trail crosses another wooden bridge, goes up a slight rise, and turns right. Red and white oak, ash, shagbark hickory, hop hornbeam, bur oak, sugar maple, beech, and birch grow in the rich clay. Some very large, old oaks are scattered in the woods, some still standing, others mere skeletons.

The trail jogs back and forth over a tangle of roots. A yellow birch with spectacular roots is on the left. The understory waxes and wanes inversely with the hemlocks in the canopy.

The trail passes through a white pine plantation near the edge of the Thorp Brook swamp. Next to the swamp a huge old bur oak (Quercus macrocarpa) stands with a diameter of nearly 3 1/2 feet. A stately tree indeed!

The trail bends to the left keeping the swamp on the right. The canopy is mostly hemlocks and white pine. A wolf tree, a white pine that grew wide branches in a field, is on the left.

The trail emerges from the dark coniferous woods to mixed woods again. Basswood, another indicator of fertile soils, and shagbark hickory join the other hardwoods.

The trail makes a number of turns and crosses several small bridges before it rejoins the outbound trail for the last few minutes.

Coyote, white-tailed deer, and wild turkey are plentiful in these woods. Look for scat, prints, feathers, browsed twigs or the animals themselves.

OLD TREES

New England's rigorous climate makes it difficult for trees to grow to old age as wind, snow, ice, lightning, and pathogens conspire against longevity. Many native species have life spans of three to four hundred years, eastern hemlock, northern white cedar, eastern white pine, and white oak among them.

What, then, are old trees and what constitutes old growth?

The term old growth implies a lack of human disturbance- no logging, pasturing, tilling for crops, or roads at their feet, although such trees may be victims of natural calamities. Experts disagree about where old growth trees exist in Vermont but that there are some old trees is certain. Williams Woods has some oaks that may approach two hundred years of age.

EUROPEAN BUCKTHORN

An introduced species that escaped cultivation, buckthorn (Rhamnus cathartica) is spreading like a weed through New England woods. Its seeds spread by birds, buckthorn squeezes out plants that provide benefit to a wider range of wildlife. One competitive advantage of the buckthorn is its ability to photosynthesize for a longer season than many of its competitors. It is one of the few plants in the woods holding its leaves through November.

ABOUT CLAY

Clay soil, the waterlogged underpinning of Williams Woods, owes its fertility to its small particle size and the many negatively charged ions on its surface. Important minerals for healthy plant growth, like calcium and magnesium, are positively charged and attach to the clay molecules while remaining accessible to the plants.

GETTING THERE

From the north take Rte. 7 south and turn right at the stop light in Charlotte, Ferry Road or F-5. There are signs for the ferry to New York State. Drive 0.3 mile to the stop sign. Turn left on Greenbush Road. After two miles you will swing to the left- be careful! Greenbush Road continues, paved, to the south. (If you cross the railroad, turn back. You missed the turn.) After 1.0 mile you will find a wooden sign, tucked under the trees on the right, for Williams Woods. Pull to the side of the road to park.

From the south on Rte. 7, turn left at Stage Road in North Ferrisburg. The Ferrisburg Post Office on the southwest corner. Drive 1.0 mile to Greenbush Road. Turn right. The entrance to Williams Woods will be 1.0 mile on the left.

FOR MORE INFORMATION

The Nature Conservancy- Vermont Chapter
http://www.nature.org/wherewework/northamerica/states/vermont/

20 Pease Mountain Natural Area

A prominent hill in the Champlain Valley with a rich diversity of plants and a large flock of wild turkeys. A great place to snowshoe.

CHARLOTTE, VT
LOWER WALK: **1.5** MILES, **200** FOOT ELEVATION GAIN
1 HOUR
UPPER WALK: **2.5** MILES, **400** FOOT GAIN
TO SUMMIT RIDGE
1.5 HOURS
MODERATE WITH SOME ROCKY FOOTING
DOGS MUST BE LEASHED AND STAY ON
TRAILS AT ALL TIMES.
CLEAN UP AFTER PETS.

A SERIES OF NEWSPAPER ARTICLES written in the 1890s by William Wallace Higbee provide historical texture to many local haunts. His collected writings were compiled by the Charlotte Historical Society in *Around the Mountains*, and from it we glean some details about Pease Mountain.

Higbee writes that Pease Mountain was twice "denuded of its forestry" in the nineteenth century. Its trees fed the boilers of the Rutland and Burlington Railroad, yet by 1897 the land was once again forested. So it is with forests in Vermont.

The 800-foot high mountain was home to the town's first settled minister who built his house on the sunny, southeast side of the mountain. In 1841, Charlotte Town Selectmen leased a large section of the mountain to George Pease for 999 years. The family returned that generosity in 1949 when trustees of the Pease estate donated 180 acres to the University of Vermont (UVM).

Pease Mountain is a UVM Natural Area. Forestry students use it for plant identification and mapping exercises. Students at Charlotte Central School observe nature in this outdoor laboratory. A new housing development on the northern flank of Pease Mountain has resulted in a relocation of the trail but public access has been maintained. The UVM Natural Area is unchanged.

Two walks are pleasant options. The lower walk leads to two rocky outcroppings, both good picnic spots. One has seasonal views to the Lake and the other

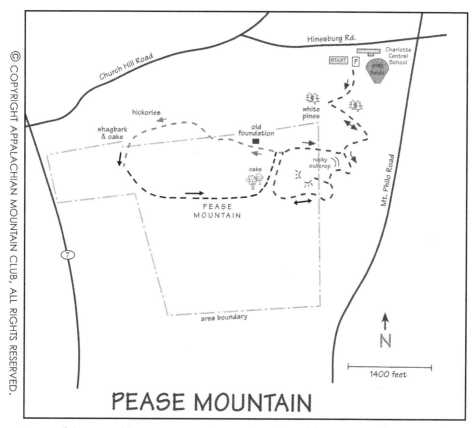

PEASE MOUNTAIN

is a restful stop and home to many interesting plants. The upper walk rises to a loop around the summit. In winter there are views to the west, south, and east. Both walks use the same access trail.

• • • • • •

Walk south across the playing fields to the right of the backstop. Climb the slope to the trailhead at the edge of the woods.

The trail begins in a dense stand of white pines. Because of abundant runoff at the base of the mountain, these well-watered trees have grown quickly, erasing grazing and agricultural fields. Notice that many of the pines have multiple trunks. The white pine weevil probably infested the young trees. (See page 78.)

The trail turns left and climbs gradually. Partridgeberry and purple-flowering herb Robert peek from beneath lush ferns. Sensitive ferns are abundant here indicating moist ground. Several young black birches, moderately shade tolerant trees, grow beneath the white pines. Their leaves and twigs taste of wintergreen and the sap can be used to make birch beer.

The trail is never blazed but is worn and obvious. It makes several S-curves as

White trillium are among the lush wildflowers on Pease Mountain.

it gains elevation leaving the pines in favor of hardwoods and a rich collection of wildflowers. We begin to see bitternut hickory saplings with vertically striped bark and relatively few stubby, alternate branches. Bitternuts buds are unmistakable, large saffron-colored swellings already conspicuous in August for the next spring. Its compound leaves fairly explode from the bud with as many as eleven leaflets. Bitternuts are only found in fertile soil.

These woods are home to a wide variety of deciduous trees, among them paper, yellow and black birch, red oak, American beech, hop hornbeam with its shreddy bark and lacy twigs, elm, poplar, maple, white ash, basswood, and bitternut and shagbark hickories. Among the shrubby trees, we find serviceberry, striped maple, and the occasional blue beech. Many of these trees are generalists and will grow in a variety of conditions but basswood and bitternut hickory are indicators of fertile soil. In early May a bounty of wildflowers bloom in the rich soil including white trillium, hepatica, trout lily, spring beauty, and bloodroot.

After a right turn the trail slopes slightly downhill. It is circling the rocky outcropping (our destination), making a series of left curves and turns. One section descends in step-like fashion, as if the quartzite was once quarried. When a small trail forks to the right, stay on the main trail to the left. We pass through several patches of invasive honeysuckle. Its bright, prolific berries are attractive to birds.

When you reach a three-way intersection, go left for the lower walk and right to the summit loop. First, we will go left to the lower walk.

Keep curving left (you will have made much of a circle) on a wide and well-worn section of trail. It rises over rocky surface and immediately a small trail, not well marked, goes steeply up scrabbly rock to the left. Clamber uphill on the worn trail through woods dominated by shagbark hickory and hop hornbeam trees. On the right is a four-trunked red oak that sprouted from a stump after logging. The central trunk, measured from the center of each sprout, would have produced a huge piece of timber. The ground is littered with paper birches that may have died due to lack of sunlight. There's also a patch of the yellow-flowered barren strawberry.

The trail rises over rosy quartzite outcroppings. The bedrock of Pease Mountain is very old metamorphic rock. This Monkton quartzite, called redstone, was used in many local buildings in the nineteenth century. The quartzite formed when sandstone was subjected to enormous heat and pressure. This process does not alter the mineral content and the quartzite has the same calcareous or limy characteristics as the original sedimentary rock.

Tidy, evergreen polypody ferns.

When glaciers melted at the end of the Ice Age, much of the Champlain Valley was inundated, first by freshwater Lake Vermont and later by the salty Champlain Sea. (See Button Bay, page 158.) Thick deposits of sediment left by these bodies of water became the rich, clay soils of the valley. Only the islands that stood above water, including Pease Mountain, Mt. Philo, and Snake Mountain, are not mantled in clay.

Another unmarked but worn trail goes left, uphill. Near the top of this short stretch you will see a number of serviceberry trees (Amelanchier canadensis), with wavy vertical lines on their smooth gray bark. These early-flowering trees never grow beyond thirty feet. As early as April five, long white petals burst forth. The name refers to the time when burial services could be held for those who had died in winter (when the ground was frozen). Its other names, shadbush and Juneberry, also refer to the season: the spawning of shad and the tree's June-ripening fruit.

You will reach the first outcropping with winter views north to the lake. Returning from this short detour turn left to continue to the second, larger quartzite outcropping. The soil here is very thin so please stay on the bedrock. This is a lovely place to tarry, a place of color, texture, and bird song. The soft, gray-green tufts of reindeer moss, really lichen, grow in pretty patterns on the maroon quartzite. Sun-loving plants, tolerant of the dry conditions on this shallow soil, are low and compact: lowbush blueberry, huckleberry, and juniper. Pease Mountain is a great place to see and hear spring warblers.

When you have had enough of this plateau, retrace your steps, down the steep section, and turn right. You are walking back toward the three-way intersection. Trees are taller here than on the outcropping because more moisture is available in the deeper soil. The trail curves gradually to the right passing patches of red and white trillium. They both prefer rich, moist soils. White trillium are more common in the Champlain Valley and red in the higher elevations.

At the meeting place of three trails, you may turn right and retrace your steps to the bottom (20-30 minutes) or turn left and take the upper walk.

Immediately you will pass a sign for the Pease Mountain Natural Area and moments later a trail comes in from the left. Do not take the left- we will return from here. We climb gently for a few minutes and the trail is often wet. Look for an old redstone foundation on the right. This may have been the home of Charlotte's early minister. This once-sunny location would have been protected from the prevailing south winds and several springs for water are nearby.

It's about a fifteen-minute walk uphill to the summit ridge. When the leaves are off the trees there is a view to the lake. Dry conditions produce early spring wildflowers here. Hepatica bloom early in April, one of the first joys of spring. Its flowers, on hairy stems, range from deep purple to white and evergreen leaves are three-lobed. The ability of evergreen leaves to use every ray of spring sunshine contributes to the plant's early flowering.

The summit forest is a lovely mix of hickories, oak, ash, sugar maple, and hop hornbeam. The trail, named Paradis Loop by UVM students in honor of their professor Rick Paradis, is well worn if not well marked. It curves gently to the left around the summit to make a loop. You may catch a view of Mt. Philo to the south and the Green Mountains to the east even in summer. As you descend you will pass through seas of white trillium before rejoining the trail where you left it.

When you reach the trail, turn right, pass the Pease Mountain sign, and stay left to return to the parking lot.

TURKEY TROT

A maze of wild turkey tracks covers the winter snows on Pease Mountain. These three-pronged prints appear gigantic, six inches from front to back and three inches from side to side, as melting snow exaggerates their dimensions. The stride, distance from one print to another, is about a foot.

The wild turkey (Meleagris gallopava) was nearly hunted to extinction before habitat management, controlled hunting seasons, and calculated reintroduction helped reestablish the giant bird. The male averages 48" from beak to tail, the female 36". The turkey is predominantly brown and white, with many beautiful, striped feathers.

Ground nesting makes turkeys vulnerable to predators. They lay ten to fifteen eggs in a shallow leaf-lined depression in the vegetation.

GETTING THERE

Take Rte. 7 to Charlotte. At the stop light, the intersection of Ferry Road to the west and Church Hill Road to the east, turn onto Church Hill Road. At the stop sign in 0.7 mile, turn right on Hinesburg Road. Turn right in 0.3 mile to park in the lots west of Charlotte Central School.

FOR MORE INFORMATION

University of Vermont
Environmental Program
http://www.uvm.edu/~envprog/?Page=naturalareas/default.html

21   Mount Philo State Park

The view from Mt. Philo is special any month of the year. Its geology is intriguing and visible and its spring wildflowers spectacular.

CHARLOTTE, VT
1.75 MILES, 600 FOOT ELEVATION GAIN
1.5 HOURS
MODERATE WITH SOME STEEP SECTIONS
DOGS, ON LEASH, ARE PERMITTED ONLY IN
CAMPGROUND AREA.

MT. PHILO IS VERMONT'S oldest state park. The 968-foot summit has lovely, gentle views of the Champlain Valley. Its spring wildflowers are early and prolific. Hawk viewing is excellent and there's a great sledding hill.

Owners of the Mt. Philo Inn built the original carriageway in 1903. In the 1930s, the Civilian Conservation Corps (CCC) constructed the current road that makes Mt. Philo's summit so accessible. Young, old, and the physically challenged can enjoy the same view. When April turns the countryside to a sea of mud the pavement leads to a bounty of wildflowers and the songs of migrating warblers.

In January 1998, northern New England experienced an epic ice storm. Damage was localized according to elevation and Mt. Philo was devastated. Hundreds of trees, many of them part of the 1930s plantations (see photo on next page), crashed to earth. The park was closed for months as trees were removed. The scarred earth and shattered trees broke our hearts.

Today most of the damage is invisible to a casual visitor. However, openings in the canopy have produced a splendid display of wildflowers- better than before the Ice Storm of 1998.

Hiking trails in the park are not for everyone and certainly not for every season. Maintained for summer use only, they are steep and often muddy. They can be icy in winter. The road is passable much of the year, open to cars in season and foot traffic year round. The asphalt access is an off-season gift so we will take it.

• • • • • •

The road wastes little time in beginning its climb, which continues steadily to the top. On the lower slopes, plantations of conifers were planted by the CCC in the 1930s to reforest the bare hillsides. Look for tamaracks or larch, Scotch and red pine, and Norway spruce. The short needles of Scotch pine, usually less than two

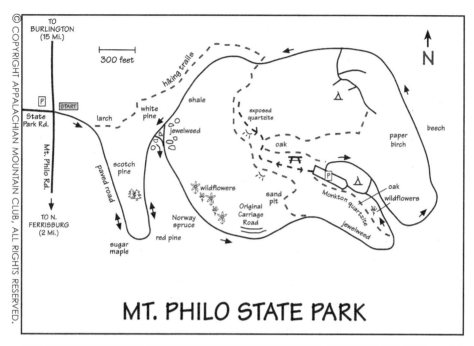

TO
BURLINGTON
(15 Mi.)

300 feet

P

START

State
Park Rd.

Mt. Philo Rd.

TO N.
FERRISBURG
(2 Mi.)

paved road

larch

white
pine

shale

hiking trails

jewelweed

scotch
pine

sugar
maple

red pine

Norway
spruce

wildflowers

Original
Carriage
Road

sand
pit

exposed
quartzite

oak

Monkton quartzite

jewelweed

P

oak
wildflowers

paper
birch

beech

N

MT. PHILO STATE PARK

The park was closed after the 1998 ice storm for removal of downed trees.

inches long, are in bunches of two. The upper bark on the trunk glows a salmon color, like a perpetual sunset. Red pines also have bunches of two needles, but they are long, dark green, and brittle. The mature trunk has rosy patches peeking from beneath brown scales of outer bark. Tamaracks, or larches, are our only deciduous conifer. Other evergreens keep their needles from three to ten years and shed them gradually. Tufts of short, bright green needles give tamaracks a soft look. In late autumn they glow butterscotch yellow. Norway spruce, with drooping boughs, looks altogether different. Its short, spiky needles are not bunched but arranged spirally around the twig.

The road makes one switchback before coming to a fork within ten to fifteen minutes. In late April or early May bloodroot blooms here. A member of the poppy family, the plant gets its name from the red-orange juice in its roots and stems. Native Americans used it as an insect repellent and dye. Its eight to ten white petals surround a golden-orange center and a single leaf curls around the stalk. The blossoms open in full sun and close at night.

A delightful panorama for all: those who come on foot and those who drive to the summit.

Maidenhair fern grows in the damper, rich soil of the north side.

At the fork go uphill to the right, around a boulder field. Chunks of maroon Monkton quartzite have fallen from the top of the mountain (more about this shortly).

Any time from late fall until mid-spring, Mt. Philo is a great place to learn the basics fern identification. Four evergreen ferns grow on Mt. Philo. With no other leaves, flowers, or summer ferns as a distraction, the task is quite manageable. Warning: Do not try this in summer; it's overwhelming! (See Fern Identification Made Simple, page 145.)

The common polypody fern, a once-cut fern, favors rocky sites. Rarely more than twelve inches high, the leathery, bright green fronds may have up to twenty pairs of tiny leaflets. Christmas fern, also once-cut, has deep green, leathery fronds up to two feet in length. Its lobed leaflets resemble a Christmas stocking. Marginal woodfern is twice cut and grows to two feet. Its fruitdots, on the underside of the frond, are conspicuous along the margins of the leaflets. Hence its name. The thrice-cut spinulose woodfern has lacy, foot-long fronds and its fruitdots are clustered near the veins on the underside of the leaflet. It is most easily identified in comparison with the marginal woodfern.

This stretch of road blooms in May with early meadow rue, hepatica, white trillium, columbine, spring beauty, and Dutchman's breeches. A rich mix of deciduous trees includes sugar maple, white ash, paper birch, hop hornbeam, shagbark hickory, black cherry, butternut, and basswood. To the left is the original carriageway, it base on boulders built into the hillside.

Walk about fifty feet into an entrance marked Service Vehicles Only. An open sand pit gapes on the left, the remains of a glacial kame. (Piles of brush remain after the Ice Storm clean up.) As glacial ice melted, sand accumulated against the hillside and remained after the ice was gone. This is the origin of many local sand and gravel pits.

The paved road gets steeper. While catching your breath, admire a huge patch of jewelweed on the left flourishing in the damp soil. In early spring this is home to Dutchman's Breeches.

Look up at the towering cliff. Notice that the quartzite is layered, the color changing at irregular intervals. This rock was laid down as sedimentary rock, a sandstone, and then subjected to heat or pressure to become the harder, metamorphic quartzite. At the base of the mountain, softer shale crumbles beneath its weight and chunks of quartzite break off. This flank of Mt. Philo is littered with chunks of quartzite. We will see the best exposures of shale on the walk downhill.

Along the last stretch before the summit another sea of spring wildflowers blooms: hepatica, spring beauty, trout lily or dogtooth violet, white trillium, and sessile bellwort. Pink lady's slipper also flowers in these woods.

The summit is home to mature northern white cedars in addition to red oak, shagbark hickory, and hop hornbeam, trees at home in the thin, drier soil on the summit. Oaks prefer warm, well-drained sites. In the Champlain Valley they often grow on south and west-facing slopes. The quartzite bedrock has a calcareous component favored by the cedars. (See the walk in Leicester Hollow, page 210.)

Walk to the farthest observation point on a rocky outcrop facing west. Notice the quartzite underfoot- it is sloping uphill toward the west. In a tumultuous earth-building event, about 350 million years ago, the older Monkton quartzite was thrust westward over younger, softer shale. It is this sloping layer of erosion-resistant quartzite that gives the local sheepback mountains their characteristic shape.

Now look south to similar profiles of Buck and Snake Mountains. They share the same gradual eastern flanks and sharper drop-offs to the west.

The road starts down from the parking lot, next to the sign recognizing the CCC and State Forester Perry Merrill. The more gradual eastern slope has deeper soils and retains more moisture and nutrient runoff than the west-facing cliffs. Trees are taller and plant diversity greater. You will find several indicators of rich or limy soil, including maidenhair fern, herb Robert, and basswood. Large clumps of American beech grow in the woods. They prefer soil that never dries out. There are few oaks here.

After a grove of paper birch, the road rises slightly. On the left, just beyond a culvert, three of the evergreen ferns grow together on left: Christmas fern, marginal woodfern, and spinulose woodfern.

Beyond the lower campground, as the road curves to the left, look for exposed shale. The thin, brittle layers slump visibly beneath the weight of the overriding quartzite.

The roads rejoin at the fork where another massive patch of jewelweed flourishes on the left.

FERN IDENTIFICATION MADE SIMPLE

Fronds are divided into four categories of leaf structure. Imagine a flat palm frond and a pair of scissors. If you cut from the edge of the leaf to its mid-vein, you create simple leaflets (once-cut). If you take each resulting leaflet and repeat the procedure, cut it from its edge to its middle, the leaf is twice cut, into subleaflets. If the subleaflets are cut yet again, a lacy leaf or thrice-cut fern results. Thus we have once cut, twice-, or thrice-cut ferns. The fourth category includes ferns with unusual or non-fernlike leaves.

Next, determine the shape of the frond or leaf. There are three types: broadest at the base- a triangle; semi-tapering to base; and tapering to base. These last are pointed at both ends.

With the leaflet type and frond shape established, the spore cases positively identify the species. These organs, also called fruitdots, are usually found on the underside of the leaflets, although they sometimes occur on separate stalks (even easier to identify).

The Vermont Department of Forests, Park, and Recreation distributes a free booklet, Common Ferns of Vermont, at state parks. It is clear, simple, and very helpful.

WHICH WAY TO THE BEACH?

Lake Vermont and the Champlain Sea, the bodies of water that filled the Champlain Valley at the end of the Ice Age, left behind many shore-and lake-level indicators. Mt. Philo was an island in Lake Vermont and near the shore of the Champlain Sea. So, which way to the beach?

While vegetation hides much of the surface geology, some evidence is visible. Beach gravel from the Champlain Sea straddles State Park Road where it joins Route 7. Pebbly sand from Lake Vermont begins at the park gate and grades into beach gravel as the access road climbs toward the switchback. On the east side, downhill from the park road, are deposits of lake sand and boulder strewn lake sediments.

A detailed map is included in a booklet describing the geology of three state parks, D.A.R., Mt. Philo, and Sand Bar. It is available at many state parks or from the office of the state geologist. (See Bibliography.)

GETTING THERE

From the stop light on Rte. 7 in Charlotte, drive south on Rte. 7. Turn left on State Park Road at the blinking light, 2.5 miles. The park gate will be in front of you in 0.6 mile.

FOR MORE INFORMATION

Vermont Department of Forests, Parks, and Recreation
http://www.vtstateparks.com/index.cfm

22 Copp-Welch Loop

Cathedral of mature hemlocks, towering hardwoods, hidden meadow, and wetland pond in a quiet corner of Hinesburg. This conserved land is testimony to the power of volunteers to make a difference in their community. Great for cross-country skiing and snowshoeing.

HINESBURG, VT
1.7 MILES
1 HOUR
EASY
DOGS SHOULD BE UNDER CONTROL AT ALL TIMES.

IN THE DECADE SINCE this book was originally published the Hinesburg Land Trust (HLT), working with other volunteer groups, has conserved significant acreage. In addition to this property, now owned by the Department of Fish and Wildlife, HLT has protected an adjoining farm that includes brood trees for the endangered Indiana bat, a working farm and sugar bush in the heart of the village (see In the Area at the end of this chapter), and additional conservation lands across town.

This property feels remote at the edge of the state's most populous county. A wildlife corridor, it connects to another recently conserved parcel, the New Town Forest, which includes the headwaters of the LaPlatte River.

• • • • • •

The trail begins behind a chain intended to exclude wheeled vehicles. Two short stonewall segments flank the gravel path as its rises up a slight grade into the woods. Trout lilies bloom here early in the spring. Very soon dirt replaces gravel. The wide path is smooth and carpeted with leaves and needles. Footing is good and the trail is blazed at frequent intervals with white paint.

Mixed hardwoods with few side branches tower overhead. Where sunlight reaches the forest floor wild cucumber, trillium, Canada mayflower, and twisted stalk flower beneath a shrub layer that includes beech saplings, striped maple, and the occasional hobblebush.

After about ten minutes on this access trail we reach the Copp-Welch Loop. We bear left (and will return from the right).

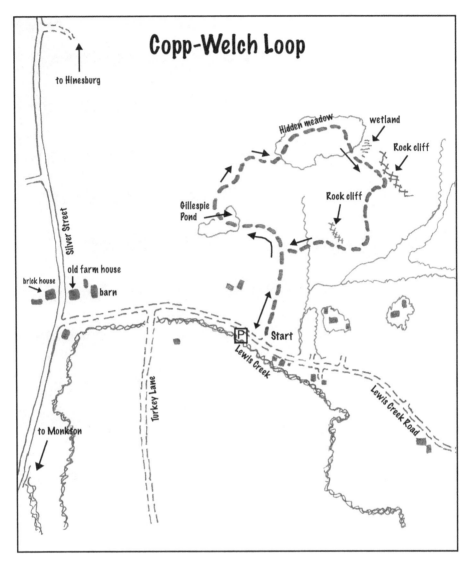

Copp-Welch Loop

to Hinesburg

Hidden meadow   wetland

Rock cliff

Rock cliff

Gillespie
Pond

Silver Street

old farm house

brick house

barn

P   Start

Lewis Creek

Turkey Lane

to Monkton

Lewis Creek Road

The trail continues to rise gently. Many beech trees here are afflicted with beech bark scale disease that will eventually kill them. Fortunately the shrub layer is thick with healthy young beech trees. As the larger tree sickens it sends up numerous root sprouts. This strategy insures a population of beech after the death of the main tree. Hemlocks increasingly join the hardwoods as we continue and these evergreens exclude sunlight. As a result fewer wildflowers grow. On the right a steep rocky hillside is littered with blow downs. A large patch of white trillium enjoys the resulting sunshine beneath openings in the canopy.

Within ten minutes we arrive at a small meadow. A shapely pair of white cedars stands in the middle of a sea of sensitive ferns. If our shoes haven't already done so, these ferns tell us it's wet underfoot. To the right is Gillespie Pond, marshy and lined with cattails. The trail curves right, wrapping around the far side of the pond and returning to the woods.

Some white pines mix with young deciduous trees and within ten minutes we arrive at a three-way intersection, clearly marked. The Copp-Welch Loop goes right. The trail is generally flat through mixed woods of hemlocks and young deciduous trees.

In about five minutes we reach another intersection. The Ravine Trail goes right. This short, 0.25-mile connector returns through mixed hemlock and deciduous woods to the access trail from Lewis Creek Road. (In wet seasons this would be a drier route.) We will instead turn left to continue the Copp-Welch Loop. We immediately enter the Hidden Meadow.

Forestland surrounds this lovely island of grass and wildflowers. Walking clockwise around it we pass some shrubby trees at its edge, among them shadbush, red-osier dogwood, and some very thorny hawthorns, all a rich source of fruit for birds. Within five minutes two trails depart from the edge of the meadow: the 0.37-mile access trail to Gilman Road and the 0.55-mile Bissonette Loop. The latter connects

Keep your eyes open for this diminutive bloom, Canada mayflower.

149

to the LaPlatte Headwaters Town Forest. See For More Information at the end of this chapter.

We continue to circle the meadow. Very soon the trail exits the open space and return to the woods. The ground is damp and as a result tree roots, seeking more oxygen, sprawl underfoot. Mind your footing! Hemlocks increasingly dominate these woods although a steep ridge rises on the left where deciduous trees grow. Within five minutes we approach another access trail going left to Lower Gilman Road, 0.48 mile. We turn right on the Copp-Welch Loop.

As more deciduous trees mix with the hemlocks we see the miracle of light. Wildflowers return: white trillium, wild cucumber, and twisted stalk among them. The trail turns right and goes steeply down a muddy stretch, crosses a stream on logs, and climbs back to the height of land. Shortly the Ravine Trail comes in from the right (Do not take it.). In about 100 feet the Copp-Welch Loop completes its circuit. We turn left on the access trail and follow it back to Lewis Creek Road.

GETTING THERE

From the stoplight at the intersection of Charlotte Road and Route 116 (in front of Lantman's Market), drive south 0.2 mile on Rte. 116 to the intersection. Silver Street goes right or south, while Rte. 116 swings to the left. Take Silver Street 2.8 miles. Turn left on Lewis Creek Road- this turn is hidden so slow down. Drive 0.5 mile on Lewis Creek Road- it is dirt, to a pullout on the right. If there is not room to park, return to Turkey Lane and park near the bridge.

FOR MORE INFORMATION

Town of Hinesburg, Recreation Office
10632 Route 116
Hinesburg, VT 05461
482-4691
http://www.hinesburg.org/hart.html
La LaPlatte Headwaters Town Forest
http://www.hinesburg.org/btf/btfmap.pdf

•ALSO IN THE AREA •

RUSSELL FAMILY TRAILS

Two miles of foot trails traverse a working farm in Hinesburg Village. They rise from Lyman Park through woods and fields. The Village Overlook Trail loops off of the Perimeter Trail. The trailhead is located at the north end of Lyman Park fields where you will also find parking. Lyman Park Road is opposite Hinesburg Community School on Rte. 116 just south of the village.

Southern Champlain Valley

23 Kingsland Bay State Park

A forested peninsula on Lake Champlain with lovely views of lake and mountains. Beautiful wildflowers.

FERRISBURG, VT
0.6 MILE
45 MINUTES
EASY BUT THE FOOTING CAN BE UNEVEN
DOGS NOT PERMITTED.

NOT MANY OF LAKE CHAMPLAIN'S 587 miles of shoreline are publicly accessible. Much of that public land has a recreational purpose and has been cleared for swimming, boating, or fishing access. A lakeside walk through a quiet forest of old, gnarled trees is a rare pleasure indeed.

MacDonough Point has many cool and shady spots from which to enjoy the sights and sounds of the lake. On a quiet day you may hear fish flopping and loons calling. The gnarled northern white cedars paint a picture of survival, their tortured roots and contorted trunks testimony to an ambiance of wind, waves, and ice.

The 264-acre Kingsland Bay State Park was until quite recently a summer camp. The lovely stone Hawley House dates from 1790. The park warden can give you a key to see a newly installed exhibit of maritime history.

• • • • • •

The walking trail begins near the shore, to the north of the swimming and picnic areas. It immediately disappears into the woods. In May, thousands of white trillium bob in the breeze. Large-flowered trillium (Trillium graniflorum), members of the lily family, prefer deciduous woods with neutral soils. The three-petaled flower, which turns pink before it fades, sits atop a whorl of three leaves. Picking the flower will almost certainly kill the plant because there are no other leaves to manufacture food.

The trail rises and descends gently on a bluff above the water. As the trail approaches the lake you will feel a chill in the spring and warmth off the water in the fall. This shoreline microclimate means that flowers and leaves near the shore are slow to emerge in the spring and they are the last to succumb to frost at the end of the season.

After a few minutes you will see woodpecker excavations on a white cedar to

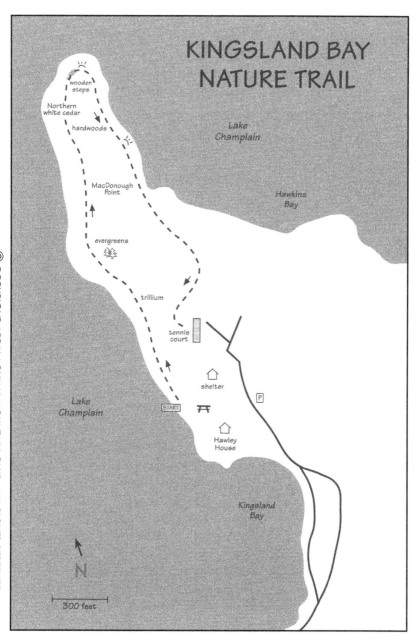

KINGSLAND BAY
NATURE TRAIL

Lake
Champlain

Hawkins
Bay

wooden
steps

Northern
white cedar

hardwoods

MacDonough
Point

evergreens

trillium

tennis
court

shelter

P

Lake
Champlain

START

Hawley
House

Kingsland
Bay

N

300 feet

the left of the trail. Only the pileated woodpecker makes holes of this size while searching for carpenter ants or making a nest cavity for its family. These huge woodpeckers, nearly eighteen inches from beak to tail, are quite shy of humans. You may hear them drumming in the distance or find the heap of wood chunks at the base of a tree. If you see the enormous bird there is no mistaking it: huge red crest on its head, long beak, black body with bold white stripes on the head and the long, strong tail with which it props itself against trees.

White cedar trees cling ferociously to the rocky shore.

These woods are home to four evergreen conifers, the northern white cedar being dominant. The white cedar (*Thuja occidentalis*) has scales rather than needles and its bark often shreds in vertical strips. These trees hug the edges of the cliffs, often with dramatic result.

The familiar white pine, with its five long needles (w-h-i-t-e), has dark gray bark that makes it easy to distinguish from the red pine. Red pine needles are longer than those of the white pine and are bunched in twos. You won't be able to see that on tall trees so look instead at the rosy trunk. The bark of a mature red pine is a beautiful thing, thick rosy plates beneath a layer of brown.

The fourth conifer is the hemlock, with short, flat needles. Its shallow root system enables it to survive on this thin soil. The bedrock, which keeps appearing underfoot, is never far from the surface.

Where evergreens are thick few plants survive beneath them. The ground is covered with fallen needles, mosses, and the occasional fern.

On the hillside to the right of the trail, in the center of the peninsula, deciduous trees grow, a mixture of shagbark and bitternut hickory, oak, maple, ash, birch, and hop hornbeam. Before these trees leaf out, a riot of wildflowers unfolds beneath them: trillium, trout lilies, false Solomon's seal, and hepatica among them.

On a quiet day in May a pair of loons paddled by nearby. (For more information on Loons, see next page.) Swallows swooped for insects just above the water's surface, fish splashed, and three Baltimore orioles flitted at the edge of the woods.

The trail turns right and descends a set of wooden stairs built into the hillside before returning on the eastern, or bay side of the peninsula. Immediately you will notice that the trees are taller, protected from the wind and weather of the open lake. Several oak and ash trees have grown to a good height. Above a moss-covered rocky outcropping on the right side of the trail is a remarkable sight. A grape vine must have wound around a paper birch when it was young. The tree has a series of diagonal stripes making it look like a barber's pole.

The trail hugs the shore, which is eroded in places. Across Hawkins Bay you will see Camel's Hump, Vermont's most distinctive mountain. Mt. Philo in Charlotte is on the left in the foreground.

On the right side of the trail are several clumps of American yew or ground hemlock (*Taxus canadensis*), a low, shade-loving plant. Its needles are yellow green in contrast to the darker blue green of the eastern hemlock. In the late summer yew produces an almost translucent red berry with a cylindrical hole right to the seed in its center. These berries are poisonous to humans.

The trail turns away from the shore and returns to the parking area.

LURE OF THE LOONS

Notwithstanding the six billion birds summering in the United States, Vermont's small population of black and white common loons (*Gavia immer*) has captured a disproportionate number of hearts. Although the state's loon population is slowly growing, pairs abandon their nests when humans venture too close. Please enjoy them from afar, at least 300 feet.

With their big feet and torpedo-shaped bodies, loons can dive to one hundred feet where they may fish for over a minute. An especially designed rib cage forms an overlapping lattice that prevents compression of the loon's lungs under pressure.

Loons cannot walk and with dense bones are poorly designed for flight. Their wing area to weight ratio makes it hard for them to soar even after a long run and shallow climb. Remarkably, once airborne, they can fly as fast as 100 mph.

Loon eggs, usually two, hatch one day apart in June. Like most ground-nesting birds, the chicks are sufficiently developed to leave the nest quickly and can soon swim.

If a storm erupts or a predator threatens, parents will lure away the firstborn chick and abandon the second. Predators include northern pike, muskellunge, or snapping turtles from below and hawks or eagles from above. Cold is a greater threat than predation, perhaps the reason adults give chicks rides on their backs in the first few weeks of life.

Loons may live to be thirty years old. Perhaps the key to longevity is their shoe size. Extrapolated to humans it would be 45 triple R!

VERMONT LOON RECOVERY PROJECT,

www.vinsweb.org/cbd/VLRP.html, works to support and protect the population through education, monitoring, and management.

GETTING THERE

From Rte. 7 in Ferrisburg, turn west on Little Chicago Road- coming from the north this will be a right turn, from the south a left turn. The Town Clerk's office is on the corner. Follow this road across the river and the railroad track. At 0.9 mile, turn right onto Hawkins Road. It meanders through farmland and along the Otter Creek. The entrance to the State Park is on the right at 3.4 miles.

FOR MORE INFORMATION
Kingsland Bay State Park
787 Kingsland Bay State Park Road
Ferrisburg, VT 05456
802-877-3445
Department of Forests, Parks, and Recreation
http://www.vtstateparks.com/index.cfm

• ALSO IN THE AREA •

ROKEBY MUSEUM

A stop on the Underground Railroad, Rokeby was the sheep farm of Quaker abolitionists. Family home to the Robinsons for nearly two centuries, Rokeby reveals the life and times of this unusual family.

Rokeby is on Rte. 7 in Ferrisburg.

24 Champlain Nature Trail, Button Bay State Park

A lakeside walk through an old forest atop some of the oldest fossilized coral in the world. A Nature Center for all ages.

Remember, fossil collecting is not allowed on state lands.

FERRISBURG, VT
1.6 MILES
1 HOUR
EASY WITH OCCASIONAL ROUGH FOOTING
DOGS, ON LEASH, ARE PERMITTED ONLY IN
CAMPGROUND AREA.

BUTTON POINT IS A QUIET wooded peninsula with magnificent views. It also has some stately old oaks, hickories, and pines. Button Island, just off the Point, is part of the oldest coral reef in the world. Coral formations are visible on the far side of the island.

As the earth's plates shifted over its molten center, some 450 million years ago, great pressure converted the organic debris- coral, shells, and ocean sediment to limestone and shifted it to its current location. The reef surfaces again in the Champlain Islands (see In the Area).

In more recent geologic time, the Champlain Valley was inundated by a fresh water lake and a saltwater sea. Clay deposited by these waters lies thick across the valley and in Button Bay it took on some unusual shapes, many like buttons. These flat, donut-like disks inspired British soldiers to dub the area Button Mold Bay.

In the late 1800s, Samuel Putnam Avery bought the land from the state in order to build a summer home on Button Island. The property stayed in Avery's family until the 1970s when his niece, Amy Welcher, sold it back to the State of Vermont.

The Nature Center was Amy Welcher's summer camp. A self-taught naturalist, Welcher built the camp with lots of windows and doors to bring nature indoors. The fireplace is built from local stone including fossils, concretions, and two polished pieces of coral. Look at it carefully when you visit the Center.

• • • • • •

Begin walking west along the gravel road. Within ten minutes you will come to the nature trail on the right. Stay left on the gravel road toward the nature center. We'll return along the nature trail.

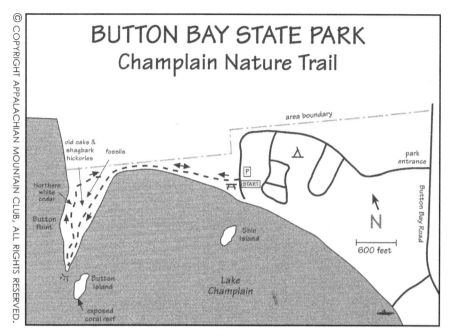

BUTTON BAY STATE PARK
Champlain Nature Trail

area boundary

old oaks & shagbark hickories

fossils

Northern white cedar

Button Point

park entrance

Button Bay Road

P

START

N

600 feet

Ship Island

Button Island

Lake Champlain

exposed coral reef

As you enter these woods, look up! You'll miss the majesty of these old trees if you don't. They are a mix of very old hickory, oak, white and red pine, hemlock, and white cedar.

Button Point has exquisite views at nearly every bend. The first vista is to the east. Ship Island is in the foreground and Snake Mountain rises to the right. The ridgeline of the Green Mountains is in the distance. Straight ahead is the Sugarbush Range, its tallest peak Mount Ellen is tied with Camel's Hump as the state's third highest mountain at 4,083 feet. To the right, further south, is the Middlebury Range.

Patches of trout lilies thrive beneath the oaks. Their yellow bells dangle over spotted green leaves that resemble trout.

The trail continues toward the point through a dense understory of white cedar, hemlock, and white pine saplings beneath towering red and white oak, white cedar, and red and white pine. Notice the beautiful patches of rosy bark on the red pines.

The bedrock is exposed at Button Point and you can see striations scraped onto its surface by glacial ice. Rocks frozen into the massive glacier scraped, from northeast to southwest, over the relatively softer limestone. (See page 160, Ice Age in the Champlain Valley.)

Across the lake the Adirondacks rise quite abruptly from the shore, a striking contrast with the wide Champlain Valley of Vermont.

Don't forget to stop at the Nature Center. The trail returns along the west or lake side of the point. The trees are scrubbier near the open lake where they are more exposed to winter winds and year-round storms. Many old white cedars cling tenaciously to the shore as the trail continues over rocky ground. Gnarled oaks tower overhead and the gray bark of aged sugar maples peels away from the trunks. A few flowering plants and ferns find enough sunlight among the trees: hepatica, false Solomon's seal, trout lilies, polypody fern, and marginal woodfern.

Several snail-like fossils, Maclurites magnus, appear in a prominent limestone outcrop to the left of trail. They look like faint circles in the rock, several inches in diameter. These snails lived in tropical waters about 500 million years ago. Shells form the limestone bedrock and contribute to the highly fertile, limy soil.

The trail bears to the right. There are several large specimen trees, a shagbark hickory, a few hemlocks, and a cluster of white pines. One of these pines has a diameter of over two and a half feet. The trail crosses the peninsula back to the trailhead through a final patch of trout lilies on left.

ICE AGE IN THE CHAMPLAIN VALLEY

The Ice Age is a recent blip in geologic history, a science that counts time in millions and billions of years. The last large glacier of the Ice Age, the Wisconsin glacier, flowed over New England between 18,000 and 20,000 years ago. One mile thick in places, the ice sheet covered Vermont's highest mountains, smoothing their peaks and removing soil deposited by earlier glaciers.

As the earth's temperature rose, between 10,000 and 12,000 years ago, the Wisconsin glacier slowly melted. Thawing ice combined with precipitation and runoff to create a series of lakes dammed to the north by ever-present glacial ice. Many lakes formed, sometimes merging as more ice melted and sometimes separating as accumulating water breached dams and shorelines. Glacial lakes reached beyond the Green Mountains where water followed the finger-like valleys of the Lamoille, Winooski and Missisquoi Rivers.

Lake Vermont, the largest of these bodies of water, filled the Champlain Valley far beyond the reaches of the current lake. While the Green Mountains were above lake level, only the highest of the valley hills- Mt. Philo and Pease Mountain in Charlotte and nearby Snake and Buck Mountains were islands in Lake Vermont.

All bodies of water leave behind evidence of their shorelines. These lake-level indicators may include ridges of sand or gravel left by waves, terraces at the high water level, and wave cuts and deltas of sediment where streams entered. Lake-level indicators from Lake Vermont remain on each of these mountains. (See Which Way to the Beach on page 146.)

As the glacier continued to melt, receding to the north, water flowed from Lake Vermont northward into the St. Lawrence Valley. The level of Lake Vermont lowered significantly. But the melting glaciers caused the ocean level to rise and eventually the tide turned. Salt water now poured southward. Freshwater Lake Vermont was turned into the Champlain Sea as icy Arctic waters filled the Champlain Valley. The Champlain Sea never reached the size of its freshwater predecessor and much of Middlebury, Charlotte and Hinesburg stood above water.

Fossils of marine life have been found in the clay soils deposited by the Champlain Sea. Along the shoreline of Button Bay, east of the nature trail, layers of clay in the cliff faces occasionally reveal marine artifacts including clamshells related to contemporary Arctic species. In Charlotte, not far from today's shoreline, an 11,000-year-old Beluga whale fossil was uncovered during the building of the railroad in 1849.

The buttons, for which Button Bay was named, are formed from glacially deposited clays. Because of calcium in the lake water, they solidify like concrete into a variety of interesting shapes, called concretions, about an inch or two in size. Al-

Look for several fossils of the maclurites magnus.

though the process continues, plant growth along the water's edge keeps them from drifting to shore. It is rare to see a button along the shore today.

HOURS, FEES, FACILITIES

The Nature Center is open from mid-June through August. The Center is closed while the resident naturalist leads nature walks and activities. Call in advance for a schedule.

GETTING THERE

From Rte. 7 in Vergennes, take Rte. 22A south. After you pass through the town of Vergennes you will cross the Otter Creek. Take a right onto Panton Road 0.3 mile past Otter Creek. Follow Panton Road 1.4 miles to Basin Harbor Road and turn right. After 4.4 miles you will turn left onto Button Bay Road. The entrance to the park is 0.7 mile on the right. Follow signs to the picnic shelter, 0.7 mile. Just beyond the stop sign park on the left. (Handicapped parking is located at the trailhead.) Continue on foot along the gravel road following signs to the nature center.

FOR MORE INFORMATION

Department of Forests, Parks, and Recreation
Park Ranger
802-475-2377
Nature Center
802-475-2375
http://www.vtstateparks.com/htm/buttonbay.cfm

• ALSO IN THE AREA •

LAKE CHAMPLAIN MARITIME MUSEUM, BASIN HARBOR

Just minutes from Button Bay, the lake's maritime history unfolds in very tangible ways. Replicas of historic boats are constructed based on underwater archaeology. Maps of shipwrecks, models of historic crafts, and artifacts fill the lakeshore exhibits. Open early May to mid-October. 802-475-2022, http://www.lcmm.org/

CHARLOTTE THE WHALE

Charlotte the Whale, Vermont's State Fossil, resides at the Perkins Geology Museum at the University of Vermont, Burlington.

802-656-8694
http://www.uvm.edu/perkins/

FISK QUARRY, ISLE LA MOTTE PRESERVATION TRUST

The same ancient, 480-year-old coral reef has been preserved at Fisk Quarry in Isle La Motte. At the northern end of the Champlain Islands the preserve is open from dawn to dusk year-round. See Lake Champlain Land Trust in Appendix B, Organizations.

http://www.lclt.org/guidefiskquarry.htm

25 Dead Creek
Wildlife Management Area

Vermont's largest waterfowl management area attracts thousands of migrating geese and shorebirds.

ADDISON, VT
TWO WALKS, EACH LESS THAN ONE MILE, PLUS DRIVING,
EACH WALK LESS THAN ONE HOUR
EASY
DOGS OKAY.

THE LAZY WATERS of the Dead Creek flow northward to the Otter Creek through the flat agricultural lands of Addison County. The Vermont Department of Fish and Game manages over 2,800 acres, providing an aquatic habitat for nesting, brood rearing, and stopovers for migratory waterfowl. In addition the department lowers the water level in impoundment areas to encourage diverse plant growth and to attract migratory wading and shorebirds.

Visit Dead Creek with binoculars and a bird book. Raptors soar overhead, attracted by open fields and thermal currents near Snake Mountain. Each October tens of thousands of Canada and snow geese feed and rest at Dead Creek. Shorebirds wade in the shallows and red-winged blackbirds spend the summer in cattail marshes.

Peak viewing season is generally the first two weeks in October for Canada geese and the third week in October for snow geese. Other waterfowl, birds, and wildlife can be seen from early spring until late fall.

. . . . . .

You may visit several locations. The refuge headquarters, on the north side of Rte. 17, is home to much of the preserve's infrastructure: grain storage buildings, a garage for boats, trucks, and farm equipment, an incubator, and brooder house. Please stay in your car.

Continue west on Rte. 17, passing a 70-acre refuge on the right where geese nest and are banded. A native breeding population was developed here in the 1950s when few Canada geese stopped on their annual migration.

On the south side of the road is a large viewing area, generally packed with photographers on October weekends. Further west on Rte. 17, just before the

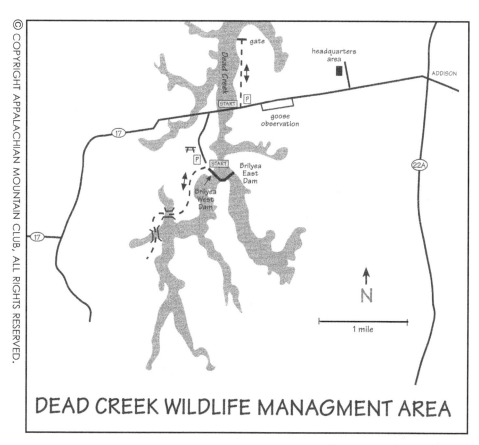

DEAD CREEK WILDLIFE MANAGMENT AREA

creek, there's a boat access on the right. A dirt road parallels the creek to the north for about a half-mile. This is a particularly good vantage point for spring viewing of waterfowl and a nice place for a short walk.

Great blue herons, the largest shorebirds of the region at up to four feet, fish here. With long legs and neck and a yellow, dagger-like beak, the slow motion of their wings in flight defies gravity. These carnivores eat fish, frogs, insects and in the shallows. Otter, muskrat, and mink as well as ducks, rails, gallinules, and green herons frequent the creek. Bald eagles, osprey, and peregrine falcons have occasionally been spotted.

Drive west on Rte. 17 a few hundred feet, cross Dead Creek, and turn immediately left on a dirt road. The creek is on the left and agricultural fields to the right. Beavers have gnawed several oaks along the road.

The parking area for Brilyea East Dam is at 0.8 mile, at the edge of an oak-hickory forest, once commonplace on the clay soils of the Champlain Valley. If left undisturbed these young shagbark hickory, red, white, and swamp white oak

165

trees could grow to great size in this warm, fertile plain. The trees have potential lifespans of more than three hundred years.

This is a nice spot for waterfowl viewing, lunch, or a walk. Snake Mountain is to the east, with its maroon quartzite cliffs. A farm road leads south along the creek, crossing several more dams. A leisurely stroll to the end of the road and back takes less than an hour.

Walk past the orange gate on the dirt road. Dead Creek is dammed on the left and there is a small swamp on the right. A row of young, scrubby trees grows along the creek and immature woods are on the right. Raptors often float overhead, riding air currents. In addition to the huge number of raptors seen during spring and fall migrations, kestrels, red-tailed hawks, and marsh hawks spend the summer in the area.

Within ten minutes another gate blocks the road at a second dam and a cattle guard keeps livestock in the fields. Buttonbush grows at the water's edge. After passing through another wooded stretch, the path crosses a third dam with water on both sides. Wood duck boxes dot the perimeter and a splendid view of Snake Mountain looms to the east, on the left.

The trail rises up a slight slope, passes through woods, meadow, and woods in succession before ending at the boundary of the preserve. Retrace your steps to return.

Be Aware: This area is used in the early fall for training of hunting dogs. Blank shots, shrill whistles, and barks punctuate the tranquility as dogs are trained to respond to hand and whistle signals.

A BIT ABOUT THE BIRDS

CANADA GEESE
Canada geese are known for their honking and V-shaped flight formations during spring and fall migrations. Lake Champlain is part of the Atlantic flyway, the eastern route followed by migratory waterfowl as they journey between their summer and winter homes. Tens of thousands of geese stop at DCWMA for rest, food, and water.

The Canada goose is a large brown bird, with a long black neck and head and a white cheek patch. The male and female look nearly identical except that the male is larger. Geese mate for life and are very protective of their territory. While there are goslings in the nest, they will chase away other geese or humans who venture too close.

Adult Canada geese molt once each year in mid-summer. For several weeks they cannot fly. By the time the adult flight feathers have grown back, the young are also ready to fly. By late summer the geese gather into large flocks for their annual migration.

GREATER SNOW GEESE

The greater snow goose is also a migratory waterfowl, generally white, and in the process of a comeback from reduced numbers.

Snow geese are multiplying at a troubling rate. The population of the Atlantic Flyway, now estimated at one million, has increased twenty-fold since the 1960s. While this makes for some beautiful October days on Dead Creek, the enormous flock is taking a toll. Their breeding ground on the Arctic tundra cannot support

Shagbark hickories thrive only in the Lake Champlain lowlands in our region.

these numbers and has difficulty recovering because of the harsh climate and short growing season. In addition, in 1996, farmers in Quebec filed $1 million (Canadian) in claims for hay and alfalfa crops lost to snow geese.

While the Fish and Game Department allows hunting of snow geese, they are difficult to hunt. They always travel in flocks so it's difficult to place decoys. Adult birds, as old as fifteen, recognize human tricks and will take flight with an entire flock in tow. As one official explained, "It's hard to fool those 15-year-old eyes."

REDWING BLACKBIRDS

One of the first signs of spring is the return of red-winged blackbirds. With bright red epaulets and black feathers, the males return several weeks in advance of the females. They frequent marshes and generally nest in cattails, shrubs, or grasses.

Males are territorial will scold those who venture too near a nest. Some are polygamous and will defend as many females as have nests in their territory.

Redwings raise several broods annually, each in a different nest. Toward the end of summer they disappear to a secluded marsh for their annual molt. In September, with new feathers, they flock together to feed and roost before beginning their annual migration.

In the spring redwings gobble insects by the thousand but later in the season they may eat crops. When they congregate for winter roosting, by the hundreds of thousands, they can be very destructive.

GETTING THERE

From the north, take Rte 22A south from Vergennes (about 6 miles). At Addison, turn right on Rte. 17 west. The headquarters buildings are 1.0 mile on the right. Another 0.4 mile on the right is the refuge, used seasonally. On the left or south side of the road is a long stretch for parking, viewing, and photography.

FOR MORE INFORMATION

Vermont Department of Fish and Wildlife
http://www.vtfishandwildlife.com/

26   Snake Mountain Wildlife Management Area

One of Vermont's loveliest views and a great spot to see hawk migrations. A gratifying hike for children. Wear hiking boots and bring binoculars.

ADDISON/WEYBRIDGE, VT TOWN LINE
3 MILES ROUND-TRIP WITH AN ELEVATION
GAIN OF 900 FEET
2–3 HOURS
MODERATE/DIFFICULT
DOGS PERMITTED

AN ABANDONED CARRIAGE ROAD is the route up Snake Mountain, located in the 1,215-acre Snake Mountain Wildlife Management Area. The land, including an eighty-acre parcel owned by the Nature Conservancy, is managed by the Vermont Department of Fish and Wildlife.

Called Grand View Mountain by locals, Snake truly has a grand view. It was the site of the Grand View House, one of many mountain top hotels in Vermont at the end of the last century. Imagine, as you pace along in hiking boots, carriages full of women in fancy hats and voluminous petticoats bouncing up the same path!

Snake Mountain takes its name not from an infestation of reptiles but from its shape. Four summits stretch along a serpentine ridgeline. One of several sheepback mountains in the Champlain Valley, Snake has a gently sloping east side and a precipitous western drop. (Picture a sheep munching grass, its head low and its back rising to an abrupt backside.) Sheepback mountains were smoothed by the flow of glaciers during the ice age but they owe their underlying shape to the durability of the quartzite on their summits. Thrust from east to west over a softer shale, their eastern flanks of quartzite determine their shape. This is very clear on the summit of Mt. Philo. (See page 140.) Nearby Buck and Pease Mountains have similar shapes.

Observers flock to the west-facing cliffs to view spring and fall hawk migrations. On the perfect September day, it is possible to see more than 1,000 migrating hawks. From the summit we can look down on huge flocks of migratory geese at a favorite resting and refueling spot, Dead Creek Wildlife Management Area. (See page 164.) As many as 14,000 geese a day may tarry at Dead Creek in October. Snow Geese, which outnumber Canada Geese three to one at DCWMA, look from a distance like masses of shifting snow.

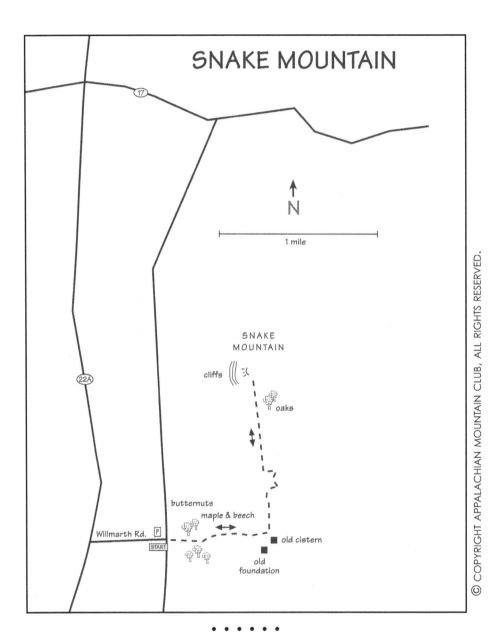

• • • • • •

The wide trail starts behind an orange gate at the end of Willmarth Road. The roller-coaster trail has been bulldozed to discourage wheeled vehicles. In minutes you are in the woods. Beech trees and sugar maples dominate the long-abandoned farm fields. The smooth gray bark of the beech makes them easy to distinguish in any season. Shagbark hickory also scatter through these woods, long vertical strips of bark peeling away from their trunks. We once filled our pockets with hundreds of shagbark hickory nuts and then turned to Euell Gibbons' *Stalking the Wild Asparagus* for inspiration. The resulting thick soup tasted rich before a bitter aftertaste nearly choked us. Hats off to the pioneers who used these nuts to sweeten their corn cakes and hominy!

Other denizens of this rich soil include ash, hop hornbeam, bitternut hickory, basswood, large-toothed aspen, and paper birch trees. A large red oak on the right side of the trail has a diameter of three and a half feet and the occasional maple has extensive side branches, indicating it grew in a field rather than the woods.

After about twenty minutes the trail arrives at a T-intersection with the original carriage road. If muddy boots haven't already done so, a thick cluster of jewelweed confirms perennially moist soil. These leafy plants with succulent stems can grow to five feet by late summer and their seedpods are irresistible. When touched, even gently, the ripe pods explode tiny seeds in every direction leaving behind only an empty green curlicue. (See page 173, Seed Dispersal.)

Turn right for a short detour. About a hundred feet from the intersection, remnants of an old farm hide in the ever-thickening woods: an open cistern ringed in flat stones is on the left side of the trail; to the right a collapsing foundation, piles

Bloodroot takes its name from the red-orange liquid in its roots and stem.

of chimney bricks, rusted farm or household implements, a stone wall and a tree stump which grew around barbed wire.

Sheep farms and apple orchards were mainstays of the local economy in the nineteenth century. In 1837, Addison County, home of Snake Mountain, boasted a population of 260,000 sheep. When Australia entered the wool market sheep farming collapsed and small farms like this one failed and were consumed by encroaching woodlands.

Turn back and continue uphill on the main carriage trail. A small stream flows on the left as the trail climbs steadily. Deciduous woods like these host many flowering herbs. Trillium, false Solomon's seal, large-flowered bellwort, sweet cicely, hepatica, herb Robert, early meadow rue, and bloodroot grow along the trail.

Keep your eyes open for turtles. One late summer day an enormous map turtle (Graptemys geographica), nearly a foot in length, surprised us by the side of the trail. It was, however, not startled by us and didn't budge or blink. Of the large native tortoises only map turtles are known to range far from water during summer.

In late summer and early autumn we have seen large praying mantises and even the elusive walking stick. The latter had found camouflage on a white pine, the ends of its green legs mimicking exactly the tree's needles. Large insects like these, fully mature and ready to lay eggs, are most visible as their summer camouflage dies back.

After about twenty minutes, the trail becomes steeper, leading uphill to the right and then swinging to the left. The carriageway is lined with beech trees across a small plateau, many bearing carved initials. Striped maple, its candy-striped green and white trunk and huge leaves, is an abundant shrub.

After the plateau, the trail goes steeply uphill to the right and then turns sharply to the left. One more sweeping right turn and the road climbs gently to the summit. Clumps of beautiful moss grow along both sides of the path. Serviceberry trees, with sensuous gray curves on their bark, are common and a number of red oaks tower overhead. Partridgeberry leaves are thick on the ground. After fifteen minutes, the trail leads left to the abrupt edge of the mountain where it ends at an incongruous cement slab.

Hawks and turkey vultures often float on thermal air currents below the cliffs. It's a powerful feeling to look down on a dozen or more soaring raptors. At your feet is some of the finest farmland in Vermont, a patchwork of corn and hay fields dotted with Holstein cows. Lake Champlain stretches north and south and the voluptuous layers of the Adirondacks provide the western backdrop. There may be more expansive panoramas from the higher peaks, but the scale and scope of this view from Snake Mountain is very special.

Retrace your steps to return. It will take less than an hour. Don't miss the right turn onto the spur near the bottom. Both the carriage road and the spur are wide and well worn and it is easy to walk beyond this turn toward Willmarth Road.

SEED DISPERSAL: HITCHHIKERS, PARACHUTES OR TASTY TREATS?

While the ultimate mission of a plant is to reproduce, creating viable seeds does not guarantee survival of its offspring. Seeds need to germinate far enough from their parents to avoid competition for water, sunlight, soil, and nutrients.

Since plants can't travel, how do they disperse their seeds?

Coconuts float far from home to give baby palms a distant germination point and pussy willows drop their seeds into waterways beside which they grow.

Squirrels, chipmunks, birds, and even humans are unwitting participants in another travel scheme as they transport fruit to eat or store. Sometimes edible seeds are left behind; forgetful squirrels and chipmunks bury nuts a perfect distance below ground for safe germination. Birds drop seeds far from where they were consumed, passing berry seeds and cherry pits through their digestive systems intact. Neither apples nor cherries can germinate until the flesh is removed. Humans, too, carry fruit from place to place. Tomatoes did not float to Europe unassisted.

On a blustery day, dandelions, cattails, and milkweed demonstrate their parachutes. Other flyers include the winged carriers of maple, ash, and elm seeds, lightweight with a large surface area to catch the wind. Hitchhiking seeds with hooks or barbs attach themselves to passersby. Have you or your dog brushed up against a burdock lately?

Last but not least are exploding pods that launch ripe seeds away from the parent plant. This is how jewelweed, also known as touch-me-nots, got its nickname.

GETTING THERE

Take Rte. 22A south from Vergennes. From the crossroads at Rte. 17 in Addison, continue 3.0 miles farther on Rte. 22A to Willmarth Road, a dirt road on the left. This road ends in 0.5 mile at Mountain Road. Turn left to the parking area 0.1 mile on the left. The trailhead is at the intersection of Willmarth Road. Don't miss the butternut trees as you walk along Mountain Road.

FOR MORE INFORMATION

Department of Fish and Wildlife
http://www.vtfishandwildlife.com

27 Mount Independence, State Historic Site

A National Historic Landmark, the least-disturbed site of the American Revolution. Lovely lake views. The strategic location and historic remains are best viewed when the trees are not in full leaf.

ORWELL, VT

BALDWIN AND ORANGE TRAILS

3.1 MILES, MINIMAL ELEVATION CHANGE

1.5 -3 HOURS PLUS TIME AT THE VISITORS CENTER

EASY WITH OCCASIONAL ROUGH FOOTING

ALL PETS MUST BE LEASHED.

THIS RUGGED PENINSULA sits across a narrow stretch of Lake Champlain from Fort Ticonderoga. In June of 1776, American troops began clearing trees from this four hundred acre site. Surrounded by natural barriers- cliffs, the lake, and a marshy creek, the Mount offered several strategic benefits. It has a commanding view to the north, the feared invasion route of British troops coming from Canada. Mount Defiance, another British stronghold, sits just across the lake. And Fort Ticonderoga could easily be reached a few hundred yards over water.

By the fall of 1776, with camps, batteries, and a fort accommodating more than 12,000 soldiers and their families, Mount Independence had nearly as large a population as Boston. When British General Guy Carleton considered an assault on the position he quickly abandoned the idea and retreated to Canada for the winter.

Many American troops returned to their homes that winter and those who remained struggled against cold, hunger, and disease. In July of 1777, as British General John Burgoyne's forces moved into the area, the Americans abandoned the Mount and withdrew. That summer witnessed confrontations at nearby Hubbardton, Bennington, and finally the American's decisive victory at Saratoga. British and German forces stayed at Mount Independence until November when they learned of the British surrender at Saratoga. In a parting gesture, they burned and destroyed the site.

Today archeologists gently peel back the layers of time. A wide array of artifacts in the Visitors Center helps paint a picture of domestic and military life: a ship's cannon, fishing paraphernalia including hooks, weights and fish vertebrae,

MOUNT INDEPENDENCE

N

0.25 mile

Orange Trail

Orange Trail

East
Creek

Lake
Champlain

Orange Trail

Baldwin Trail

START

Visitor
Center

P

TO ORWELL &
ROUTE 22A

pots, bowls, ammunition, medicine vials, knives, hoes, axes, spades, buttons, pipe stems, shoe soles, keys, cufflinks, and belt buckles.

No reconstructions have or will be made. Bring your imagination on this walk through history. Make sure to pick up a map.

More than six miles of walking trails thread across the Mount. The Baldwin and Orange Trails give the flavor of the history and beauty of the spot. The Baldwin Trail is a handicap-accessible gravel path with impressive boardwalks and bridges. Interpretive signs provide details of Revolutionary life and military constructions. If you choose not to walk the longer Orange Trail you will still get a good sense of the history and the site. I recommend packing a lunch and stopping at one of many picnic tables along the route, most with spectacular lake views. Don't miss the Visitor Center.

• • • • • •

Walk up the slope behind the Visitors Center to an information kiosk. The Baldwin Trail is a loop with three out-and-back fingers. Begin to the left.

The first stop is a view over the lake. Continue to the only identified grave-

Hepatica bloom in early spring, its flowers can be white, blue, pink or purple.

stone on the Mount, dating from 1760, before the defenses here were built. Two thousand soldiers are presumed buried here in unmarked graves.

Stop 3 is a kiosk. The interpretive signage along the Baldwin Trail paints a rich picture of the lives of soldiers in addition to military strategy and lore.

Walk toward Stop 4, likely the foundation stones of officers' quarters as enlisted men's accommodations did not have foundations. The trail continues to Stop 5, a lookout across the lake to Mount Defiance and Fort Ticonderoga. Returning through the intersection you arrive at Stop 6, the general hospital. Even today, a 600-bed hospital sounds impressive. The Americans clearly anticipated heavy casualties. Remains of the stone foundation are visible as well as excavations for an addition. The building was begun in the April mud of 1777, and was still under construction when the Americans evacuated in July. Disease was as much an enemy as the invading armies, taking a high toll on the 2,500 soldiers who wintered here in 1776-77. Do not take the Blue Trail on your left.

You will pass Stop 7, the site of the Third Brigade encampment, before turning on to the Orange Trail. It passes through woods of mature white cedar, sugar maple, hop hornbeam, and shagbark hickory. Many of the shagbarks and hop hornbeams are large. A member of the birch family with characteristic lacy branches, the Eastern hop hornbeam (Ostrya virginiana) has very hard wood, hence its other common name ironwood. The fruit of the hop hornbeam are nutlets in a papery brown cover, resembling hops. Its bark is shaggy in narrow vertical strips and the tree never grows above fifty feet. The invasive buckthorn is thick in the understory. (See Williams Woods, page 129.) In early spring hepatica bloom.

You arrive at an opening where the barracks of the Star Fort were located on the highest point of land. The earth was so heavily pounded by marching feet that even today trees do not grow here. The one exception is the cedar at the presumed location of the whipping post. Legend has it that the tree is nourished by spilled blood! Archeologists unearthed hundreds of musket balls with tooth marks in them, presumably bitten by soldiers as they were being whipped. Records have been found with victims' names, dates, and number of lashes.

The trail goes left to where a crane was used during the Revolutionary era to unload boats 200 feet below.

Retrace your steps until the trail goes left. Several shop foundations are on the right as the trail leads toward the end of the peninsula. At Stop 4, the remains of the horseshoe-shaped battery can be seen, the location from which cannons commanded the lake to the north. With the heavy growth of trees it's difficult to see that these gun placements pointed straight up the lake. The shore battery, at Stop 5, had even heavier firepower.

Along the shore, just beyond the battery, is Stop 6 where the floating bridge once connected to Fort Ticonderoga. The bridge was twelve-feet wide and had twenty-two sunken piers. Twenty-one cribs remain in the lake.

The trail goes uphill to the left on the old road. At Stop 7 the ship masts for Benedict Arnold's fleet were stepped, a nautical term for fixing the mast. The foundations here show traces of mortar, the only such evidence on the Mount. French occupiers at Fort Ticonderoga used mortar.

Cross the battery again and enter the woods. Imagine this entire plateau devoid of trees. Stop 8, an L-shaped foundation, overlooks East Creek, another important component of the Mounts' defenses. Many broken wine bottles were excavated from three-sided watch huts, the sentry outposts just down this bank.

The final stop along the trail, also close to the creek, is a rectangular foundation, perhaps a blockhouse. A large area of black chert, a low-quality flint, is nearby. It was used by Native Americans for tools and weapons and during the Revolution for gunflints.

Turn right and rejoin the Baldwin Trail. Turn left if you want to see the Amer-

Fort Ticonderoga from Mount Independence.

ican Blockhouse. Otherwise, jog right and continue through the junction to Stop 10, location of a storehouse. Stop 11 was the British Blockhouse. The final junction is at Stop 12 where you can return to the Visitor Center or take a final detour to the Southern Battery Overlook, a powder magazine, and a German hut.

HOURS, FEES, AND FACILITIES

The Visitors Center is open daily, late May through mid-October, 9:30 a.m. to 5:00 p.m. Admission $5, ages 15 and older. Pets must be on a leash. Cross-country skiers are welcome.

GETTING THERE

From the intersection of Rtes. 22A and 73 in Orwell, take Rte. 73 west. In 0.4 mile the road forks. Go straight while Rte. 73 goes right. After 3.0 miles you will fork right on Mt. Independence Road. After 1.8 miles take a sharp left uphill. The Visitors Center and parking are at 0.1 mile.

FOR MORE INFORMATION

Mount Independence State Historic Site
Orwell, VT 05760
802-759-2412
http://www.historicvermont.org/mountindependence/

• ALSO IN THE AREA •

FORT TICONDEROGA

Across the lake in Ticonderoga, New York, the reconstructed fort has daily reenactments of eighteenth century events. Built by the French in 1755, Ft. Ti was later controlled by the British and eventually taken by the Americans.

FORT TICONDEROGA FERRY

Crossing on an irregular basis as early as 1759 and in scheduled operation since 1799, the Ft. Ti Ferry is one of the oldest in the country. It crosses the lake using underwater cables. Don't miss the Incomplete History of the Fort Ticonderoga Ferry, available onboard. The ferry operates between Larrabee's Point, Shoreham, Vermont and Ticonderoga, New York.

Central Green Mountains and Valleys

28 Green Mountain
Audubon Nature Center

A variety of hillside and valley habitats with views of Mt. Mansfield and Camel's Hump. The Sensory Trail is roped for the visually impaired with Braille signs and an optional audiotape.

HUNTINGTON, VT

SENSORY TRAIL, HIRES TRAIL, BROOK TRAIL, WHITE PINE TRAIL, AND HEMLOCK SWAMP TRAIL

1.5 MILES

1.5 TO 2 HOURS

MODERATE

DOGS ALLOWED ON LEASH

TWO HUNDRED AND FIFTY-FIVE ACRES of the Green Mountain Audubon Nature Center are tucked in the Huntington River valley six miles upstream from the Winooski River. Rich soils attracted farmers to this fertile kame terrace left by melting glaciers of the Ice Age. Until the 1940s, much of this land was a working farm with open, hilly pastures.

In 1966 the Nature Center was established on land donated by Christine L. Hires (after whom the Hires Trail is named). Over five miles of trails weave through forest, field, swamp, and marsh, past ponds, streams, and river. A working sugarbush has 800 taps and produces hundreds of gallons of maple syrup each spring. Visitors are welcome on Sundays in March for sugaring. Tasting is, of course, part of the process.

Year-round workshops, classes, and programs explore environmental and nature topics. Day and overnight camp programs are offered for children in summer. The staff is active in bird research and monitoring projects. The Audubon chapter is expanding its outreach to local high schools and court diversion programs as well as the general public.

Signage is better on some trails than on others. Make sure to pick up a map and get oriented before setting out. Beavers are active and sections of trail may be impassable. Check at the office for current information.

• • • • • •

I did my best to appreciate the Sensory Trail as it is intended. Roped along its entire 2/3 mile, the path crosses several habitats allowing visually impaired visitors to

Sherman Hollow Road

Sherman Hollow Brook

Brook Trail

Hemlock
Swamp

Huntington Road

Huntington River

White Pine Trail

Beaver
Pond

Brook Trail

Hires Trail

Fern Trail

P

Visitor
Center

START

Peeper
Pond

N

250 feet

Sensory Trail

GREEN MOUNTAIN AUDUBON
NATURE CENTER

touch, smell, taste, and hear the sounds of fields and woodlands. Twenty Braille and
large-print interpretation signs line the trail.

The woven rope starts at the bottom of the steps at the Visitor Center and
leads to a raised herb garden. Touch these plants and smell your fingers. I was surprised at how many scents were unmistakable, many etched in childhood memory:
marigold, basil, parsley, oregano, chives, and bee balm. One plant has sticky stems,
another long trumpet flowers, and a third fuzzy leaves.

Pick up the rope again on the left. Young mixed woods are on the left and a
backyard habitat on the right includes raspberry and blueberry plants, lilacs, and
fruits trees.

Stop and listen for a moment. In the spring dozens of migrating birds sing in the early morning hours while the ovenbird and American redstart sing all day long. The wind rustles the nearby white pines and the valley echoes the sounds on nearby Huntington Road.

Tactile sensations at the edge of the woods include thorns on hawthorn and black locust trees, small, woody alder cones, and beady fertile fronds of sensitive ferns. Raspberry and blackberry canes are prickly.

Raspberries, blackberries, and thimbleberries are brambles, members of the rose family whose stalks or canes live for two seasons until they produce their fruit. (The rose family also includes apple, pear, plum, cherry, strawberry, almond, and

Beavers at work.

spirea.) Angular stems with stout prickles can distinguish blackberry. Red raspberry has round bristling stems and purple-flowering raspberry, often called thimbleberry, has hairy stems. Thimbleberry leaves resemble maples while other brambles have compound leaves with three to seven elliptical leaflets. The fruit of the thimbleberry is not as sweet and succulent as its cousins but it is a favorite of wildlife.

The trail enters the woods, old pastures planted in white pine. The overgrown woodlot wasn't previously managed and the Center is now thinning the pines as fuel for sugaring. If too many trees are cut at once the remaining ones will be vulnerable to wind. Listen for chickadees which nest in the snags.

Close your eyes again. Needles are soft underfoot and the cool, dark woods are damp and smell of pine. If you touch a tree it may be sticky with resin.

The trail climbs to a ridge through mixed woods and descends through more white pines before bending right and returning to the open meadow. A final right turn brings us to the beginning of the trail.

Look behind the Visitor Center for the Hires Trail. Walk uphill and then to the right. In summer the hillside is lush with ferns. The woods are a mixture of paper and yellow birch, maple, and hop hornbeam. Rock outcroppings are covered with moss, ferns, and young hemlocks. Partridgeberry, Clintonia, and clubmoss are underfoot.

Stay right when the Hires Trail meets the Brook Trail. The Brook Trail climbs and descends gently for about ten minutes before reaching the road.

An ideal itinerary is to turn left on the road to continue on the Brook Trail. However, active beavers have swamped the lower section of the Brook Trail and blocked this route. If you have the time and inclination, you might walk at least a stretch of the beautiful and interesting Brook Trail. It tangos with two brooks as it slopes downhill through mixed northern woods rich with maple, poplar, yellow birch, hop hornbeam, hemlock, white pine, and basswood. The wildflowers and shrubs are luxuriant as well: Canada Mayflower or wild-lily-of-the-valley, Clintonia, red trillium, twisted stalk, Solomon's seal, wood sorrel, ferns, and hobblebush. Deer and moose have nibbled the hobblebush.

The trail follows Sherman Hollow Brook, over a wooden bridge and onto a sandy bed of spring overflow. This oxbow is now separated from the brook except during high water. The trail rises to higher ground along the edge of the brook and crosses it. Note the erosion of its banks and the piles of sediment, sorted by size. As the flow of water slows, the river has less carrying capacity. It drops bigger stones first, then smaller ones, and finally sand. Fine silt usually settles at the mouth of a river.

Beaver lodge

You may need to turn around unless the beavers have relocated.

Another route to the lower trails is via the White Pine Trail. Returning along the dirt road in the direction of the Office, turn left on the White Pine Trail. You will descend toward the beaver pond, peeper pond, and hemlock swamp.

Follow signs to the Hemlock Swamp. A boardwalk, about sixty feet long, leads through the spring-fed swamp. Uprooted trees covered with moss, ferns, and young saplings lean across the swamp and duckweed coats the open pools. Hemlock, swamp maple, green ash, and yellow birch are numerous. Look for both yellow birch and hemlock growing on stilts. These trees can geminate on nearly any moist surface and often do so on stumps. When the stump rots away the tree roots support a tree several feet off the ground. On higher ground several shrubs adapted to cool, damp conditions thrive. Both hobblebush and winterberry produce a bonanza of red berries. Deer have browsed striped maple and hobblebush here. Look for painted trillium that prefers a cool, acidic environment. It more often produces two flowers per plant than either its red or white cousins.

Cold climate plants grow on mounds of sphagnum moss: goldthread, wood sorrel, Clintonia, partridgeberry, red and painted trillium, starflower, and wintergreen. Marsh marigolds, five-petaled yellow spring blooms, dot the swamp in May.

The trail crosses another section of boardwalk. Hummocks of sphagnum moss and tree roots elevate less water-tolerant trees, like the birches, above water level.

At the west side of the Hemlock Swamp beavers reign. New ponds have flooded a wide expanse and newly cut stumps poke into the air. Audubon uses beaver baffles to regulate the water level and they have also protected some trees with fencing.

Return to the White Pine Trail and climb to a plateau. From this perch the panorama of beaver ponds, dams, lodges, and newly shorn trees stretches at your feet.

Follow signs to return to the Visitor Center.

KNOWING THE TREES

To begin identifying trees, start with one you already know, perhaps a sugar maple, and describe it: simple leaves with five pointed lobes, branches which are opposite each other, paired seeds with wings, and, on old trees, gray, furrowed bark. You will make similar observations as you identify other trees.

There are about thirty hardwood trees in the area, many of these in families like the oaks, maples, poplars, and birches. If you learn one new tree on each walk in this book, the job will be done!

Most local trees exhibit alternate branching where leaves and branches sprout alternately, first on one side then on the other, along a branch. For those with opposite branching, an acronym helps: MADCapHorse, for maple, ash, dogwood, Caprifoliaceae (the family including viburnum, honeysuckle, and elderberry), and horse chestnut.

Leaves are simple or compound. A compound leaf is divided into many leaflets. Ash, hickory, locust, butternut, and horse chestnut have multiple leaflets where maple, oak, and poplar trees, among others, have a single, undivided leaf. The shapes of many of these leaves are familiar, the lobed leaf of oaks and maples, the oval of birch and elm leaves, and lance-shaped willow leaves.

A tree guide points out further distinctions: bark, flower, and seed descriptions; thickness of twigs (a great winter guide); habitat (sugar maples do not grow in swamps); size. Shape can be misleading if a tree grows in the woods where it develops few side branches.

HOURS, FEES, FACILITIES

Trails open from dawn until dusk daily. No admission fee but donations are welcome. Restrooms in the Visitor Center open Monday to Friday, 9:00 a.m. to 4:30 p.m. Leashed dogs are welcome on the property.

GETTING THERE

From the stoplight on Rte. 2 in the village of Richmond, turn south on Bridge Street. Pass the historic Round Church on the left, and follow the main road that bears right. You will travel 5.2 miles to Sherman Hollow Road, a dirt road on the right. Turn right and follow signs toward the Audubon Nature Center and the Birds of Vermont Museum. The parking area is 0.3 mile on the left.

FOR MORE INFORMATION

Green Mountain Audubon Nature Center
255 Sherman Hollow Road
Huntington, VT 05462
802-434-3068
http://greenmountainaudubon.org/

• ALSO IN THE AREA •

The Birds of Vermont Museum is located 0.6 mile beyond the Visitor's Center on Sherman Hollow Road. Open May 1 through October 31.

Life-like carvings of hundreds of birds are presented in their native habitat with nests and eggs. Founded by artist and carver Bob Spear, the non-profit museum informs and enchants through the beauty of nature's creatures and the skill of the artist.

http://www.birdsofvermont.org/

29 Mad River Greenway

Dairy farms, a meandering river, and mountain views in a river valley. Great for cross-country skiing or snowshoeing.

WAITSFIELD, VT
5.5 MILES
3 HOURS
EASY
DOGS MUST BE LEASHED.

THE NON-PROFIT MAD RIVER PATH ASSOCIATION (MRPA) has created a network of trails linking the towns of the Mad River Valley. The Mad River Greenway wends its way through lush agricultural land along the banks of the Mad River.

Today the river provides a scenic venue for walking, kayaking, or trout fishing. Not long ago the river defined life in the valley, providing water, fish, gravel, ice, recreation, and power. Bucket by bucket gravel was removed for use on the roads. Ice, a cash crop, was cut several times each winter. The Mad River's steep grade was well suited to mills and many were built: cider, grist, and sawmills. Recreation centered on the river as well: skating in winter, swimming in summer, and fishing between times. Removal of gravel made for better swimming holes, too!

The river dictated the rhythm of life. Many farmers worked subsistence hill farms and then put in hours at the mills. When water filled the pond behind the dam, work began at the mill and lasted for several hours until the water was depleted. Then back to the farm while the pond filled again.

Not always beneficent, the Mad River occasionally fills the valley. The Flood of 1927 destroyed bridges, mills, houses, and cattle and the 1938 Hurricane flooded many homes and farms. As recently as the 1990s, the river has overflowed its usual floodplain during heavy rains.

Reminder: This is not public land! Don't forget as you walk, snowshoe, or ski, that private landowners have generously allowed non-motorized use of their properties. Yield to farm equipment and please be careful. Dogs must be leashed.

• • • • • •

The trail begins to the left of the parking area. White, plastic-covered rolls of hay,

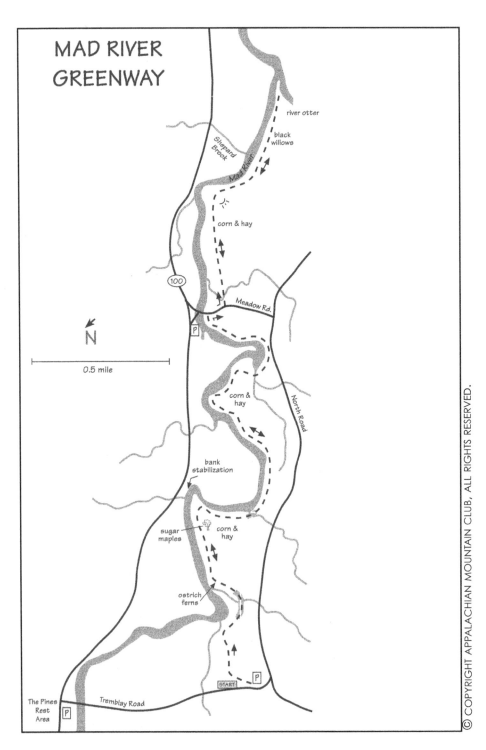

MAD RIVER GREENWAY

river otter

black willows

Shepard Brook

Mad River

corn & hay

100

Meadow Rd.

N

0.5 mile

corn & hay

North Road

bank stabilization

sugar maples

corn & hay

ostrich ferns

START

The Pines Rest Area

Tremblay Road

like giant marshmallows, dot the farm fields that stretch to the river. Beyond, farm-houses, barns, and ski trails rise into the mountains.

A thicket borders a stream on the right. Wild grape, virgin's bower (*Clematis virginiana*), and wild cucumber entwine paper birch along the bank. With leaves like a maple, the wild cucumber (*Echinocystis lobata*) produces an inedible fruit covered with weak spines. The hollow, fibrous shells remain on the vine into winter. Speckled alder, sensitive fern, box elder, and willow are all indicators of damp soils, while basswood and common elderberry prefer both wet and rich soil.

Within ten minutes the trail reaches the end of the field and goes right across

Red elderberries sparkle in the woods in July.

a wooden bridge into woods dominated by yellow birches. The trail crosses another wooden bridge and immediately turns left. Hay and cornfields stretch to the right and young woods border the stream on the left, a mix of sugar maples, speckled alder, ash, linden, and some scraggly butternut. (Butternut trees across the northeast are dying from a fungus.) Ostrich ferns and jewelweed are big and lush in the damp, fertile soil. Ostrich fern can grow to six feet in river bottoms and open, wet woodlands. The twice-cut fronds taper to both the base and tip and may have as many as forty pairs of narrow, pointed leaflets.

The trail approaches the slow-flowing Mad River on the left. On the bank, a hawthorn tree is a parasol of vines as it struggles for survival against a wild grape vine, its diameter about half that of the tree.

After about thirty minutes of walking, a sign of the Lake Champlain Basin Commission and Friends of the Mad River explains efforts to stabilize the riverbanks. Dormant willow posts are interspersed with saplings. In the wet soil the willows sprout and their roots add to the anchoring power of the saplings. Live stabilization, more aesthetic and less expensive than stone rip rap, has additional benefits. Shade cools the river and insects fall from the trees to feed fish. While, in geological time, the river will ultimately prevail, meandering back and forth across valley floor, these efforts protect farmland and buildings important to the economic health of the valley.

Detour left into the riverbed, across sand, and onto the gravel bar. We are on the inside of the curve, the shortest distance water must travel. The river drops its sediment as it slows, depositing sand and gravel. On the opposite, outer bank, erosion takes place as fast moving currents cut into the bank.

Return to the trail and turn left to continue. The river has turned almost ninety degrees. Corn and hayfields are on the right. The river soon meanders left again.

In a few minutes an arrow marks a left turn and the trail crosses a wooden bridge. A stone bench is on the right. In winter this is the intersection of two major snowmobile routes. Signs indicate distances, directions, and amenities on the network of trails. The local snowmobile club, the Mad River Ridge Runners, works in concert with the MRPA in routing trails and building bridges.

We continue to walk at the edge of hay and cornfields. In summer, the corn is as high as an elephant's eye- eight to ten feet. A bench overlooks eroded bedrock in the river before the trail arrives at Meadow Road, about an hour into the walk. Another parking area is across the river.

The path continues north through a thicket of young trees until it meets a farm road where it turns left. Several basswood or linden trees have dropped their fall load of thousands of gray pea-sized nuts. Continue following the river as agricultural fields stretch to the right.

Stately trees shade a grassy stopping place. Its back to the water, a bench faces the mountains over the fertile fields, houses, and barns.

Several huge, gangly black willows preside over the last stretch of trail. Deeply ridged and furrowed bark covers their Medusa-like trunks and limbs. Across the Mad River, Shepard Brook enters from the west.

The mowed path enters young woods where it ends at the tip of a peninsula. Look for otters frolicking here.

At a leisurely pace, the outbound walk takes about an hour and a half to two hours. The return, with fewer stops, takes about an hour.

MEANDERING RIVER

The slightest obstruction can shift a river's current against one of its banks. The current is then deflected to the opposite bank. Erosion takes place on the outside of each bend and deposition usually occurs on the inside of the next bend, where the water moves most slowly.

As the river makes bigger and bigger swings, the difference in the water's rate of flow (between the inner and outer curves of the meander) increases, which in turn increases the erosion and deposition. This process continues for hundreds or thousands of years until the curves meet. The channel then flows again along a straight path and the meander- now called an oxbow, is abandoned.

GETTING THERE

From Waitsfield take Rte. 100 north from Bridge Street for 1.2 miles. At the Pines rest area, turn right onto Tremblay Road. A small parking area is on the left at 0.7 mile.

From the north, take Rte. 100 south. Tremblay Road is on the left, 3.1 miles south of the junction of Rtes. 100 and 100-B.

FOR MORE INFORMATION

Mad River Path Association
P. O. Box 683
Waitsfield, VT 05673-0683
802-496-PATH (7284)
www.madriverpath.com

30 Robert Frost Interpretive Trail
Green Mountain National Forest

A walk through Robert Frost country enhanced by his poetry. Great on snowshoes and with children. Part of the trail is wheelchair accessible.

RIPTON, VT
1 MILE, MINIMAL ELEVATION GAIN
1 HOUR
EASY
DOGS MUST BE LEASHED.

PART OF THE 335,000-acre Green Mountain National Forest, this unusual trail unites the poetry of Robert Frost with the landscape that inspired it. Frost spent twenty-three summers in a small cabin less than a mile from here. Many of his poems are posted along the trail.

The forest service actively maintains the open areas to keep them from reverting to forest. Logging, brush cutting, and prescribed fires are used to maintain the fields, blueberry bushes, and views. Many plants are identified along this walk, even a few obscure ones. There are lots of benches in settings that tempt you to stay awhile.

The trail has a figure-eight shape, the near loop being wheelchair accessible.

Flooding in August 2008 washed out an important bridge on this trail. In 2009 only the wheelchair accessible gravel loop is available. The bridge will be designed and engineered in 2009 with rebuilding scheduled for 2010. Check my website—www.NatureWalksVermont.com—or the Green Mountain National Forest website, or phone the Middlebury Ranger Station for updated information on bridge construction.

• • • • • •

Begin to the right. Many black cherry trees line the path. You can recognize them by their curled plates of dark, peeling, and bitter-tasting bark. The trail leads to a bench at the edge of a swampy area and the poem, The Pasture.

We cross the swamp on a wooden bridge. A wood duck box is on the right. The path turns left and passes through a thicket of red raspberries and speckled alder, which is identified. The alder is a shrub that thrives at the edge of streams and in swamps. Its strong matted roots help to stabilize banks along waterways. Tiny, woody cones cling to the branches through winter and can be seen in com-

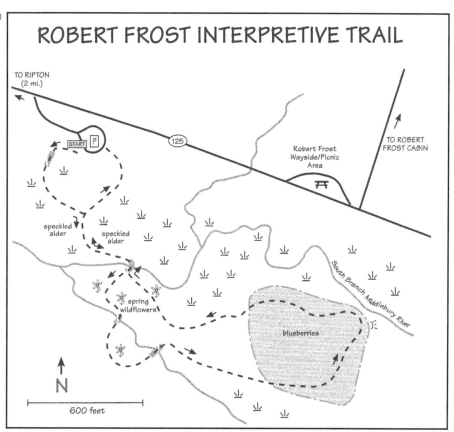

ROBERT FROST INTERPRETIVE TRAIL

TO RIPTON
(2 mi.)

START P

125

Robert Frost
Wayside/Picnic
Area

TO ROBERT
FROST CABIN

speckled
alder

speckled
alder

spring
wildflowers

South Branch Middlebury River

blueberries

N

600 feet

pany of its catkins and leaves the following spring. The bark has conspicuous white lenticels, horizontal lines across the bark that admit air into the branches. The poem, "A Winter Eden," is about a winter garden in an alder swamp.

Very shortly we come to a T-intersection and turn right. The trail crosses the river on a wooden bridge (washed out in 2008) and is no longer wheelchair accessible. Hemlocks hug the riverbank. The poem, Come In, welcomes us to the deeper woods. As the trails diverge we turn right by the poem, The Road Not Taken. The trail climbs slightly as we pass an identified red spruce. It is easier to distinguish red from black spruce by location than by looks. Black spruce are smaller trees usually found in bogs, swamps, and high latitudes. In drier, mountainous habitats, red spruce grow to seventy feet.

The trail meanders to the left, past a wooden bench and a large yellow birch. Hobblebush is identified, an easy shrub to recognize. In winter its huge yellow buds look ready to burst open and in summer its opposite, heart-shaped leaves lie nearly horizontal, like a row of saucers along the stem. Partial to cool woods, this viburnum family-member re-roots when its branches touch the ground, hobbling the unsuspecting passerby. Also known as witch-hobble, it is a favorite food of deer and moose.

The trail makes a right turn, crossing a stream on a small bridge. The poem, "Spring Comes First," reminds us that spring comes to the forest floor first and works its way toward the canopy. The understory here is thick with spring flowering plants, Canada mayflower, Clintonia, bunchberry, wild sarsaparilla, trillium, and wood sorrel.

The trail rises slightly and the American beech tree is identified on the right. This is one of the easiest trees to recognize by its smooth gray bark. Beech trees sprout from the roots and here you can see a circle of beech saplings around an older tree. Sugar maple trees are dominant as we rise towards an intersection with the Watertower Trails on the right. We bear left. Hayscented fern is identified on the left. When crushed this fern smells like freshly mown hay.

There's a bench on the right and the poem, "In Hardwood Groves." The trail slopes gently down towards the brook. On the left is a hospitable glacial erratic, home to a striped maple sapling, ferns, grasses, and moss.

The trail crosses the bridge and turns right. Bracken fern is identified on the left but was in short supply when I visited. Sometimes called the laid-back fern, its three nearly horizontal fronds arch backwards. Its leaflets are quite lacy and delicate. Unlike most ferns that prefer damp, rich locations, bracken ferns thrive in full sun on poor, barren or burned-over soil.

On the left is an unusual tree, the blue beech (*Carpinus caroliniana*) with its rather splotchy-colored but smooth bark, thin twigs and buds, and alternate branching. It never grows over 30 feet in height. A member of the birch rather than the beech family, this tree has many names and is often confused as a result. It is also known as water beech (perhaps because it looks water-marked), musclewood, ironwood, or American hornbeam.

Here's the confusing part. Also in the birch family is the American hop hornbeam (*Ostrya virginiana*), with shreddy, shaggy bark. It is also known as leverwood or ironwood. Although the trees look very different their names are used interchangeably.

The trail soon leaves the woods and crosses a meadow. Lowbush blueberries and meadowsweet are low shrubs, the latter a spirea with a reddish stalk of flowers at the end of each stem.

The trail turns left when it arrives at the South Branch of the Middlebury River. A sign explains the US Forest Service burn policy, used to perpetuate lowbush blueberries. Another panel offers a good explanation of why fields are tem-

Hobblebush flowers resemble viburams, to which they are related.

porary, describing the fate of pioneer plants that alter the environment for their off-spring. It's hard to imagine most of the Green Mountain National Forest as open fields.

At the edge of the meadow the trail enters a tunnel of trees. On the right black cherry is identified. There's a good example of the deeply curled, mature bark on a tree several feet into the woods.

A mix of red spruce, hemlock, birch, and red maple thrive on the bluff over the river. We turn right and cross the bridge. Once again a thicket of speckled alder borders the gravel path. We bear right at the final intersection, and the poem Stopping by Woods, to complete the loop. The poem, "Reluctance," appropriately ends the trail.

BIRCHES

(Don't miss Frost's poem, "Birches.")

Four types of birches grow in northern Vermont, and their names, if not the trees themselves, are often confused.

There's no mistaking the sweet birch (Betula lenta), also called the black or cherry birch, with its dark brown to black bark. The crushed twigs and leaves are fragrant and taste of wintergreen.

The other three birches, all with whitish bark, have overlapping characteristics and names. Bark characteristics are used, not always precisely, to describe them.

The paper or canoe birch (*Betula papyrifera*), often called white birch, was used by Native Americans to make canoes. The creamy bark peels off in large sheets like paper. The tall, single-trunked tree favors rich, moist soils and ample sunlight and can live as long as two hundred years.

The gray birch (*Betula populifolia*), also dubbed white, is a short-lived tree that usually grows in clusters. It rarely exceeds 30 feet, prefers full sun, and will grow on poor, sandy, or overgrazed soil. Its flexible limbs bend to the ground under the weight of ice, often snapping. While its bark is a grayish-white, it does not peel like the bark of paper birch. There is often a dark triangular scar beneath the branches. Gray birch, also called wire or old-field birch, is a pioneer of old, depleted fields.

The last of this trio is the yellow birch, occasionally called gray or silver birch (*Betula alleghaniensis*). Its bark has a rich bronze cast and peels into narrow strips. Yellow birch is a big tree, growing as tall as 100 feet. It may live over three hundred years. Like black birch, its mature bark becomes reddish-brown and fissures into scaly plates and its twigs and foliage may have a slight aroma of wintergreen.

HOURS, FEES, FACILITIES
Pets must be leashed. The near loop of the trail is gravel and is wheelchair accessible. There is a year-round toilet at the trailhead.

GETTING THERE
From Middlebury, drive south on Rte. 7 to the intersection of Rte. 125 east, about 4 miles on the left. Take Rte. 125 through East Middlebury and Ripton to the Robert Frost Interpretive Trail on the right, 6.3 miles from Rte. 7.

FOR MORE INFORMATION
Green Mountain National Forest
Middlebury Ranger District
802 388-4362
http://www.fs.fed.us/r9/forests/greenmountain/

• ALSO IN THE AREA •
An impressive cooperative effort has established the sixteen-mile Trail Around Middlebury (TAM), a recreation path crossing parks, Middlebury College, public preserves, and an assortment of public and private lands. The foot path is a remarkable asset to the Middlebury Community. For information contact the Middlebury Land Trust (see Organizations).

www.malt.org

31 Abbey Pond Trail, Green Mountain National Forest

Abbey Pond is in a wilderness where bear, moose, deer, and bobcat roam. Great blue herons regularly nest at Abbey Pond. In years when they nest the trail is closed from May to July. Great on snowshoes

RIPTON, VT

3.8 MILES, ROUND TRIP, 1160-FOOT ELEVATION GAIN

2.5 -3 HOURS

MODERATE/DIFFICULT

DOGS ARE PERMITTED.

In August 2008, flooding damaged a bridge along this trail. The less nimble might choose to avoid this trail until it is repaired. Check my website, www.Nature-WalksVermont.com or the Green Mountain National Forest website or phone the Middlebury Ranger station for information about nesting and bridge repairs.

. . . . . .

The trail begins on an unmarked logging road bordered by sprouting stumps. Within five minutes the road enters the woods, a mixed northern forest of yellow, paper, and black birch, hemlock, American beech, maple, ash, hop hornbeam, and cherry. The first blue blaze is at the edge of the woods.

In the spring mud I followed moose tracks along this road, the stride over two feet in length, the print four inches wide and six long. Deer tracks, similar rounded troughs, are tiny by comparison, about three inches long.

The trail rises and turns left, passing over Roaring Branch at the sign-in ledger. Be careful of slippery and rotting wood on the bridge. The rushing water spills over picturesque falls to the right.

The trail makes a right turn and climbs, sometimes steeply, before leveling off. The rocks underfoot can be slick as the trail passes beneath a thick tunnel of hemlocks. Hemlocks preclude most growth in their deep shade. In winter, evergreen ferns peek through a cascade of icicles on a rocky outcrop to the left of the trail.

We cross Roaring Branch again on a bridge of boulders and turn left. A logging road rises quite steeply. Pale jewelweed thrives on the damp banks along with asters, nettles, jack-in-the-pulpit, and bloodroot.

Hobblebush and striped maple, called she-moosewood and he-moosewood, respectively, thrive in the cool, dark woods and are heavily browsed in winter. Striped

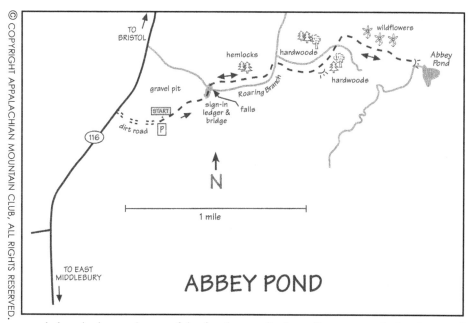

maple has the largest leaves of the family, usually from five to seven inches long and four to five inches wide. This is characteristic of understory trees which receive less light as it is filtered through the canopy. They need disproportionately large leaves to capture adequate sunlight. These striped maple, with bright green and white striped trunks, are unusually large with diameters of five inches.

A mossy outcropping on the right is covered with clubmoss, bright green even in winter. Its tiny branches resemble spruce with pointed leaves in a spiral around the entire three-inch stem.

Spikenard flourishes along the trail. Growing to five feet, the shrub-like member of the ginseng family has heart-shaped leaflets, as many as twenty-one on a branch. Its fruit resembles a bunch of tiny grapes, turning from green to dark purple in September.

The trail climbs moderately but steadily. On the right, when the leaves are off the trees, you can glimpse the lake and the Adirondacks.

The trail bends right then left. A beech tree on the left shows scars of bear claw marks. Beech nuts are high in protein and are a favorite food of bears as they bulk up for winter. Other inhabitants of these woods include chipmunks, red and gray squirrels, and the lumbering porcupine. This clumsy rodent is generally nocturnal, girdling trees to dine on their bark. While spruce and hemlock are preferred, birch is another favorite. Black birch grows along the trail, its leaves, twigs, and smooth, dark bark taste of wintergreen.

The trail continues to rise very gradually past many herbs of the northern forest: starflower, partridgeberry, trillium, jack-in-the-pulpit, wild sarsaparilla, and Clintonia.

The trail crosses the Branch for the third and last time on large rocks in the streambed. There are several large white ash and an increasing number of red maple as we walk over soggy ground. A few of the older specimens have very shaggy bark. Several old paper birch dot the hardwood forest. There is scarcely a conifer to be seen.

These woods were once half spruce but were logged repeatedly over the centuries for softwoods. A sawmill on Roaring Branch made shingles and, in the late 1800s, hardwoods were taken for charcoal. The last landowner continued to log birch, ash, basswood, and poplar into this century. Most of the land along the trail was purchased by the federal government in 1935.

In November 1950, a non-hurricane windstorm ripped through Vermont with gale force winds. South of Abbey Pond the devastation was great and these blow-downs are the most recent cause of widespread forest upheaval.

Goldthread has bright orange roots from which it derives its name.

Hobblebush grows profusely along the last section of trail as well as a riot of spring wildflowers: starflower, Indian cucumber-root, wood sorrel, goldthread, and jack-in-the-pulpit. Patches of princess pine provide year-round greenery and sensitive fern attests to the high level of moisture.

Abbey Pond is a tranquil sanctuary in the woods. The twin peaks of Robert Frost Mountain rise to the south. Bracken fern and heaths prosper in the sunshine. A dam and lodge are evidence of beaver activity. This is a nice place for a picnic before returning on the same trail.

BUSY BEAVERS

For all of the evidence they create- dams, lodges, ponds, and pencil-sharpened stumps, beavers are not easy to spot. A nocturnal laborer, the beaver (Castor canadensis) works at night and sleeps all day. Your best chance is in summer, very early or late in the day, as their construction spills over into daylight hours.

Like all rodents, the beaver has incisors which never stop growing. If a rodent doesn't gnaw it will die as its teeth grow into the opposite jaw. Poplar, willow, and birch are preferred before the harder oak and maple. Evergreens are rarely gnawed. Family groups work together, chewing a groove around a trunk until it falls. They drag their quarry to a dam site, adding smaller sticks, mud, and rocks to complete construction.

As the dam backs up water into a pond, the beavers build their lodge next, a platform of sticks and saplings covered with a dome-shaped mound. Shredded and chewed plants make a soft carpet and water drains out through the floor. Underwater entrances keep the beavers' home safe from predators. Winter food rafts, leafy branches anchored to the pond bottom, are also protected by water and ice.

Winter confinement suits beavers. They can be heard chatting in the lodge while they groom each others' fur with special waterproofing oil. A beaver may occasionally gnaw a hole in the ice near the dam allowing water to escape. With the lower water level beavers can enjoy meals at the raft without returning to the lodge to breathe.

Beavers have some remarkable adaptations: lots of body fat for warmth, nose and ears with special valves to keep water out, a special protective eyelid for seeing in water, and huge cheeks which close behind the teeth so she can work underwater without choking. Five-fingered front feet are dexterous like those of a raccoon and the rear feet are webbed paddles for swimming. The leathery flat, oval tail is used as a balancing prop when gnawing, a sculling oar for swimming, and for slapping the water to warn of danger.

Beavers have a dramatic effect on their neighborhood. A dammed stream creates a pond which attracts frogs, deer, fox, otters, bobcats, ducks, and turtles. As sediment fills the pond it becomes swamp and no longer provides protection to beavers. When they move upstream to build another dam, the swamp fills with plants and begins its passage through wetland succession. (See Ethan Allen Homestead, page 70.)

Beaver pelts were currency of early Dutch settlers and beaver fur was a fashion statement in Europe for years. Trapped nearly to extinction, first in Europe and later in the States, the animals were endangered everywhere at the end of the nineteenth century. They were reintroduced and have successfully colonized in every state but Hawaii. They are no longer endangered.

GETTING THERE

From the intersection of Rtes. 17 and 116 west of Bristol, take Rte. 116 south. At 7.3 miles, just beyond the entrance to a gravel pit, look for a brown Forest Service sign to Abbey Pond on the left. The dirt road forks immediately but the forks rejoin. The right fork is better maintained. Follow it 0.4 miles until several dirt tracks intersect. Park off the road and do not block it. The trail begins on the logging road, the continuation of the road you have driven.

FOR MORE INFORMATION

Green Mountain National Forest
Middlebury Ranger Station
802 388-4362
http://www.fs.fed.us/r9/forests/greenmountain/

Leicester Hollow and Chandler Ridge Trails

This is an unconventional itinerary for a beautiful and interesting walk. Leicester Hollow is a cool, damp limestone valley where a rich variety of moisture and lime-loving plants flourish. A few hundred feet to the west, on a quartzite ridge running parallel to the hollow, a completely different cast of acid-loving plants thrives in drier conditions. The contrast between these two trails speaks volumes about habitat.

GREEN MOUNTAIN NATIONAL FOREST
BRANDON, VT
3-4 MILES
2-3 HOURS
MODERATE
DOGS ARE PERMITTED.

WHILE A CIRCUIT of trails makes a seven mile loop, that walk is longer than the parameters of this book. It is possible to see the areas of greatest contrast by walking north on each trail less than a mile and then returning.

Leicester Hollow, a shady valley nestled between two ridges, is cool and damp at all times. Chandler Ridge, three hundred feet above the hollow, has sweeping views east to the Green Mountains and west to the Adirondacks. The ridge of Cheshire quartzite is sunny, dry, and quite open.

Depending on the type of day and time of year, you might chose to take this walk in reverse order.

Flooding in the summer of 2008 wrecked havoc with Leicester Hollow. Some spots closest to the river are boulder fields, with no trail remaining. It is nonetheless a place of spectacular beauty. Until repairs are completed the Chandler Ridge Trail is the easier and safer option. Consider investigating the flora of Leicester Hollow only if your energy, balance, and mobility are equal to the challenge. Check my website—www.NatureWalksVermont.com—or the Green Mountain National Forest website, or phone the Middlebury Ranger Station for updates on trail conditions.

Walk around the gate that marks the beginning of the Leicester Hollow Trail. This dirt road once led to the Silver Lake Hotel. Be alert for beech trees with bear

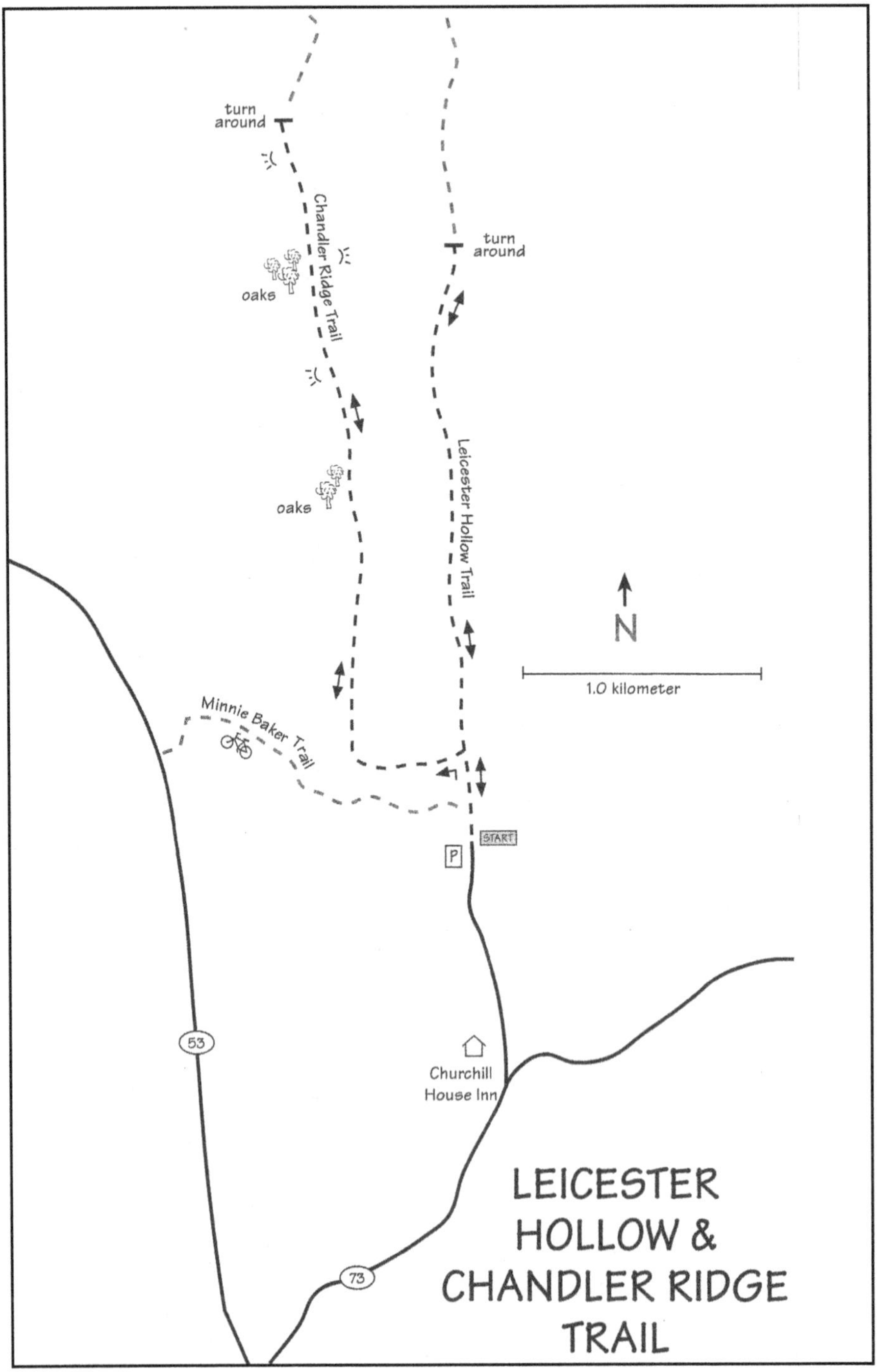

turn
around

Chandler Ridge Trail

oaks

oaks

turn
around

Leicester Hollow Trail

N

1.0 kilometer

Minnie Baker Trail

START

P

Churchill
House Inn

53

73

LEICESTER
HOLLOW &
CHANDLER RIDGE
TRAIL

claw marks. The smooth, gray bark scars readily when bears climb to their favorite fat and protein-rich nuts. The scars grow with the tree, leaving the impression of very large bears!

A glacial erratic on the right is home to a sizable yellow birch with three trunks. Within five minutes the Minnie Baker Trail (to Rte. 53) is on the left. Shortly thereafter a cross country ski trail climbs to the right.

Within ten minutes of the parking area, the trail crosses Leicester Hollow Brook. Immediately, the Chandler Ridge Trail goes left, stone steps rising steeply up a blue-blazed trail. We will take this trail.

The trail heads south initially and after five minutes bears right to continue westward up onto the ridge. Finally it turns northward. Red and white oaks share the canopy with hop hornbeam, the occasional basswood, elm, ash, sugar and red maple, yellow and paper birch, and beech. Beech saplings sprout from the roots of larger trees.

Many of the herbs and shrubs tolerate dry or acidic conditions: Canada mayflower, starflower, Clintonia, partridgeberry, trailing arbutus, and wintergreen. The dominant fern is bracken fern which generally grows in sunny, dry conditions on poor soil. Low-bush blueberry, huckleberry, and witch hazel are among the shrubs.

The woods are peppered with moss-covered glacial erratics hosting a giddy array of plants: reindeer moss, ferns, clubmoss, blueberry, mountain maple, and trailing arbutus, among others.

The canopy thins and a vista opens to the west. Red and white oaks dominate and the thin, dry soil atop the ridge keeps them from reaching great size. Many red oaks have double trunks, reminders of a logging past. The footing is quite rocky. Witch hazel (Hamamelis virginiana), a shrub or small tree with wavy-toothed, un-even-based leaves, flourishes. A favorite of dowsers or water witches, the shade-tolerant plant grows to twenty-five feet. Only after its leaves fall in autumn do spidery yellow flowers appear, four long, crinkly, narrow petals about 3/4 inch long. The petals curl back into a bud when the temperature drops and open again in warm weather. Its small, orange-brown fruit explodes sending seeds up to thirty feet. Extract of the bark and leaves is used as a topical astringent while its seeds, buds and twigs are eaten by pheasant, bobwhite, ruffed grouse, white-tailed deer, cottontail rabbit and beaver.

Extravagant in the fall are Indian cucumber-root, whose deep blue berries sit atop of a whorl of red leaves. Purple and white asters bloom luxuriantly, pink lady's slipper hides its seed in a brittle leaf-like hood, and false Solomon's seal produces a cascade of pink or red berries. Look for the pendulous red berries of wintergreen

Bear claw marks on a beech tree.

and tiny bright orange-red partridgeberries.

A ridge rises on the right- the east. The soil is deeper and there are fewer rock outcropping along the trail. The understory is thicker with saplings, especially striped and red maple. There is still a splendid view to the west of the Champlain Valley and the Adirondacks.

When the trail makes a right turn and descends into a damp ravine, turn around. The return to the trailhead is a gradual descent and will take 30-45 minutes. Blue blazes are frequent in both directions.

As you descend the ridge you meet the cool of the hollow. Turn left on the Leicester Hollow Trail.

The hollow was created over thousands of years as erosion and naturally acidic rainwater dissolved the soft limestone. The alkalinity of the bedrock produces fertile, limy soil and its high fertility supports an unusual assortment of plants.

Maple, yellow and paper birch, basswood, ash, and beech grow tall in the hollow, thriving in deeper, fertile soil with more moisture. In late May or early June, this is a wildflower paradise. Moisture-loving plants include jewelweed, ferns, nettles, and Indian pokeweed, its long, thin leaves growing sheath-like around a central stalk. Plants partial to limy soil abound including maidenhair fern, blue cohosh, Herb Robert, and bulblet fern. Despite its fernlike leaves, Herb Robert is a flowering plant with a delicate pink-purple bloom. Red trillium and jack-in-the-pulpit, both partial to rich soils, grow to great size.

Look for Clintonia and Canada violet with a pansy-like flower, its petals white on the inside and purple outside. Ramps, or wild leek, are fragrant. Virginia waterleaf, named for the mottles on its leaves, produces a cascade of purple or white bell-like flowers on tall stalks towering above the five- to seven-lobed leaves.

The streambed and boulders on the valley floor are pale-colored limestone or marble. The trail crosses the brook a total of six times while rising gently. Two of the bridges are wooden and can be very slippery. Tread carefully!

The 800-foot elevation and cool temperatures are hospitable to hobblebush, a prolific shrub of the northern forest. Its large, heart-shaped, opposite leaves lie nearly horizontal along the stems which often reroot, hobbling the unsuspecting.

Stinging nettles are a fact of life in the hollow. Late in the season, when the plants are huge, stick to the center of the trail to avoid them. Heart-shaped, opposite leaves grow on plants up to four feet. Stinging bristles on both the leaves and stems deliver an acid which causes a burning skin irritation. Flowers are tight white clusters which appear in the leaf axils.

You will cross the sixth and final bridge in less than an hour. From here the valley between the ridges widens and the hollow is less pronounced. The land was once farmed and you may see apple trees, day lilies and other evidence of civilization.

Retrace your steps to return to the trailhead.

CALCAREOUS BEDROCK (AND WHY WE CARE)

Why do different plants grow on different bedrock? Plants survive in a given location because of a number of factors: extremes of temperature, moisture, sunlight, wind, favorable sites for seed germination, and available nutrients.

The limestone bedrock in Leicester Hollow has a high pH, an important factor in soil fertility. The presence of lime, or calcium carbonate, keeps the pH high making the necessary elements, especially calcium and magnesium, available to plants.

Water constantly leaches away nutrients needed for healthy plant growth. Thus soil becomes more and more acidic over time, making fewer nutrients accessible to plants. Limestone hillsides, located over a long-term source of calcium carbonate, do not become as acidic as many other soils do. The fertile soil is home to environmental indicators like maidenhair and walking fern, bloodroot, and basswood and butternut trees in addition to the usual array of less particular plants.

GETTING THERE

Rtes. 53 and 73 meet about 3 miles east of Brandon. Take Rte. 53 east for 0.8 mile. Immediately past the Churchill House Inn, take the unmarked dirt road which forks left. Follow this narrow road, Brandon Town Road 40, 0.6 mile to a small parking area where the trail begins.

FOR MORE INFORMATION

Green Mountain National Forest
Middlebury Ranger District
802 388-4362
http://www.fs.fed.us/r9/forests/greenmountain/

Moosalamoo Partnership
c/o Brandon Area Chamber of Commerce
P. O. Box 267
Brandon, VT 05733
802-247-6401
http://www.moosalamoo.com/

33 Texas Falls

A pretty, plunging river in woods with luxuriant spring wildflowers. An interesting walk for children.

GREEN MOUNTAIN NATIONAL FOREST, HANCOCK, VT
1.2 MILES
1 HOUR OR SLIGHTLY MORE
MODERATE
DOGS OKAY

THIS IS A BEAUTIFUL SPOT to enjoy the northern woods. We have left the warmer Champlain Valley for the slopes of the Green Mountains. Trees, shrubs, and wildflowers of the northern forest thrive here. Gone are the oaks, hickory, and white trillium of the lowlands.

In recent years the trail has not been maintained and flooding in August 2008 washed out the access road and the pedestrian bridge that accesses the trail. Road-work should be completed in 2009 with bridge design and engineering to follow. The hope is that the bridge will be rebuilt in 2010. Check my website—www.NatureWalksVermont.com—or the Green Mountain National Forest web-site, or phone the Middlebury/Rochester Ranger Station for updated information on this trail.

Why include this damaged walk? Books are updated at long intervals and Texas Falls and its woodlands are so beautiful that it seems a shame to exclude them. This trail has the feel, smell, and flora of the mountains and yet is accessible and not a difficult walk. As our nation grapples with financial difficulties money may not flow quickly to fund such repairs. Yet the joy we experience on such a beautiful walk is invaluable.

· · · · · ·

The trail begins across the road. Stop to admire the beautifully sculpted bedrock of Hancock Branch. Thrust up at an angle, its different layers have been unevenly eroded over the years. Potholes have been scoured by the abrasive action of whirling water and stones. At one time the water level was higher, leaving potholes above the current flow of the river. Notice the isolated pool on the near-shore filled by seasonal high water.

Several trees cling perilously to the opposite bank. The river has eroded soil from around their tenacious roots.

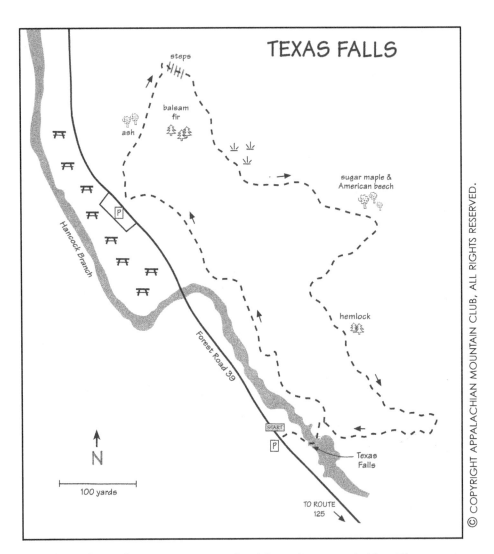

TEXAS FALLS

steps

balsam
fir

ash

sugar maple &
American beech

hemlock

Hancock Branch

Forest Road 39

START

P

Texas
Falls

N

100 yards

TO ROUTE
125

The trail goes down some steps to the right and crosses a bridge. The water is aquamarine in color. Look upstream at the deep cut made by the water over time.

Be careful not to trip over tree roots. Hemlocks and yellow birch, both with wide-spreading, shallow root systems, anchor themselves horizontally on this shallow soil. Their seeds can germinate in nearly any moist place and saplings often begin life in unlikely places including boulder and stumps.

Follow signs to the Nature Trail although it is no longer maintained as such. Turn left to walk upstream with the river on your left. A shaded bench overlooks the falls, a nice perch for admiring spring wildflowers. Both painted and red trillium grow here in addition to wood anemone and Clintonia. Clintonia has a pair of thick oval leaves. A cluster of yellow bell-like lilies, turning to deep blue berries, is at the end of a single stem.

Shrubs that prefer cool or shady locations flourish here, including American yew, hobblebush, and striped maple, these last two both heavily browsed by moose and deer.

Less than ten minutes into the walk the trail becomes a wide gravel path and climbs away from the water. Yellow and paper birch, beech, maples, and white ash dominate the woods. The river disappears across the road and the woods are quiet except for birds and chipmunks. Within five minutes the trail slopes down and approaches the river again. A picnic area is across the road with covered tables.

The trail turns right and climbs easily but steadily. There is a large ash on the left with a triple trunk; the diamond pattern of its bark makes it easy to recognize. Water bars have been built to prevent erosion. We pass red trillium, jack in the pulpit, tall meadow rue, false Solomon's seal, wild sarsaparilla, and more heavily browsed hobblebush. Many beech saplings are sprouting from the roots of more mature trees.

A ten-minute climb brings us to a right turn and steps built into the hillside. The understory is lush with deciduous saplings, striped maple, hobblebush, and young hemlock. The trail is very easy to follow. On the inside of a right turn is a huge black cherry tree with characteristic "burnt potato chip" bark, one of the largest I've seen on my walks. There are occasional red spruce as we gain elevation, with short, spiky gray-green needles. The other boreal or northern tree making an appearance is the fragrant balsam fir. If you remember the adage that fir is friendly and spruce is spiky you won't have trouble distinguishing the trees. Particularly in the spring, the new, yellow-green growth of the balsam fir feels like feathers. Later in the year balsam distinguishes itself with upright cones, like candles.

Spring flowers are everywhere: painted trillium, Clintonia, wild lily-of-the-valley, Indian cucumber, starflower, and Solomon's seal. In May I saw pink twisted stalk in bloom, a delicate pink bell dangling from each axil. The plant resembles Solomon's seal but is much smaller.

The trail crosses a series of small rivulets in a swampy stretch with many blowdowns. Waterlogged soil forces a tree to extend its roots along the surface to get adequate oxygen. Trees with shallow root systems are more easily uprooted. Some shaggy-barked, old sugar maples prevail in the company of smooth-barked American beech, with distinctive blue-gray coloring. Although shallow, the beech's root system is extensive which may enable it to endure strong winds.

On the right side of the trail is a nurse log. Seeds often germinate on the moist, rich surface provided by rotting stumps. This log is home to moss, ferns, and a

The dainty painted trillium favor cool locations.

cluster of jack-in-the-pulpit.

The trail bends to the right and begins a gentle descent. A small stream rushes in the distance. Many small, round holes dot the earth, leading to chipmunk burrows. Their complicated tunnels can be thirty feet long yet may reemerge only a short distance from another entrance. Food is stored there and a leafy nest is fit for winter slumbers and spring litters of young. Its most-feared predator, the slim weasel, can pursue the chipmunk throughout its burrow.

Three wooden bridges cross small streams in rapid succession. Ash trees are frequent again and the hemlocks begin to thicken. Not much grows beneath the hemlocks except the occasional fern.

Walk carefully down a stairway built into the hillside. The trail continues on the level for a few minutes. We cross another bridge before bending to the left and descending again.

The hillside and trail are reinforced against erosion as the descent becomes steeper. We pass a beech tree on the left with beech blister, a canker disease that is killing a large numbers of the trees. A few more turns and steps bring us to a final vista of the falls and its pools. The trail returns to the parking area.

TRILLIUM THREE

There are three types of trillium in our area. The name of the plant tells much of the story: three leaves, three petals, three sepals.

Near Lake Champlain the large-flowered trillium (Trillium grandiflorum) flourishes. Its large, white flower stands above a whorl of three broad leaves. The plant can be as tall as 18 inches. The blossom lingers for several weeks and turns pink before fading. In rich woodlands with neutral or basic soil, trillium bloom before the trees leaf out.

Growing in coolers hills and mountains, purple trillium (Trillium erectum) are a deep red or maroon. The flowers and leaves are generally smaller than those of the white trillium and the leaves are net- rather than parallel-veined.

Painted trillium (Trillium undulatum) is the least common in our area. Its blossom has a central V of deep pink that bleeds slightly toward the tips of the petals. Painted trillium favor moist acidic woods and swamps.

Trillium have a symbiotic relationship with ants. The red berry-like covering of the trillium seed is delectable to ants. The ants drag the seed to their underground colony where they devour only its covering. They leave the bare seed to germinate in this ideal location. It still takes seven years from germination until a trillium produces a flower.

GETTING THERE

From Rte. 7 south of Middlebury (about 9 miles) turn left onto Rte. 125 east towards Ripton. You will pass the Bread Loaf Campus of Middlebury College and the Middlebury Snow Bowl. After cresting the Green Mountains the road descends. At 13.1 miles turn left at a sign for Texas Falls Recreation Area, Forest Road 39. The parking area is 0.4 mile on the left. Additional parking is available at the picnic area another 0.2 mile.

From Rte. 100 in Hancock, take Rte. 125 west for 3.0 miles. Turn right at the sign for Texas Falls, Forest Road 39.

FOR MORE INFORMATION

Green Mountain National Forest
Middlebury Ranger District
802 388-4362
or
Rochester Ranger Station
802-767-4261
http://www.fs.fed.us/r9/forests/greenmountain/

Montpelier Area

34 Rock of Ages Granite Quarry

Home of Vermont's two-century-old granite industry. Fascinating for kids.

GRANITEVILLE, VT
MINIMAL DISTANCE
1 HOUR
VERY EASY
NO PETS.

THE GRANITE QUARRIES are too interesting and awe-inspiring to overlook even if there's really no walk here. The quarries also provide an excuse to look at geologic history- in case you fell asleep during that class. How did such an impressive quantity of granite find its way to Vermont?

Barre granite has been quarried since shortly after the War of 1812, although surface stone was used in the late 1790s for fence posts, doorsteps and boundary markers. The state capitol in Montpelier was built of Barre granite in the 1830s, unfortunately a money-losing project for the quarry owners. It cost more to transport the stone twelve miles using horses and rollers than the suppliers were paid! It was only with the arrival of the railroad to Barre in 1875, that the granite industry began to flourish.

The hardest rock known to man, granite is very durable. The local stone has a uniform color and medium-grained texture. Granite is an igneous rock whose main components are quartz, contributing hardness, feldspar determining its color, and mica, allowing finished stone to take a high polish.

The majority of the granite from these quarries is used for monuments. Huge rollers, used in the manufacture of paper and for grinding cocoa nuts, are cut from unusually large pieces of stone weighing about 200 tons. Granite is also used in scientific work including space missions. Scraps and imperfect pieces are crushed as a bed for road pavement or cut into curbstones.

Gray granite is quarried elsewhere in Vermont, in Hardwick and Woodbury, while white granite is found in Bethel. Elsewhere in the world granite exists in shades of pink, green, black, and red.

The 2009 *Star Trek* movie, *Quantum of Solace*, includes a car chase scene. The

The Rock of Ages Granite Quarry is fascinating for both children and adults.
Photo courtesy of Rock of Ages Granite Quarry.

car flies off a cliff into a digital recreation of Rock of Ages' Smith Quarry, the one you will visit.

• • • • • • •

Behind the Visitor's Center there is an abandoned quarry. The water is 200 feet deep indicating the depth to which stone was removed.

You will ride a bus to the active Smith Quarry during working hours. Grout piles, the Scottish word for waste, cover the hillsides enroute. Today unused pieces are returned to old quarries to reclaim them. Before mechanized transportation, debris was dumped as close as possible.

This active quarry, opened in 1880, covers 50 acres and is 795 feet deep. There are about twenty-five workers in the quarry each day. Because the pit is so deep, crane operators on the rim cannot see their cargo and signalers must communicate between granite workers and the cranes.

In recent years, steel derricks have replaced 150-foot Douglas firs and capacity has increased fivefold from the original fifty-ton capacity. Worker safety has improved and productivity has increased in many ways. Jet torches, burning at 4,200 degrees Fahrenheit, have replaced explosives for most of the cutting and wet drilling has eliminated stone dust, cause of the lung disease silicosis. Yet dangers still exist. The quarried stones, averaging ten by ten by five feet, each weigh twenty-five to thirty tons.

This granite mass has been measured sonically at two by four miles on the surface and ten miles deep. At the current rate it can be quarried for 4,500 years!

GEOLOGY OVERSIMPLIFIED

Geology is very complicated. Scientists examine our landscape and try to reconstruct billions of years of history. Geological theories continue to evolve with advances in technology, new means of dating, continued archeological excavations, and even space exploration.

This simplified geological history breezes through the millennia in an effort to make the very basics clear. Several references are listed in the bibliography and I encourage you to explore them. Like recognizing birds, ferns, leaves, or animal tracks, knowing about rocks adds to the enjoyment of being outdoors.

The earth was once a mass of molten materials. As this liquid cooled a crust formed on the surface, not unlike the skin on hot milk. The crust broke into pieces as it floated over the liquid center. These pieces are called plates and their movement plate tectonics.

These plates moved (and still do) back and forth over the earth's molten core. In bumping into one another they pushed up mountain ranges. One of the oldest exposed mountain ranges on earth is the Adirondacks, believed to be two billion years old. The Adirondacks were on the east coast of a major plate, ancestral North America, and over millions of years the mountains eroded and their sediment built up along the east coast of the continent.

Meanwhile the plates of North America and the European/African continent, separated by an early Atlantic Ocean, were drifting apart. Then, around 445 million years ago, the plates reversed direction and began to drift toward one another. A chain of volcanic islands, a bit like today's Hawaiian Island chain, had been building beneath the Atlantic Ocean. These volcanoes, called the Bronson Hill volcanic arc, got pushed against the coast of North America.

As the plates closed against each other, these volcanoes were subjected to great pressure. The magma or liquid rock in these volcanoes couldn't reach the surface and cooled slowly beneath the earth's surface. The resulting rock is granite, but we'll get back to that later.

The continents continued to move closer together until they collided about 350 million years ago. The Bronson Hill volcanoes were no longer on the east coast of the North American continent but in the middle of a huge land mass called Pangea.

Around 200 million years ago the tides turned and the continents drifted apart. When the land masses separated some of the European continent remained attached to North America. This European fragment is now much of New Hampshire and Maine. The remains of the volcanic arc are the White Mountains and the mass of granite seen at the quarries around Barre.

With this information we can visualize, from west to east, the ancient Adirondacks, sediment from ancient seas which constitutes much of Vermont's western valleys, the Green and White Mountains, and the foreign appendage of New Hampshire and Maine.

HOURS, FEES, FACILITIES
The Visitors Center is open from mid-May to October 31, from 9:00 a.m. to 5:00 p.m., Monday to Saturday, and Monday to Sunday from mid-September to October 31. Quarry tours are conducted between 9:15 a.m. and 3:35 p.m., Monday through Saturday with the addition of Sundays from mid-September. The facility is not open on July 4 but operates on the Sundays of Memorial and Labor Day Weekends. Tour cost is $4.00 for adults with reductions for children and seniors. Water, restrooms, and a snack bar are located at the Visitors Center. Visitors may also purchase a ticket to sandblast some granite in the factory next door. You will leave with an item of your own creation.

GETTING THERE

Take I-89 Exit 6. Follow Route 63 to the bottom of the hill. Go straight through the light following overhead signs to "Graniteville/Granite Quarries." Go straight, up Middle Hill road. The Rock of Ages Visitors Center is on the left.

FOR MORE INFORMATION

Rock of Ages Corporation
558 Graniteville Road
Graniteville, VT 05654
877 225-7626
http://www.rockofages.com

• ALSO IN THE AREA •

ROCK OF AGES INDUSTRIES

Next to the Visitors Center, the Rock of Ages Manufacturing Division handcrafts the monuments that have made Barre granite famous. A free, self-guided tour allows visitors to watch the cutting, sculpting, and polishing from an observations deck above the work areas. Business hours are 8:00 a.m. to 3:30 p.m.

HOPE CEMETERY

Just north of Barre on Rte. 14, Hope Cemetery is a monument to monuments. From the early days of local stonecutting, immigrant sculptors carved statuary to remember their loved ones. Hope Cemetery has dozens of remarkable carvings from local granite.

35 # Hubbard Park

A wide range of habitats within the city limits of Vermont's capital. Cross-country ski trails are groomed in winter.

MONTPELIER, VT
1.5 MILES
1.5 TO **2** HOURS
EASY TO MODERATE
DOGS OKAY

THE CITY OF MONTPELIER is blessed with two significant natural areas, Hubbard Park and North Branch River Park. While the two parks are connected by a right-of-way open much of the year, each merits a visit.

Hubbard Park, 185 acres of meadow, swamp, and woodland, was established in 1899 by a gift from the estate of John E. Hubbard. A winter cross-country ski destination, the park bustles with summer activity on its trails, softball diamond, recreation fields, Paracours fitness trail, the tower, and picnic shelters.

Various benefactors have contributed additional land or funds for improvement over the years. In 1915, work began on a 50-foot stone observation tower, constructed from nearby crumbling stonewalls. The tower, completed in 1930, has stunning mountain views.

During the Depression, the Civilian Conservation Corps built and improved roads, buildings, and fireplaces throughout the park. In the 1960's a nature trail was added (no longer maintained). A fitness trail was threaded through the sylvan setting in the 1980s. Hubbard Park has nearly seven miles of trails.

We will meander through woodlands, climb the tower for a spectacular view, and walk a stretch of the fitness trail beneath towering hemlocks.

• • • • • •

From the parking area at the hairpin turn, look across the road for an entrance to the nature trail, no longer maintained. The park was once treeless pastureland, now grown up with young trees. Many trails thread through these woods that are encircled by the dirt road leading to the tower. If you miss a turn- easy to do, enjoy the walk knowing that you will come to the dirt road. Wherever you join the road, walk uphill. There are numerous signs to the tower.

Sugar maples mix with hemlock and white pine, the thick canopy allowing

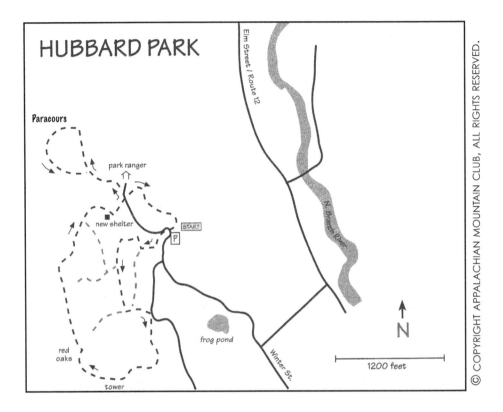

HUBBARD PARK

Paracours

park ranger

new shelter

START

P

Elm Street / Route 12

N. Branch River

frog pond

Winter St.

red oaks

tower

N

1200 feet

minimal ground cover of wild lily-of-the valley, goldthread, partridgeberry, sensitive fern, and spinulose woodfern. At a fork the trail rises. Alternate-leaved dogwood, starflower, interrupted and Christmas fern grow in the understory beneath maple, beech, hemlock, paper birch, red oak, and black cherry. Notice the characteristic curls of black bark, like burned potato chips, on the cherry trees.

Turn left. The trail rises slightly beneath red pines. Go left at a fork beneath thick hemlocks. Look for a dead red maple, damaged when it was split by frost. This threat to deciduous trees is little appreciated. With no leaves to protect it from the low winter sun, the trunk absorbs the sun's heat and expands. The darker the color of the bark the greater the absorption. When the sun dips below the horizon frigid air contracts the wood. The outer bark cools more quickly than the insulated pulpwood. The bark cracks to relieve pressure creating an opening in the tree's protective layer. Organisms enter the wood and the tree begins to rot. This tree shows attempts to heal around the wound before it succumbed. Insects and diseases kill more trees each year than spectacular forest fires.

The trail crosses a small brook on a boardwalk. On damp ground spirea grows in the only available sunlight.

The trail turns right before passing through an evergreen plantation dating from 1937. It includes the droopy-boughed Norwegian spruce and red pines. A glacial erratic sparkles with mica beneath a cover of moss.

The trail dips downhill and the golden bark of yellow birch glows in the sunshine. The trail turns right around a large red oak with three trunks, then bends right around a large white pine. At a T-intersection, turn right and then to the left shortly thereafter. When the trail reaches the dirt road, go right. When the road forks go right to climb the dirt road, with red oaks towering overhead, in the direction of the tower.

A steep five to ten minute uphill brings us to the tower. In early spring clouds of tiny bluets surround the base. Sixty-five steps climb past beautiful stones with varied colors, textures, and striations. On a clear day the views stretch west to Camel's Hump, east to New Hampshire's White Mountains, and slightly west of north, to Hunger Mountain in the Worcester Range. Trees have grown up preventing a view of the golden capitol dome.

When you come out of the tower turn left on the dirt road. Huge red oaks share the woods with both red and sugar maple. Red maple leaves tend to have three lobes and there is a V between the central and side lobes. Sugar maples have five lobed-leaves and the angle between the central and side lobes is rounded, like an old sap bucket. Sugar maple leaves have smooth edges while reds are serrated or toothed.

The road passes an old stone gatepost. You may stay on the dirt road or detour briefly into the woods by turning left on a small trail near a picnic table. In this moist ground there are beech and many birch, maple, and oak with multiple trunks. We pass a stonewall with very large rocks. The understory is lush with ferns, goldthread, wild lily-of-the valley, partridgeberry, Clintonia, and wintergreen, its white flowers like tiny bells. Indian pipes are abundant in the dead leaf litter on both sides of trail.

When the trail arrives back at the dirt road, go left. Just before the park gate take a dirt road on the right (to stay in the park). Hemlock, oak, and Norway spruce dominate, box elder and birch mix in. Do not take the trail that crosses the road; continue on the road. It leads slightly downhill, crosses a bridge and approaches the New Shelter. Look to the right for a chair sculpted from a tree trunk. Bear left to cross the open, grassy area and turn left at the dirt road.

Along this road, young basswood sprout from the base of a parent tree on the left. Hemlocks dominate the canopy. In the swamp on the left hobblebush is abundant beneath black ash, birch, and maple. Do not take the first left onto the fitness trail (you will return from here) but continue on the road until it curves left

The tower was built from the remnants of stone walls.

and rises. Several log benches sit in the shade and a bank on the right is covered with luxuriant moss. Several ski trails go off to the right.

Turn left at the fitness or Paracours trail marked by a large green arrow on a white square. These are rich northern woods, a mix of yellow birch, ash, hemlock, black cherry, hobblebush, striped maple, and sugar maple. The herb layer is lush with ferns, jewelweed, trillium, jack in the pulpit, and sassafras.

The bark path is silent and soft underfoot. The trail turns left at Stop 15. Hobblebush is solid in the understory, its heart-shaped leaves lying parallel to the ground. A large hemlock is peppered with rows of sapsucker holes. With its brush-like tongue this woodpecker laps at the sap that oozes from the holes and also consumes the insects attracted to it.

The path crosses a stream on a bridge. At Stop 18 a rotting trunk on the right, a nurse log, is home to tendrils of moss, goldthread, wood sorrel, starflower, and spinulose woodfern. The trail crosses another wooden bridge. Follow the green arrows for the Paracours along the road briefly and then into the woods again.

The trail goes uphill and to the left, past Stops 13, 20, and 21. (The trail is going in both directions here.) Follow the path to the right. When the trail forks, go right or straight (not left), past Stops 12 and 22 on a plateau. A beech tree on the left has sprouted lots of saplings from its roots near Stops 11, 23, and 24. Past Stops 10, 25, and 26, the trail leads to a picnic table and fireplace overlooking the open meadow at the parking area.

CONIFERS, IN BRIEF

Conifers are trees with woody cones (hence the name) and needles or scale-like leaves. Pollen and seed cones are generally found on the same plant and rely on wind for pollination.

The tamarack, or eastern larch, is the region's only deciduous conifer, loosing its leaves each fall. Its bright green one-inch needles occur either singly or in large bunches.

The pines, four native and two introduced species, have bunches of needles. Red and gray or jack pine have clusters of two needles, pitch pine three per cluster, and white pine five. The two non-native pines, Scotch and Austrian, each have two needles per cluster. Needle length and bark coloration aid in identification.

Vermont has four spruces, three native and one introduced, plus one native fir. Red, white, and black or swamp are the native spruces, Norway the introduced species; balsam the fir. If you grip a branch of these trees, the spruce will feel "spiky" and the fir "friendly."

HOURS, FEE, AND FACILITIES

Hubbard Park is open daily, year-round from 7:00 A.M. to 9:00 P.M. Gates may be locked around dark. There are no fees. Restrooms and water are available seasonally. Scoops and pits for dog waste in several locations.

GETTING THERE

From I-89 take Exit 8 and follow the exit road to the first stoplight, 1.3 miles. Turn left on Bailey Avenue. Just over the bridge turn right onto State Street, 0.1 mile. Beyond the capitol building turn left at 0.4 mile on Elm Street. Turn left on Winter Street at 0.4 mile. Winter Street enters Hubbard Park at 0.1 mile. Drive up the dirt road; bear right at the fork and park in designated area on the right 0.3 mile from park entrance.

FOR MORE INFORMATION

Montpelier Park Commission
39 Main Street
Montpelier, VT 05602
802-223-7335
www.montpelier-vt.org/parks/hubbard.cfm

36 North Branch Nature Center and North Branch River Park

River and hillside with variety of habitats, connection to Hubbard Park. Good wildlife viewing.

MONTPELIER, VT
NORTH BRANCH NATURE CENTER
0.6 MILE
45 MINUTES
EASY
CONNECT TO NORTH BRANCH RIVER PARK
1.5 MILES
1.5 HOURS
MODERATE, HILLY TERRAIN
WALK ON BOTH PROPERTIES
2+ MILES
MODERATE
DOGS MUST BE LEASHED.

A GRACEFUL PEDESTRIAN BRIDGE links two riverside preserves in northern Montpelier, making them a single destination for walking, skiing, and snowshoeing. On the west side of the North Branch of the Winooski River is North Branch Nature Center (NBNC). On the eastern bank and extending into the hills is North Branch River Park, a municipal park of the city of Montpelier. Trails connect from the park to Montpelier's Hubbard Park and to the East Montpelier Trail Network.

Both properties have access to a lovely, lazy stretch of the river. Otter, beaver, and muskrat make their homes here and deer, moose, and bobcat venture down from the hills. The connection to Hubbard Park (see page 223) is seasonal as the trail passes through a deeryard that is closed in winter.

The NBNC was opened by Vermont Institute of Natural Science in 1996 on an old sheep farm and in 2006 became a private non-profit with its own board of directors. NBNC offers year-round programs for all ages, nature walks, bird walks, naturalist lecture series, teen birding program, amphibian monitoring, and summer day camps. The Nature Center houses nature displays. We will begin and end our walk at NBNC.

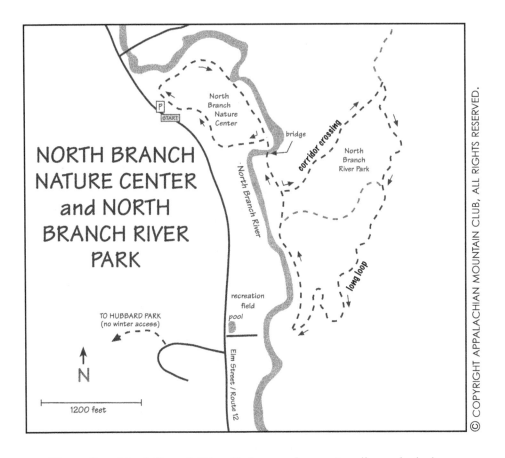

NORTH BRANCH
NATURE CENTER
and NORTH
BRANCH RIVER
PARK

North
Branch
Nature
Center

bridge

corridor crossing

North
Branch
River Park

North Branch River

long loop

recreation
field

pool

TO HUBBARD PARK
(no winter access)

Elm Street / Route 12

N

1200 feet

The trails at North Branch River Park are only occasionally marked, the terrain is hilly, and the distances are longer. If this does not sound comfortable, consider a walk in Hubbard Park (see page 223), another lovely Montpelier park.

• • • • • •

From the parking area follow the mowed trail across the meadow toward the community gardens. A loop trail around the field follows the arc of the river approaching it at several points.

In the fertile soil of the riverbank, butternut, black ash, maple, and many large white willow trees grow. Beneath them wild grape vines entangle hawthorn and apple trees, red-osier dogwood, and honeysuckle. Bluebirds have been scarce in recent years but NBNC hopes to attract them to boxes scattered across the meadow. Community gardens bustle with activity for much of the year and their seeds attract a wide range of birds.

NBNC actively manages the fields to create a range of habitats. Ragweed, birdsfoot trefoil, black-eyed Susan, cow and crown vetch, red clover, Queen Anne's

Purple or red trillium are also called "Wake Robin" and "Stinking Benjamin."

lace, wild sunflowers, and sensitive ferns create a colorful meadow. This is a great spot to see bobolinks and displaying woodcock in the spring. Part of the field is actively hayed. In another area hay is cut and left to lie, providing food and shelter for meadow moles, voles and migrating geese. Snipe, the occasional duck, and nesting red-winged blackbirds visit a wet area in the middle of the field.

Spur trails lead to the river. In spring red trillium, bloodroot, and false hellebore or Indian poke flourish. In summer a forest of ostrich ferns reigns. Huge willows dominate the riverbank along with a number of black cherry and butternut.

The river is lazy here. Look for erosion patterns on the riverbank from when the river flowed at a higher level. Harder rocks, like quartz, have resisted erosion. Several potholes are visible. Great blue heron come to dine in the river and otter scat is often found on the banks.

The trail continues along the edge of the field with detours to the river. The exposed bedrock at the turn in the river is beautiful. Paper birch and hemlock roots cling to the rock face where high water has eroded the soil.

Japanese knotweed, a non-native invasive, grows to twelve feet along the bank. Its jointed red stems produce alternate round leaves and clusters of greenish-white flowers at each axil (where the leaf grows out of the stem). Resembling bamboo, Japanese knotweed spreads aggressively and is difficult to eradicate.

Another denizen of these wet banks is spotted joe-pye weed, often growing to six feet and topped with a flat cluster of purple-pink fuzzy flowers in late summer. Its coarsely toothed, lance-shaped leaves grow in whorls of three to five.

As you cross the bridge to North Branch River Park notice the currents in the river below. Immediately on the left is a blind, a series of wooden planks spaced for viewing activities in the wetland below. Beavers are often active here.

Continue straight on the mowed grass path into a meadow where goldenrod, chicory, fleabane, milkweed, raspberry, and butter and eggs add color, texture, and variety to the grasses. Speckled alder and willow saplings are establishing themselves. Shortly you will come to a wooden directional post. The sign points left toward the East Montpelier Trails. You are not going to East Montpelier but you will turn left here to climb into the hillside trail network. The City of Montpelier online map calls this trail the Corridor Crossing although there may be no trail markings.

We pass among shrubs and young saplings as we start to climb, among them honeysuckle, hawthorn, speckled alder, sumac, box elder, willow, red maple, and basswood. In early September bright red leaves of the Virginia creeper tangle the trees.

The trail levels off between steep sections. Spruce and occasional balsam fir begin to mix with the hemlock and hardwoods. There are lots of saplings and some ferns in the understory.

After the second steep section the trail levels off and hardwoods dominate the woods. Within fifteen minutes the serious climbing is over and the Long Loop Trail goes to the right (no sign with trail names). We will take it.

The trail rises gently through the northern forest of yellow birch, ash, maple, beech, balsam fir, black cherry, spruce, and hemlock; the more hemlock the sparser the vegetation in the understory. The wide, well-groomed trail rises and falls. It crosses a number of bridges, both wooden and stone-covered culverts. There are few plants in the understory- a few red trillium, jack-in-the-pulpit, and Christmas ferns.

The trail bears to the left and starts gradually downhill and after about twenty minutes forks. A right, on the Short Loop, would return directly to the riverbank. Go left to continue on the Long Loop through more hardwood forest where only a few ferns and wild lily-of-the-valley thrive in the meager sunlight. Traffic noise tells us that Route 12 is not far away. The butternut trees are unhealthy. Follow the trail as it curves to the right and down the hill. Most likely there were farms on this hillside long ago as several apple trees struggle to reach the light by the side of the trail.

The trail alternately slopes downhill and levels out until it reaches the worn dirt path along the river. Turn right and you will be walking north, back toward the bridge and the NBNC. The path follows the river past a tangle of shrubs, young trees, and vines growing on its banks: speckled alder, red raspberry, Japanese knotweed, gray, paper and yellow birch, vines, butternut, poplar, cherry, willow, ash, elm, and box elder.

Soon you will emerge into a field and see the wooden sign where you began the hilly loop. Stay left, continuing back to the bridge. Turn left off the bridge to continue circling the meadows at the NBNC. Mowed grassy paths return to the Nature Center and parking area.

OTTER

If you are lucky enough to catch a glimpse of the river otter (Lutra canadensis), it will probably make you smile. Its broad, flat head with tiny eyes, peers from a hole in melting ice or pops out of the water at ever-changing locations, like gophers at a carnival game. A relative of the weasel, the web-toed otter lives on fish, frogs, and other small animals and has rich glossy brown fur.

Otters are shy and not easy to spot -unless you find them sliding. Otters use earthen hillsides or snow banks like toboggan runs. They must forget themselves with the fun of it all as they whiz down their slick slides.

HOURS, FEES, FACILITIES

NBNC is handicap accessible, including part of the trail. There is no admission charge. Restroom in the Nature Center, open weekdays from 9:00 a.m. to 4:00 p.m. A limited number of snowshoes are available on a first-come-first-served basis.

FOR MORE INFORMATION

North Branch Nature Center
713 Elm Street, Route 12
Montpelier, VT 05602
802-229-6206
www.northbranchnaturecenter.org

North Branch River Park
City of Montpelier
Montpelier Park Commission
39 Main Street
Montpelier, VT 05602
802-223-7335
www.montpelier-vt.org/parks

GETTING THERE

Take I-89 to Exit 8 to Montpelier. Follow the ramp, which joins Rte. 2 east, to the junction of Rte. 12 in Montpelier. Turn left onto Main Street, Rte. 12. At the rotary, 0.5 mile, go left to stay on Rte. 12. Almost immediately turn right onto Rte. 12, now Elm Street. The North Branch Nature Center is 1.75 miles on the right.

Waterbury/Stowe Area

37 Tundra Trail, Mount Mansfield (via the Toll Road)

A walk across the top of Vermont through a unique Arctic-alpine environment.

Bring warm clothes and, if you plan to walk beyond the Tundra Trail, wear hiking boots. Great place for children old enough to respect the fragility of the plants.

STOWE, VT

0.75 MILE (EXTENSION POSSIBLE)

40 MINUTES

EASY

PETS MUST BE LEASHED AND STAY ON TRAIL.

TO BORROW A PHRASE from Michelin, the Tundra Trail is worth the voyage. The Summit House, a hotel that burned down in 1964, welcomed overnight guests for over a hundred years. As early as 1922, the Toll Road accommodated their automobiles over its 4 1/2 mile distance. Rising to an elevation of 3,850, the road is by far the easiest way to get to the summit.

There are dozens of hiking trails to the summit of Mt. Mansfield but they are not for the novice. They require strength, stamina, and a certain mountain savvy. The Green Mountain Club's Guide Book of the Long Trail describes the options and includes a trail map of the area. Stowe's gondola also climbs to within a short distance of the Tundra Trail. The Cliff Trail from the gondola to the Tundra Trail is difficult and not for the inexperienced.

The Arctic-alpine zone on the summit of Mt. Mansfield is a remnant of the Ice Age. When the last glaciers receded, about 10,000 years ago, plants adapted to severe conditions began to grow in their wake. As the climate warmed these plants perished except for those on the summits of a few eastern mountains. Similar communities exist in Vermont on Camel's Hump and Smuggler's Notch, on Mt. Katadin in Maine, and in the highest reaches of New York's Adirondack and New Hampshire's White Mountains.

These plants survive despite shallow soils, high winds, low temperatures, a short growing season, and high precipitation. (Mt. Mansfield receives the equivalent of 100 inches of rain each year.) The small population and low diversity of plants conspire to limit the animal population as well.

Only six species of birds are common in this habitat. You are likely to hear

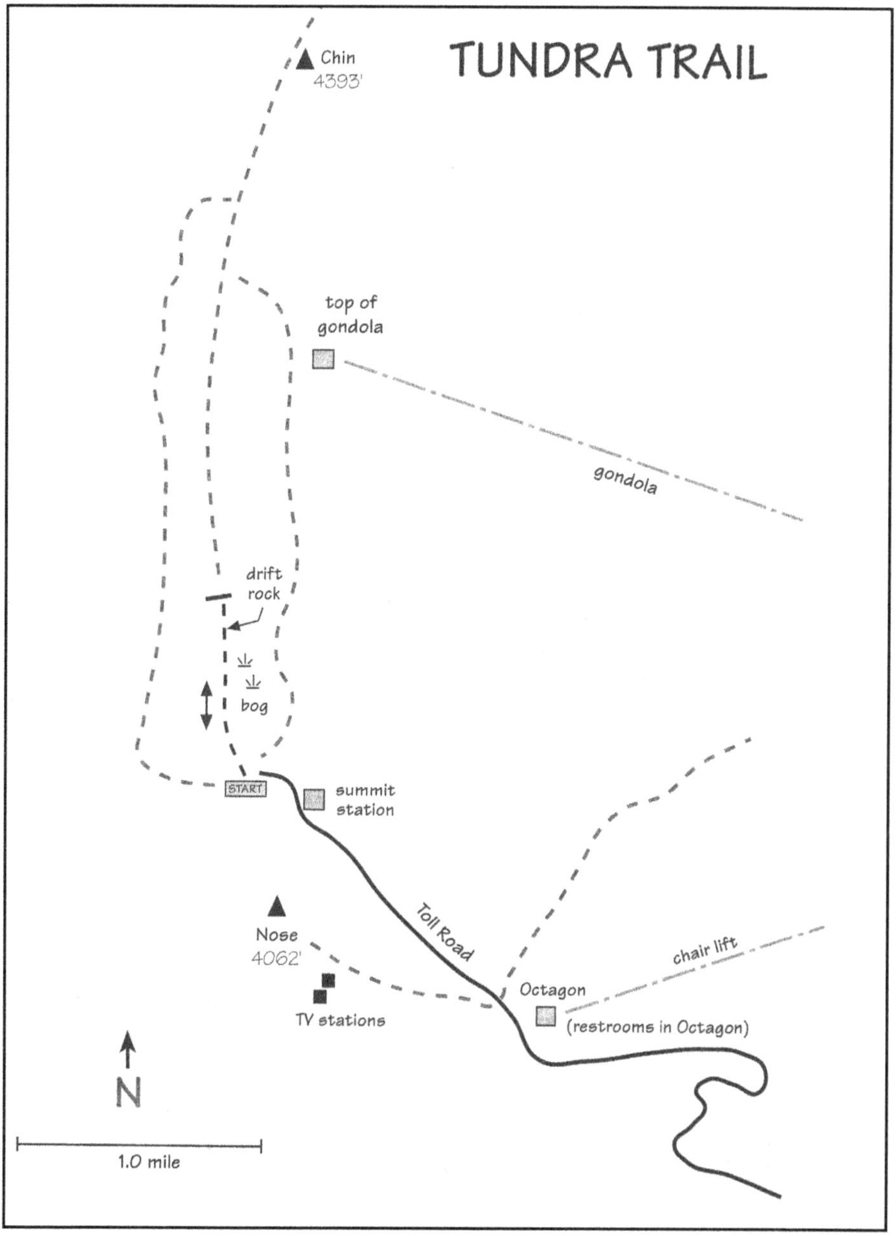

TUNDRA TRAIL

▲ Chin
4393'

top of
gondola
◻

gondola

drift
rock

↕ bog

START ◻ summit
station

▲
Nose
4062'

Toll Road

■ ■
TV stations

Octagon
◻
(restrooms in Octagon)

chair lift

↑
N

1.0 mile

two of them, the loud scolding of ravens and the mournful whistle of the white-throated sparrow.

Many of the tundra plants are in jeopardy. (In decreasing order of peril the categories used for plants and animals are: endangered, threatened, and rare.) Most of the plants are also very small. You will need to look and tread carefully. Walk only on rocks and do not stray from the marked trail. Painted markings and cairns, pyramidal piles of rocks, indicate the route.

Don't forget to admire the view!

The Summit Station houses a small exhibit that is worth a visit. You will also find trail maps and guides. A Green Mountain Club Ranger is available in the summer to answer questions.

• • • • • •

Look for the trail to the north of the Summit Station. You will see a Long Trail sign where the trail enters the trees. The Long Trail is a 265-mile footpath running the length of Vermont, mostly along the spine of the Green Mountains. Despite the sobering distance, many through-hikers walk from end-to-end each summer.

For the first few minutes the trail cuts through a forest dominated by balsam fir and red spruce. Balsam needles are flat, unlike the many-sided spruce needles, and the pale bottom of each has a conspicuous green midrib. The smell of balsam needles is sweet and may evoke memories of childhood Christmas. Notice that the trees aren't very tall as we approach the timberline.

The trail crosses a maintenance road and re-enters the trees. A scattering of birch and mountain ash grow among the conifers with the occasional Clintonia and bunchberry along the trail. The bedrock, here and elsewhere on the summit ridge, is a voluptuous whirl of colors and textures. It is metamorphic schist, sedimentary rock that changed form under intense heat or pressure beneath the surface of the earth. The rock is about 400 million years old.

Shortly we rise to the tree line and the upright trees disappear. The transitional area between the fir-spruce forest and the tundra is called the krummholz, an area where wind and harsh growing conditions combine to stunt the trees. You will see many contorted spruce trees with dead or dying branches. On a clear day you can also see the Champlain Valley at your feet with New York and Quebec beyond.

Be alert for the flowering alpine plants. The growing season is very short with July being the only frost-free month. The tiny yet beautiful flowers on these diminutive plants appear from mid-June into July. You may recognize the familiar blueberry, in a miniature version, and a similar plant, the bog bilberry. Blueberries have narrower, more pointed leaves than the more oval, bluish-green leaves of the bilberry. Blueberries grow in a clump at the end of the stalk while bilberries are scattered along the stem. You will also see mountain cranberry with its very small, shiny leaves and red fruit.

The trail rises past a huge cairn called Frenchman's Pile and continues north past a radio tower on the right. This area is called the "Alpine Meadow," with stunted balsam fir, red spruce, and the occasional heart-leaved paper birch. The predominant ground cover here is Bigelow's sedge, a glasslike plant that, although it may not look unusual, is a rare plant in Vermont. The showier blueberry, bilberry, and cranberry are interspersed. More conspicuous because of its height and large

Hare's tail cotton grass is a sedge, found in northern bogs and at high elevations.

white blooms, is Labrador tea. Its thick leaves roll downward partially concealing a brown, fuzzy underside. The plant itself may be a foot tall and its white umbrella-like blooms are abundant in late June or early July. A pleasant tea can be made from its leaves and was drunk during the American Revolution.

In just a few minutes you can make out a depression on the right. The precipitation that collects here has formed a bog. (See bogs page 91.) Sphagnum moss thrives in the acidic environment of bogs and over thousands of years forms a peat mat across the surface of the water. Growing on this mat are acid-loving plants. Several northern or boreal bog plants grow here. They are most conspicuous when in bloom: leather leaf, pale laurel, creeping snowberry, and the hare's tail cotton grass. The latter looks just like you'd expect, its seeds forming a fluffy white tuft atop an eighteen inch stem. Hare's tail cotton grass, with seeds similar to a dandelion's but whiter and denser, was abundant on a late June visit.

The Tundra Trail ends at Drift Rock, an enormous glacial erratic carried from the north by glaciers of the Ice Age. Look on the bedrock for striations caused by the scraping of this and other rocks embedded in the mile-thick mass of ice. The glacier crossed Mt. Mansfield on a diagonal, from northwest to southeast.

You may turn around here or continue walking. The footing becomes more challenging as the trail continues north.

HEATHS

Heaths are shrubs or woody perennials most of which are found on acidic soils. Worldwide they favor temperate regions, but we find many heaths in the cool bogs of northern New England.

Life is stressful for plants in a bog. It is difficult for them to absorb moisture in acidic conditions. In addition, these plants endure a short growing season, high winds, and cold temperatures.

Many heaths have evergreen leaves that enable them to utilize any available sunshine year-round. On the first spring day, an evergreen leaf uses sunlight to make sugar while a deciduous plant is using its stored energy to produce new leaves. The stiff, often leathery texture of heath leaves (not unlike the waxy coating of spruce needles) helps them to retain moisture in the unfiltered sunlight and strong winds.

Labrador tea, pale laurel, blueberry, mountain cranberry, and bog bilberry are among the heaths on Mt. Mansfield.

HOURS, FEES, AND FACILITIES

The Green Mountain Club, Vermont Department of Forests, Park and Recreation, Mt. Mansfield Company, and the University of Vermont cooperatively protect the summit of Mt. Mansfield. The Tundra Trail is a University of Vermont Natural Area. Stowe Mountain Resort of the Mt. Mansfield Company manages the Toll Road.

There is no admission charge for the Tundra Trail. There is a fee for driving up the Toll Road that includes up to six passengers. Restrooms are available at the Octagon. Dogs must be leashed and be kept on the rocks in the Arctic-Alpine zone.

The Toll Road is open from 10:00 AM to 5:00 PM from mid-May until mid-October, weather permitting. After 5:00 PM. you will need to get a gate key at the adjacent inn when you descend.

GETTING THERE

From Rte. 100 in the village of Stowe, take Rte. 108, the Mountain Road. The Toll Road is 5.9 miles on the left. The Toll Road is 4.5 miles and very steep.

FOR MORE INFORMATION

Stowe Mountain Resort
5781 Mountain Road (Rte. 108)
Stowe, Vermont 05672
802-253-3000
http://www.stowe.com/smr
http://www.uvm.edu/~envprog/

38 Sterling Falls Gorge Natural Area

A spectacular river gorge in a boreal setting with waterfalls, cascades, pools, and potholes. Perhaps the most beautiful walk in this book.

Stay on the trail and don't let children walk unattended! The gorge walls are steep. Visit on snowshoes. Ice formations are spectacular.

STOWE, VT

0.3 MILE

45 MINUTES

EASY

DOGS WELCOME IF THEY ARE FRIENDLY AND UNDER CONTROL.

THE ANDERSON FAMILY set aside this scenic section of Sterling Brook so the public could enjoy the beautiful and unusual natural features of the gorge. Sterling Falls Gorge Natural Area Trust is a public non-profit trust. The eight acres at the gorge adjoin four acres of the Stowe Conservation Area to the west. The protected 2,150-acre Watson Forest lies to the north. The Catamount Trail, a cross-country ski trail that runs the length of Vermont, also crosses the preserve.

Sterling Falls Gorge has three waterfalls, six cascades, and eight pools. (See Water Words, page 246.) The total drop of the brook within the gorge is 105 vertical feet making it one of the greatest drops of any gorge in the state.

At the end of the Ice Age, about 10,000 years ago, a series of lakes formed in western Vermont. At various times, with ice blocking the Lamoille River valley to the north, lakes filled the Stowe valley. A beach deposit of pebbly sand lies to the east of the gorge. It is assumed that ice and water combined to create the gorge.

Over the years Sterling Brook was also known as Bingham Branch, Shaw Brook, Mill Brook, and East Branch. Here, in the now defunct town of Sterling, a large sawmill operated from 1860 until 1920. In the early twentieth century nearly eighty people lived and worked in Sterling. A foundation remains from one of four mills located on Sterling Brook. The history and photographs are displayed near the overflow parking area on Sterling Brook Road.

In recent years Vermont Youth Conservation Corps helped construct a trail from the picnic area at the bottom of the gorge back upstream to the large pool at the base of the falls, protecting the steep bank from erosion. In addition, the gorge hosts ice climbing and mountain rescue squad training in winter.

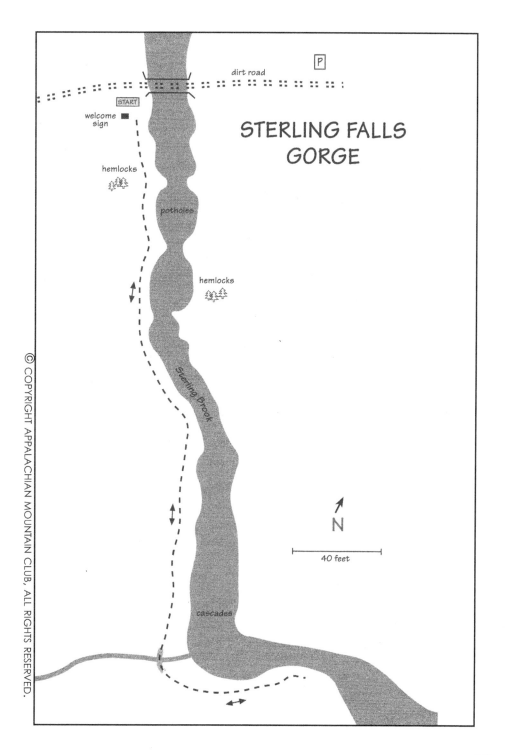

dirt road

STERLING FALLS
GORGE

welcome
sign

START

hemlocks

potholes

hemlocks

Sterling Brook

N

40 feet

cascades

• • • • • •

Walk across the wooden bridge just down the dirt road from the parking area. Some classic Christmas tree-shaped balsam firs are on both sides of the road along with several peeling paper birches. The yellow triangular marker of Sterling Falls Gorge joins the blue blaze of the Catamount Trail on the right railing of the bridge. Beyond the bridge a set of steps goes down to the left. A sign welcomes visitors and highlights the natural features. The trail begins to the left of the sign.

Enormous hemlocks dominate the shady banks of the gorge and a number of wildflowers bloom here in June: Clintonia, Canada mayflower or wild lily-of-the-valley, wild sarsaparilla, pink lady's slipper, and trillium. Trillium in this location are red and painted, not the white of the Champlain Valley. Spinulose woodfern are the dominant fern. Hobblebush thrives in the shrub layer in addition to striped maple, both favorites of deer and moose. There is young balsam fir and hemlock, too. In July, wood sorrel with its bright green shamrock-shaped leaves blooms with dainty pink and white striped flowers. The plant is only a few inches tall.

Stop 1 overlooks the brook. Thousands of years of friction from the movement of water and rocks have created potholes and smoothed the bedrock. Several potholes, including a few to the right, are above the current water level. These were formed when the brook followed a different course or flowed at a higher level.

Abrasive grinding of stones in a circular motion creates potholes. If you look straight down, keeping safely away from the edge, you can see the circular movement of water in a pothole.

As you continue walking, notice that the thicker the canopy of hemlocks the fewer plants in the understory. There aren't as many wildflowers here.

At Stop 2 the brook bends. On the inside of the turn is a pile of medium-sized rocks. The stream dropped these as it lost momentum on the inside of the turn. The faster water flows the greater its carrying capacity. Wide, slow-flowing river deltas fill with silt because the water loses its ability to carry even the tiniest particles. Sterling Brook, a narrow, rushing stream, swelled by seasonal flooding and snow melt, is able to carry large rocks until either the flow decreases, the water spreads out as the banks widen, or the brook slows down at a curve.

Huge boulders scatter across the streambed, larger than anything Sterling Brook could carry. These are glacial erratics, a common sight throughout New England. As glaciers moved south during the Ice Age, they accumulated chunks of rock. After scraping over the landscape, sometimes leaving telltale striations, the glacier dropped many erratics along the way. They usually have no relationship to the bedrock of the area.

The trail jogs left to Stop 3 where we have a good view both up and downstream. Water flowing at a much higher level has smoothed the surface of the bedrock over the millennia.

Across the gorge is a high wall of exposed rock with lines of erosion running nearly vertical. The bedrock is metamorphic rock, sedimentary rock that was exposed to heat or pressure causing some recrystallization. The result is the layered schist that makes up the bedrock of the gorge. Different minerals erode at different rates causing the wavy pattern, called schistosity, which we see here and elsewhere in the Green Mountains.

Above the rocks many large hemlocks cling to the edge of the gorge. Their shallow but sprawling root systems allow them to survive on shallow soil and in precarious locations. You would never see an oak of similar size living like this.

Enroute to Stop 4, about twenty feet into the woods on the right, is a remarkably tenacious hemlock, growing on a glacial erratic. Hemlocks can germinate on nearly any moist surface. Moss is growing on the hemlock's roots and at least one red spruce has germinated in the moss.

Ice in the gorge as the brook spills through.

At Stop 4 look back up the stream to see the schistosity or erosion of the vertical layers of bedrock.

This upland forest is composed of maple, white and yellow birch, white ash, beech, and black cherry in addition to the conifers. With an increase in deciduous trees come more wildflowers.

From the bench at Stop 5 here we can see a tranquil pool before the water flows down a series of cascades.

The trail goes left onto a bridge where Stop 6 encourages us to sit over the small stream. The schistosities in the stream are a textbook example.

The trail turns left and wood sorrel is thick again. Indian cucumber flowers here, its tiny yellowish-green flower atop two whorls of leaves. The lower whorl is larger with six to ten leaves, the upper whorl, just below the flowers, has three leaves. Native Americans ate the brittle root, tasting somewhat like cucumber. Birds are attracted to its purple-blue berries.

Stop 7 overlooks waterfalls, cascades, potholes, and the ever-deepening gorge.

The trail continues a few hundred feet to Stop 8 at the end of the gorge. The brook is no longer contained and flows downstream along a wider bed.

Retrace your steps to the trailhead.

WATER WORDS

A gorge is a section of stream channel with rock walls on both sides that are at least ten feet high. The walls at Sterling Falls Gorge range from eleven to fifty feet high at the southern end.

The distinction between a waterfall and a cascade is in how the water flows. Water must fall nearly vertically at least three feet without touching the underlying rock to create a waterfall. In a cascade the water remains in contact with the bedrock.

GETTING THERE

From Stowe, drive north 0.8 mile on Rte. 100. Turn left on West Hill Road. At 1.8 miles West Hill Road bends nearly 90° to the left (the dirt road straight ahead, Tamarack, is a Dead End). At a stop sign in 0.3 mile, turn right onto a dirt road. This is still West Hill Road. You reach a t-intersection at 2.2 miles. Turn left onto Sterling Brook Road. Stay on this narrow dirt road for 2.1 miles. At Sterling Gorge Road turn left. A sign directs you to a six-car lot for the Gorge at 0.1 mile. Walk across the wooden bridge to the trailhead.

Overflow parking is on Sterling Brook Road, location of the historic signage.

FOR MORE INFORMATION

Sterling Falls Gorge Natural Area Trust
250 Sterling Gorge Road
Stowe, VT 05672
802-253-9035
E-mail: gander07@realtor.com

39 History Hike, Dalley Loop and Hedgehog Hill Loop Trails

A walk through the remains of a nineteenth-century hill farm community.

LITTLE RIVER STATE PARK
WATERBURY, VT
4 MILES, ELEVATION GAIN **800** FEET
3-4 HOURS
MODERATE
NO PETS IN DAY USE AREAS.

THIS WALK IS A JOURNEY through time, past foundations, stonewalls, and cemeteries that are all that remain of a community once filled with life. Subsistence farms dotted these hills in the 1800s- with a few pigs, sheep, chickens, and cows in addition to gardens and apple orchards. Timber was cut and milled at local sawmills and maple sap was boiled to sugar each spring.

Unlike the flat, rich floodplain of the Winooski River Valley, these rocky hillsides were difficult to cultivate and their yield meager. Free homesteads tempted many Vermonters west in the late nineteenth century. These farms had already been abandoned when the Great Flood of 1927 inundated the valley. A second flood in 1934 spurred construction of the Waterbury Dam. Beneath the reservoir lie the remains of several similar villages.

Take your imagination on this walk and don't miss the photos of these farms in the Park's museum. When you enter the park ask for the map and brochure for the History Hike.

· · · · · ·

The trail begins on a dirt road behind a red gate. Within minutes the Hedgehog Hill Loop Trail forks to the right. Bear left to stay on the Dalley Loop Trail.

As the road climbs and crosses a brook far below, most of the trees are northern hardwoods, maple, white and yellow birch, beech, and black cherry, with a few hemlocks mixing in. You are likely to hear ovenbirds, one of the few birds that sings throughout the day.

Keep your eyes open for animal tracks. On two separate visits I found moose tracks and scat. Moose prints are cloven and shaped much like deer tracks but

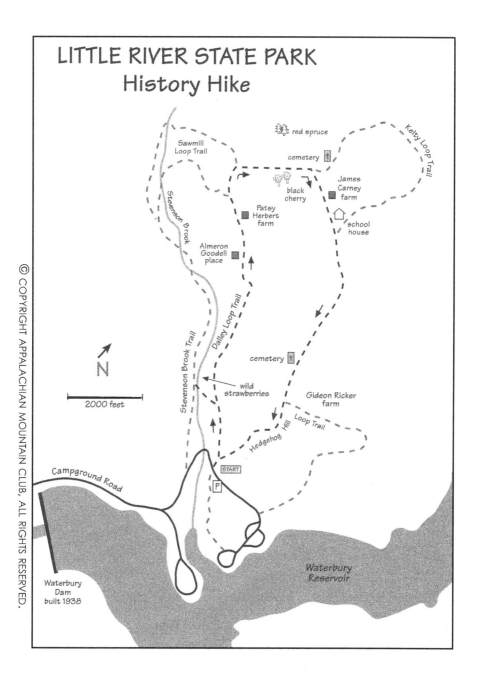

LITTLE RIVER STATE PARK
History Hike

red spruce

Sawmill
Loop Trail

cemetery

Kelty Loop Trail

Stevenson Brook

black
cherry

James
Carney
farm

Patsy
Herbert
farm

school
house

Almeron
Goodell
place

Dalley Loop Trail

Stevenson Brook Trail

N

2000 feet

cemetery

wild
strawberries

Gideon Ricker
farm

Loop Trail

Hedgehog Hill

START

P

Campground Road

Waterbury
Reservoir

Waterbury
Dam
built 1938

larger, as long as seven inches. Oval moose droppings, resembling those of deer, may be an inch long.

The largest member of the deer family, the moose weighs as much as 1,400 pounds. It has high humped shoulders, a broad muzzle, large ears and the prominent hairy dewlap on the throat. The male has broad, palmate antlers, the tines radiating from the center like fingers from a palm. The moose travels, usually alone, in spruce forests (we'll see spruce as we climb along this trail), swamps, and aspen thickets. Moose browse striped maple heavily in winter. In recent years the moose population has swelled in Vermont and a limited hunting season has been reintroduced.

After ten to fifteen minutes you'll find Stop 2, well camouflaged on the right. (Stop 1 is on the Nature Trail.) Clamber up the dirt path to a stone foundation, the remains of the farmhouse of David Hill. Butternut trees were often planted in the dooryard and the one in the foundation must be an offspring of that tree. A few lilacs and scraggly apple trees struggle with little sunlight.

Continue up the road. In a clearing on the left lush with wild strawberries, the blue-blazed Stevenson Brook Trail begins its route to the site of a sawmill.

At Stop 3, on the right, the remaining corner stones of Bert Goodell's foundations still hold firm against the earth. You may find wild ginger, an indicator of rich soils, with its two hairy, kidney-shaped leaves low to the ground. The single reddish-brown, three-lobed flower grows in the crotch between the leaves and its roots have a strong fragrance of ginger.

Local legend places the Johnson farm nearby. Although its remains have never been found, the farm was purportedly used as a sanitarium for Civil War veterans with syphilis.

Many June flowering plants line a curve in the road: yellow and orange hawkweed, devil's flower, bladder campion and yarrow. On the left there's a huge patch of horsetail.

The Almeron Goodell house, Stop 4, still stands. Until the state recently asserted its claim, descendants rented the house as a deer camp. I hiked this trail with a man whose father had stayed here for many years during hunting season. The original post and beam construction is still visible. Daylilies and lilacs crowd the dooryard and rose plants bloom near the road.

A few minutes up the road on the right is a field cleared for wildlife. Apple trees need sunlight and local bears need apples. One of the trees has many broken branches. Bears climb the trees, snap the branches, and toss them to the ground to strip later.

A clearing across the road is intended to encourage ruffed grouse. Grouse browse on buds and twigs of young trees. Few of Vermont's 323 wildlife species thrive in middle-aged or mature forests, the natural state of the land. These fields will produce a tangle of berry plants and tender shoots providing food, shelter, and camouflage.

Gaze across the valley to the Worcester Range. Each of these farms once had a similar view.

Foundation stones and rock walls are all that remain of the Patsy Herbert farm, Stop 5, on the right. Herbert was the last resident in 1910. The Sawmill Loop Trail goes left to the site of the sawmill.

Beyond the Herbert farm the Dalley Loop Trail bears right. A spur trail forks left but we continue right on the old town road. Mature maples arch overhead and stonewalls line the roadway. Spring beauties flower early in spring. Red spruce, a northern tree, appears as we gain elevation and there are many mature black cherries along the roadside. Ferns and blackberries are thick and striped maple is abun-

Spring beauties: one of the earliest wildflowers.

dant in the understory. You can recognize its green striped bark and large, three-lobed leaves.

If time is a concern, stay right on the main road and look for a basin of rocks in a tiny stream on the left (it may be dry in summer). This was probably a watering trough for animals. (A detour left leads to the well-preserved Joseph Ricker farm.)

The next stop is the Upper Cemetery, an early burial site in use from 1840 to 1860. Mary Cole's headstone tells a common story: she died at the age of 25, most likely in childbirth.

The Dalley Loop Trail goes right while the less-maintained Kelty Loop Trail departs to the left. We stay on the Dalley Loop. Stop 10, the James Carney farm, was a prosperous one with 700 maples and a sugarhouse in addition to farm animals. The solid house foundation is well preserved, in contrast to some we've seen.

A road forks to the left shortly. On the left beneath leaf litter, about 75 feet up this road, are stones marking the outlines of the schoolhouse that would not have had a foundation. Each district offered room and board and a small salary to attract a teacher to its one-room schoolhouse.

Stonewalls and foundations mark the William Clossey farm, Stop 12. From the house foundation, on the left side of the road, a well-worn path leads to the grave of onetime owner Jack Cameron. He was unable to eke a living from this hardscrabble land.

Stop 13 has succumbed to beaver activity and we pass through a soggy area before returning to the woods. Substantial stonewalls line the road as we begin to descend. Sensitive ferns like this damp ground and wild lily-of-the-valley and sessile-leaved bellwort are abundant. We pass through an area thick with spruce.

Tom Herbert's house is on the right side of the road at Stop 14. A healthy butternut tree stands in the dooryard. With as many as seventeen leaflets, butternut leaves can be thirty inches long. Farmers planted butternut trees for their beautiful wood, colorful dyes, and rich nuts.

Just a few steps away, to the left and downhill from the house, is a covered well. If you lift the lid (carefully) you will see a stone well shaft. Digging a well by hand was not easy work. A huge hole would be dug until water was found. Then a stone shaft was painstakingly built and soil returned, bucket by bucket, to support the structure until it reached ground level. No wonder so many farms located near naturally occurring springs!

As the road continues downhill there is another stone watering trough on the left. The Ricker Cemetery is on the right. White cedar trees, their Latin name arbor vitae meaning the tree of life, are a startling sight. Common in the Champlain lowlands, white cedars are not native in these hills. On the far side of the cemetery is a huge double-trunked black cherry. There are several legible head stones.

The last farm on this loop trail, Stop 16, is the Gideon Ricker farm. Portions of a barn foundation can be seen on the left side of the road, remnants of a 120-foot cow barn that had an 84-foot spruce ridgepole. There is also a stone foundation for a silo. Across the road the house foundation is the biggest in the neighborhood. (Don't miss the photos in the museum.) Thick slabs of granite, from a small quarry up the road, added a touch of class to the visible parts of the foundation.

Go right on the Hedgehog Hill Loop Trail to return to the trailhead. The trail slopes downhill crossing a stream on a very old stone bridge. You can step down on either side of the bridge to see the massive boulders supporting the angular slabs of rock. Characteristically, an old yellow birch with crusty bark and contorted roots clings to a rock next to the bridge.

The trail rejoins the Dalley Loop in a few minutes just a short distance from the parking area.

HOURS, FEES, AND FACILITIES

Daily admission entitles you to hiking but not to the recreation facilities. See In the Area.

The caretaker can let you into the small museum. There are pictures of the homes, barns, and farm families.

GETTING THERE

From the west, take I-89 Exit 11 in Richmond and follow Rte. 2 east. From the stoplight in Richmond, at Bridge Street, drive east for 11.8 miles. Turn left on Little River Road. You will pass the dam and Waterbury Reservoir on the right before arriving at the park gate 3.4 miles from Rte. 2.

From the east, take I-89 Exit 10 in Waterbury and follow Rte. 100 south to Rte. 2. Turn right onto Rte. 2 west and drive 1.4 miles to Little River Road on your right.

From the park gate turn right (you will have no choice) and then take two immediate lefts following signs to the dumpsters. This road will bear right, passing the dumpsters, before crossing a bridge at 0.4 mile. Parking for the History Trails is on the right in 0.2 mile.

FOR MORE INFORMATION

Department of Forests, Parks, and Recreation
http://www.vtstateparks.com/htm/littleriver.cfm
Park Ranger
Little River State Park
RD 1, Box 3180
Waterbury, VT 05676
802-244-7103

• ALSO IN THE AREA •

WATERBURY CENTER DAY USE PARK.

Admission to Little River State Park allows same-day use of the beach and boat launch at Waterbury Center Park. From Waterbury, take Rte. 100 north, 5.8 miles from the I-89 overpass. Turn left on Old River Road. The park entrance is 0.1 mile.

40 Stevenson Brook Nature Trail

A rushing mountain stream in woods grown up on old farmland.

LITTLE RIVER STATE PARK
WATERBURY, VT
.75 MILE
1 HOUR
EASY TO MODERATE
NO PETS

THIS LAND WAS ONCE part of a village of fifty families. Their lives unfold on the nearby History Hike. Nature has since reclaimed the banks of the Stevenson Brook.

Little River State Park is the most heavily used park in the state system and, with over one hundred sites, Central Vermont's largest campground. In addition to miles of hiking trails, the park offers campers swimming beaches and a boat launch.

Stevenson Brook is picturesque and the woods host a rich diversity of trees, shrubs, and wildflowers.

The loop trail begins and ends next to the parking area. Look for a box with trail guides.

• • • • • •

Several small black or sweet birch (Betula lenta) cluster at the trailhead, their leaves and bark tasting of wintergreen. Within a few yards you will see interrupted, sensitive, and Christmas ferns thriving in the rich soil.

Mountain maple is abundant here. A bushy tree that never grows taller than twenty feet, mountain maple loves cool, damp woods and ravines, always growing in the shade of other trees. Its leaves are maple-like, three-lobed with serrated edges. Its habitat is similar to that of striped maple but its bark is reddish brown (not green like striped maple).

Stop 1 is the stone foundation of an old farm and a good opportunity to compare barks of paper birch and yellow birch. A yellow birch is immediately on the left with its bronze bark peeling in narrow shreds. The paper birch is a chalkier white and peels in wide strips.

The trail continues toward the brook. At Stop 2, tree roots are cantilevered over

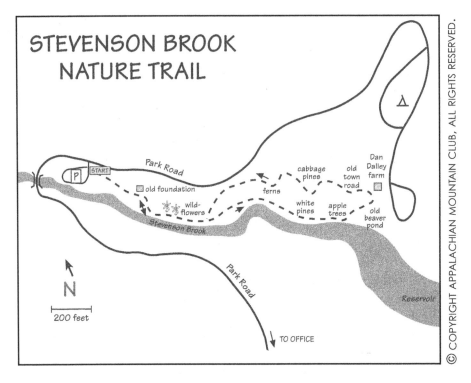

STEVENSON BROOK
NATURE TRAIL

Park Road

P [START]

old foundation

wild-
flowers

Stevenson Brook

ferns

cabbage
pines

white
pines

old
town
road

apple
trees

Dan
Dalley
farm

old
beaver
pond

N

200 feet

Park Road

TO OFFICE

Reservoir

the opposite bank. Each spring high water and ice rip at the shore and only the most tenacious trees survive along the banks.

Alternate-leaved dogwood (*Cornus alternifolia*) is at eye level. Dogwood leaves have a characteristic shape, tapering to points at both ends and the veins follow the leaf edges to the tips. Deer and rabbits often browse its green twigs and many birds, including the ruffed grouse, eat its blue-black berries.

A mix of northern hardwoods grow in this cool valley, including American beech, maple, birch, basswood, and white ash, with a number of hemlocks and red spruce. Beneath them purple trillium, jack-in-the-pulpit, and false Solomon's seal bloom in late May or early June.

We cross a sandy U-shaped depression where the brook overflows in the spring. At Stop 5, look around to see several terraces of land rising away from the brook. Over millions of years, the stream has eroded its bed only to have it lifted again by forces inside the earth. The most recent uplift occurred when the last glaciers receded about 10,000 years ago. With the heavy weight of mile-thick ice removed, the land decompressed.

At Stop 6, look for Indian pipe (*Monotropa uniflora*), also known as corpse plant or convulsion root. White and looking like a cluster of upturned pipes, the plant is a saprophyte that gets its nutrients from decaying organic matter rather than from photosynthesis. The absence of chlorophyll accounts for its color.

As the trail leaves the brook, look for wood nettles. Remember wood nettles have alternate leaves while stinging nettles have opposite leaves. Wood nettle leaves are also longer and narrower than the heart-shaped leaves of the stinging nettle.

The trail bears left onto a higher terrace. Notice the beautiful old bark on a huge yellow birch with two trunks. Stop 7 is in a dense stand of white pines in sandy soil. White pines do not like wet feet and they need sunshine.

Near Stop 8, there's a huge double-trunked basswood or linden tree on the left. Its bark somewhat resembles an ash and it has heart-shaped leaves as big as six inches across. Also called the bee tree, it is a favorite of wood carvers because it can be easily worked. Its July flowers attract bees that produce delicious honey. Basswoods are indicator trees and grow only in rich soil. (See page 210.)

Several dead apple trees and a stonewall to the left are signs of an old farmstead.

Stop 9 looks down on an old beaver pond. As plant growth thickens over what was once a pond, the water level lowers and more plants move in. Someday this will be woods again.

The trail turns left, uphill and then left again at an arrow. There is a detour to an old farm site. Up a short, narrow trail, is the stone foundation of the Dan Dalley farmhouse. Dalley was a Civil War Veteran who survived 16 battles and one capture. With his pension of $12.00 per month he bought this 68- acre farm in 1878. Picture, if you can, the house in the midst of fields with a vast view across the valley. Notice the big, rectangular foundation stones that are quite different from the more randomly shaped stones in the rock walls.

Return to the trail that follows an old road for a few minutes before bearing left into the woods. The multi-trunked white pines at Stop 11 are called cabbage trees. Because of their misshapen trunks they were unsuitable for timber. They may have been attacked by the white pine weevil. (See page 78.)

We pass a few apple trees dying for lack of sunlight. The trail turns left and then jogs right without markings. We are on the highest of the three terraces overlooking the brook. There is a huge, peeling paper birch on the left as well as a red maple with five trunks. The bark shows a bull's eye pattern characteristic of red maple. There is a large triple-trunked basswood on the left side with large, nearly round leaves. Basswood trees can sprout from the trunk even if the parent tree is alive. Look for young basswood close by.

We come to another stone wall and Stop 12. Downhill to the left is an old butternut tree, its bark deeply grooved. Butternuts are late to leaf out in the spring.

Be careful as the trail descends steps without a railing. At the base of the steps turn right along next terrace. Indian poke, or false hellebore, grows in the moist soil, its enormous leaves with parallel veins growing around a central stem. The plant may reach seven feet before the leaves wither in July.

The trail descends a ramp built into hillside and rejoins the loop at Stop 3. Turn right to follow the path back to the parking area.

GETTING THERE

From the west, take I-89 Exit 11 in Richmond and follow Rte. 2 east. From the stoplight in Richmond, at Bridge Street, drive east for 11.8 miles. Turn left on Little River Road. You will pass the dam and Waterbury Reservoir on the right before arriving at the park gate 3.4 miles from Rte. 2.

From the east, take I-89 Exit 10 in Waterbury and follow Rte. 100 south to Rte. 2. Turn right onto Rte. 2 west and drive 1.4 miles to Little River Road on your right.

From the park gate turn right (you will have no choice) and then take two immediate lefts following signs to the dumpsters. This road will bear right, pass-

The Indian poke, or false hellebore, may grow to seven feet before withering in July.

ing the dumpsters, before crossing a bridge at 0.4 mile. Just over the bridge, signs indicate the Nature Trail and parking on the right.

FOR MORE INFORMATION
Department of Forests, Parks, and Recreation
http://www.vtstateparks.com/htm/littleriver.cfm
Park Ranger
Little River State Park
RD 1, Box 3180
Waterbury, VT 05676
802-244-7103

• ALSO IN THE AREA •

WATERBURY CENTER DAY USE PARK.

Admission to Little River State Park allows same-day use of the beach and boat launch at Waterbury Center Park. From Waterbury, take Rte. 100 north, 5.8 miles from the I-89 overpass. Turn left on Old River Road. The park entrance is 0.1 mile.

New York

Ausable Chasm

A deep canyon carved by glacial ice
and the Ausable River.

AUSABLE CHASM, NY
LESS THAN ONE MILE
1 HOUR FOR THE WALK, AN ADDITIONAL
HOUR FOR THE RAFT RIDE
EASY WITH LOTS OF STEPS (DOWN)
NO PETS PLEASE.

IF YOU CAN'T make it to the Grand Canyon this year, take a day trip to Ausable Chasm. While there is no confusing Arizona's mile-deep canyon with the local item, Ausable mimics the sheer rosy, riverside cliffs of its western cousin. Eastern in scale and flavor, Ausable Chasm is spectacular in its own right.

As deep as 175 feet from rim to river, the narrow passage through multi-colored sandstone and quartzite was sculpted by glacial ice and the waters of the Ausable River about 14,000 years ago. Opened to tourists in 1870, the Chasm has been attracting visitors ever since, between 50,000 and 75,000 in an average year.

Two 1996 events demonstrated once again nature's preeminence as raging water rearranged the chasm's natural and manmade features.

Heavy rains fell during a January thaw and six feet of accumulated snow melted within hours as the temperature rose to 75 degrees. The tributaries of the Ausable River unleashed huge quantities of water and ice into the Chasm. High water under pressure uprooted sixty-foot trees, ripped out metal handrails, and tore seventy-foot steel bridges from their foundations. Some came to rest at the bottom of the Chasm; others have never been found.

New bridges with thirty inch steel beams were built and walkways reestablished. Ausable Chasm had survived a once-in-a-lifetime event and opened on schedule for the 1996 season.

On November 9, nature struck again. Heavy rains fell on already saturated ground causing unprecedented flooding. Nearby roads and bridges were destroyed and the Chasm fared no better. Two bridges that had survived the January onslaught succumbed as did the three new bridges. The volume of water raging through the Chasm was the greatest ever recorded.

Trails and bridges were rebuilt yet again, this time farther from the river, and

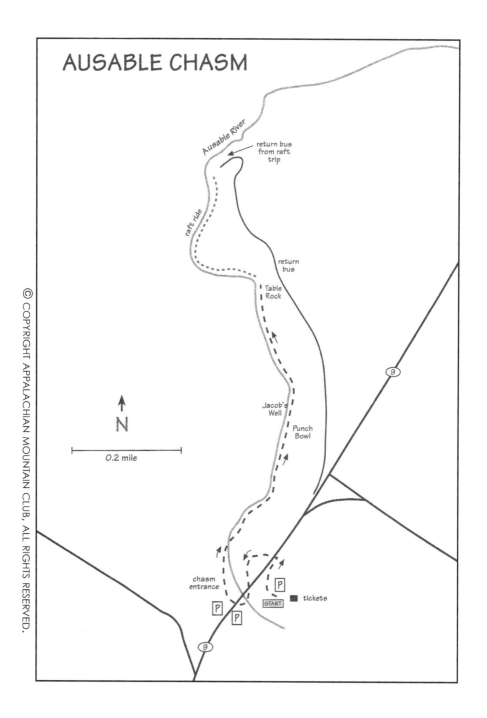

AUSABLE CHASM

Ausable River

return bus from raft trip

raft ride

return bus

Table Rock

Jacob's Well

Punch Bowl

N

0.2 mile

9

9

chasm entrance

P

P

P

START

tickets

the Chasm opened to visitors in 1997. Within the chasm, piles of debris, barren rock faces, and scarred trees attest to the events of 1996.

The Ausable Chasm Company, a private corporation that was incorporated in 1896, owns the Chasm and 823 acres. Several stockholders are descendants of the original owners.

There is a two-tiered admission structure, a fee for the walk only, with a return bus from Table Rock, and a higher charge for a raft ride through the lower portion of the Chasm. The lower Chasm is a stunning natural feature, unique in the east, and I recommend it.

• • • • • •

Use the door to the right of the ticket desk to begin the walk. Several displays are on the right including a fossil of ripple marks from the riverbed. These were left by the Cambrian Sea more than 500 million years ago. Another item on exhibit is the 1996 wreckage of a chasm bridge.

Cross under the road. You will pass a vantage point into the chasm where the visitors' walkway once descended. Walk across the highway bridge and turn right

Ausable Chasm is a natural treasure.
Photo courtesy of Ausable Chasm.

to the Chasm entrance. The walk begins on a bark trail on the west bank high above the Ausable River. Only a few ferns grow beneath a thick canopy of red and white pines and hemlocks.

A wooden walkway leads to Rainbow Vista, a view back up the river to Horseshoe and Rainbow Falls. Several times the path comes close to the edge overlooking the rushing cascades. From Rocky Point Vista you can see, far below on the opposite bank, the railing of an old walkway.

The trail meanders over occasional stretches of boardwalk through the woods. Lichen, reindeer moss (really a lichen), and polypody fern grow on rocky outcroppings. Wintergreen, huckleberry, and lowbush blueberry, all members of the heath family, grow beneath openings in the canopy on the sandy, acidic soil. Northern white cedar, the occasional white oak, and a few paper birch join the pines and hemlock.

On the right is a cleft 30-40 feet across and as deep as the chasm, called a tension joint, one of many along the route. (See Geology of the Chasm, page 266.)

The trail descends several stairways, at one point passing through a bank of dainty polypody ferns. The trail snakes along the chasm wall, so close at times you must mind your head and shoulders. In tiny soil pockets, tenacious plants anchor themselves on the rock face: herb Robert, ferns, violets, bedstraw, mullein, and asters. An extravagant yellow birch grows on almost no soil, with a fantastic web of surface roots.

Close to the river, many feet below, the twisted remnants of metal railings poke into the air at odd angles.

The trail descends to Punch Bowl vista. This large pothole was eroded by the abrasive action of swirling rocks and stones. It takes thousands of years for a pothole to form. Jacob's Well is an unusual pothole, now well above water level. A strong localized current formed this cylindrical hole, six feet in diameter and twenty feet deep.

The trail gets closer and closer to water level. We cross the 1996 flood line. Lush vegetation -mosses, ferns, saplings, and abundant northern white cedar, grows above this line. Below, plants are slowly reestablishing themselves next to the few surviving trees.

A yellow birch perches over the trail, its roots growing up, down, and sideways in search of anchor and sustenance. Bark was scoured off the tree and heaps of rocks, sticks, and stumps, are wedged behind it up the hillside.

On the left is the Cathedral, another lateral fault or tension joint the height of the chasm. Sunlight filters through its apse of arched hemlocks.

The walls of the chasm get closer together and rise high as the trail descends.

Look at the layers of sandstone and quartzite, their relative durability, changes in color and texture, and vulnerability to erosion. Don't forget to look up, too, to appreciate the height of the chasm walls.

At the end of the walkway, stairs go up to the left for the return by bus. Steps down to the right lead to a removable aluminum bridge across the river to Table Rock, departure point for the rafts.

The raft glides through the twelve-foot-wide Grand Flume. It then floats past two clefts in the chasm wall, the Sentry Box on the right and the Broken Needle on the left, the latter with a massive chunk of leaning rock. At the Whirlpool Basin the river appears to flow uphill as the striations on the rock walls play tricks with our eyes. Some gentle rapids speed the raft into a basin where the walls of the canyon disappear and the river widens. The Ausable looks like any sleepy river as it flows gently out of sight.

HOW THE CHASM CAME TO BE

More than 500 million years ago the ancient Adirondack Mountains were on the east coast of an early North American continent. Over the years, 100 million more or less, wind and weather eroded these mountains into sediment that ran down the flanks and accumulated along the ocean shore. This sediment, combined with vestiges of marine life, eventually compressed to form sandstone, layer upon layer of minerals and organic debris. Through subsequent mountain-building events, this sandstone came to the surface.

As rocks go, sandstone is relatively soft. During the Ice Age glaciers covered the area and scraped off much of the sandstone. As the glaciers melted and the Ausable River formed, it found a channel in the soft sandstone and began to erode it. The release of pressure as the weight of the ice was removed caused tension joints. These irregularities, minor faults, and differences in texture and hardness produced uneven erosion and account for the clefts along the sides of the gorge.

HOURS, FEES, FACILITIES

Ausable Chasm is open from mid-May until early October, although in recent years the owners have introduced a winter walk along the rim. The summer walking tour is self-guided and available from 9:30 a.m. to 4:30 p.m. The raft trips depart about every ten minutes. Tubes replace rafts in the warmest weeks of the year.

Admission for the walk and return bus, $16 for adults and children 12 and older. Seniors and children 5 through 11, $9. Admission for the walk, raft ride, and return bus is $25 for adults and $18 for seniors and children.

Starting at dusk, guided Lantern Tours ($20) descend 150 feet into the dark canyon along the rushing waters of the Ausable River. The evening ends with marshmallows roasting over a campfire. Lantern Tours regularly sell out. For reservations call toll free 866-RV-CHASM.

Three new daytime tours debut in 2009, each $10 for about one hour. For the agile, Upper Chasm Guided Hike visits the ruins of the 1996 floods, clambering over rock slides, venturing into Devils Oven Cave, and going close enough to touch Rainbow Falls. An Outer Rim Mountain Bike Tour offers several vantage points into the chasm that are otherwise inaccessible. Duckying, in inflatable kayaks, allows paddlers to continue beyond the end of the chasm as far as Lake Champlain, conditions permitting.

GETTING THERE

Take I-87 Exit 35 and follow Rte. 442 east for 3.0 miles. Turn right on Rte. 9 south. You cross the wide, slow-flowing Ausable River at after 1.4 miles. Continue until you cross it again as it enters the Chasm at 3.8 miles. Parking is on both sides of the bridge.

From the intersection of Rte. 9, 9N, and 22 in Ausable Chasm, take Rte. 9 north for 1.4 miles to the parking area.

FOR MORE INFORMATION

Ausable Chasm
P. O. Box 390
Ausable Chasm, NY 12911
1-800-537-1211
www.ausablechasm.com

• ALSO IN THE AREA •

CLINTONVILLE PINE BARRENS, AUSABLE FORKS.

This unusual pitch pine-heath barrens is maintained naturally by fire. The Adirondack Nature Conservancy and Adirondack Land Trust manage the property without fire. Teams of volunteers remove invasives and fast-growing white pines.

Contact the Adirondack Nature Conservancy for further information (see Organizations).

42 Coon Mountain Preserve

A short and sweet mountain to conquer with wildflowers, wild blueberries, and sensational lake and mountain views. Wear hiking boots.

WESTPORT, NY
2 MILES ROUND TRIP, ELEVATION GAIN OF 500 FEET
1.5 HOURS
MODERATE WITH A ROCKY SECTION
PLEASE LEAVE PETS AT HOME.

THIS MONADNOCK IS a compact knob at the edge of the Champlain Valley. Expansive views stretch southeast to Lake Champlain and west across agricultural valleys to the Adirondack peaks. The trail passes some impressive rock faces. Outcroppings at the summit are great for a picnic and you'll find wild blueberries in season. You may even see kettles of migrating hawks in spring and fall.

Vegetation is lush and diverse on Coon Mountain. A number of calciphiles, plants that prefer limy soil, grow on the lower slopes while the summit hosts acid-loving trees and shrubs. This is a northern outpost of red and white oak and shagbark hickory, trees that reach the northern limit of their range in the Champlain Valley.

A legend tells of the Coon Mountain panther that cried like a maiden in distress, luring local men into the deep woods. Many did not return from these forays. The panther was allegedly shot but its body never found. The last stronghold of the panther or mountain lion (Felis concolor) in the northeast was in the Adirondacks; the last credible record is from 1903. East of the Mississippi, the large, pale brown, unspotted cat lives only in the swamps of Florida.

Coon Mountain is a joint project of the Adirondack Land Trust (ALT) and the Adirondack Chapter of the Nature Conservancy. The ALT conserves working lands with a goal of protecting productive forests, agricultural land, and natural areas. The acquisition also protects ecologically sensitive and biologically rich lands, and is adjacent to the 3,700-acre Split Rock Mountain Wild Forest. The Nature Conservancy manages the property.

• • • • • •

The walk begins in young woods where none of the trees is very large or mature.

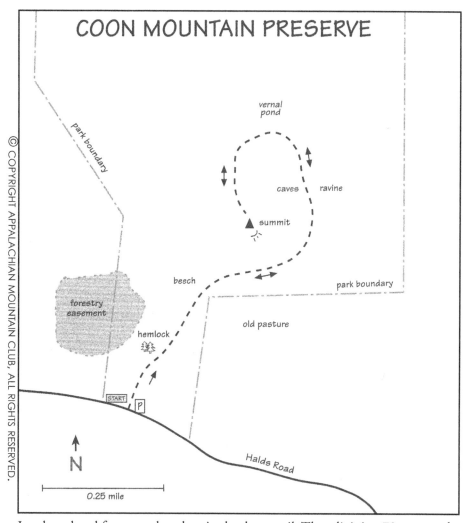

COON MOUNTAIN PRESERVE

vernal
pond

caves   ravine

▲ summit

beech

park boundary

park boundary

forestry
easement

old pasture

hemlock

START   P

N

0.25 mile

Halds Road

Jewelweed and ferns are abundant in the damp soil. The adjoining 73 acres to the west are privately owned but conserved with the ALT for preservation and forestry. Selective logging is intended to allow the land to re-seed naturally.

The woods thicken as hemlocks dominate briefly. We then pass into woods of hickory, oak, beech and maple. The red and white oaks and shagbark hickories grow only at lower elevations on Coon Mountain. Other than in the warm Champlain Valley, these trees are not found in northern Vermont. The low elevation, southern exposure, and warming influence of the lake combine to make this a hospitable location.

On the left, pale gray beech trunks stand out against the dramatic backdrop of a cliff. Look carefully at the beech bark for bear claw marks. Beechnuts, high in fat and protein, are a favorite food of bears as they bulk up for winter sleep. (See Surviving Winter below.)

A large red oak on the right, bristling with barbed wire, tells us that this was once pastureland. Some fast-growing large-toothed aspen are among the tallest trees. These trees don't grow beyond fifty feet but they do grow quickly.

As we start up a rocky scramble, jewelweed tells us the soil is damp and herb Robert and basswood trees confirm its fertility. Maidenhair fern prefers limy soil and we will see several patches of this unusual and uncharacteristic fern. Its fronds are lacy and grow in a near-circle.

When you come face to face with a rock cliff, the trail goes right. Detour just a few feet to the left for a shimmering view of Lake Champlain.

The trail is very rocky as it continues. Lichen, like peeling paint, clings to the rocky overhang and moss is thick on the wetter sections. Many of the moss-covered rocks are home to ferns, wildflowers, and saplings. The rocky caves are home to porcupines. Look for neatly gnawed irregular patches of tree bark that they have eaten.

Flowering plants are thick on both sides of the trail: false Solomon's seal, trillium, twisted stalk, perfoliate bellwort, sweet cecily, and blue cohosh. You can recognize blue cohosh by its cluster of bright blue berries and compound leaves with 27 leaflets.

The trail levels out and the footing is effortless. Striped maple and hobblebush are thick in the understory. Next year's yellow hobblebush buds are already swelling in August.

With snowmelt and abundant spring rains, vernal pools develop in several hollows here. The water evaporates later in the season but not before providing an important breeding place for frogs and salamanders.

The trail rises gradually toward the summit, always bending to the left in a near-circle. The vegetation changes to more acid-loving plants. The thin layer of soil over the igneous bedrock anchors red and white pines, juniper, and lowbush blueberries. Wild lily-of-the-valley and pink lady slipper are among the few wildflowers.

Don't miss the two summit areas, one facing west to Adirondacks and the other looking south over Lake Champlain.

SURVIVING WINTER (WITHOUT A WOOD STOVE)

How do animals survive the rigors of a northern winter? Some birds and butterflies migrate; animals may become dormant or hibernate; others simply persevere, searching for food and shelter in the snow, a stonewall, or your compost heap.

Warm-blooded mammals have little temperature flexibility. They must maintain a narrow range of body temperature in extraordinary swings of outdoor temperature. Few animals actually hibernate, a deep, long lasting sleep in which the body temperature lowers and heart rate plummets. Bats, the jumping mouse, and the woodchuck are among the hibernators. Come spring, the animals' heartbeats accelerate and their body temperatures rise until they become alert again.

Dormant animals are more active, sleeping and waking intermittently, in burrows, tree cavities, caves, and other shelters from wind and cold. On warm days they may venture out in search of food. The raccoon, skunk and chipmunk may experience some lowering of body temperature but not to the degree of the hibernators. Black bears are also dormant.

The majority of local mammals do what too many humans do—they accumulate an extra layer of fat and do their best. Fur coats thicken. Deer grow hollow hairs to retain additional body heat. Snowshoe hares and weasels turn white for camouflage against the snow. Grouse grow comb-like bristles on their toes that serve as snowshoes while extra fur serves a similar purpose for the snowshoe hare.

The leaf is "pierced" by the stem of perfoliate bellwort or wild oats.

What becomes of pond dwellers? Unable to regulate their body temperatures, cold-blooded animals slow down, their activities and metabolism stopping as they slumber through the cold with minimal needs. They generally survive if they are not encased in solid ice. Protected beneath the ice in water that never freezes, these creatures are insulated from temperatures that may plunge well below zero.

Amphibians, such as frogs and toads, may sleep through winter on land or lay eggs that will hatch in the spring whether or not they survive.

GETTING THERE

From the intersection of Rtes. 9N and 22 in the Village of Westport, take Rte. 22. Turn right on Lake Shore Road at 0.4 mile. In 2.5 miles, at Halds Road, turn left. The parking area is on the right in 0.6 mile.

FOR MORE INFORMATION

Adirondack Nature Conservancy
Box 65
Keene Valley, NY 12943
518-576-2082
www.nature.org/wherewework/northamerica/states/newyork

ORGANIZATIONS

••

NAMES AND CONTACT INFORMATION

VERMONT

Addison County Chamber of Commerce
2 Court Street
Middlebury, VT 05753
802-388-7951

Birds of Vermont Museum
900 Sherman Hollow Road
Huntington, VT 05462
802-434-2167
http://www.birdsofvermont.org/

Catamount Trail Association
P. O. Box 1235
Burlington, VT 05402
802-864-5794
http://www.catamounttrail.org/

Central Vermont Chamber of Commerce
P. O. Box 336G
Barre, VT 05642
802-229-5711

Town of Colchester
Recreation Dept.
Blakely Road
Colchester, VT 05446
802-655-0811

Ethan Allen Homestead
Ethan Allen Homestead
Burlington, VT 05408
802-865-4556
www.EthanAllenHomestead.org

Fellowship of the Wheel
http://www.fotwheel.org/

Green Mountain Audubon Nature Center
255 Sherman Hollow Road
Huntington, VT 05462
802-434-3068
http://greenmountainaudubon.org/

Green Mountain Club
4711 Waterbury-Stowe Road
Waterbury Center, VT 05677
802-244-7037
http://www.greenmountainclub.org/

Green Mountain National Forest
Middlebury Ranger District
Green Mountain National Forest
Middlebury Ranger District
802 388-4362
http://www.fs.fed.us/r9/forests/greenmountain/

Green Mountain National Forest
231 North Main Street
Rutland, VT 05701
802-747-6700

Intervale Center
128 Intervale Road
Burlington, VT 05401
802-660-3508
www.intervale.org

Keeping Track, Inc.
P. O. Box 444
Huntington, VT 05462
802-434-7000
http://www.keepingtrack.org/

Lake Champlain Basin Program
54 West Shore Road
Grand Isle, VT 05458
802-372-3213

Lake Champlain Maritime Museum
Basin Harbor Road
Ferrisburg, VT 05456
802-475-2022
http://www.lcmm.org/

Lake Champlain Islands Chamber of Commerce
Rte. 2
North Hero, VT
802-372-5683

Lake Champlain Land Trust
One Main Street
Burlington, VT 05401
802-862-4150
www.LCLT.org

Lake Champlain Regional Chamber of Commerce
60 Main Street
Burlington, VT 05401
802-863-3489

Local Motion
1 Steele Street, # 103
Burlington, VT 05401
802-652-2453
www.localmotion.org

Mad River Path Association
P. O. Box 683
Waitsfield, VT 05673
802-496-PATH (7284)
http://www.madriverpath.com/

Middlebury Area Land Trust
P. O. Box 804
Middlebury, VT 05753
802-388-1007
http://www.maltvt.org/

Missisquoi National Wildlife Refuge
P. O. Box 163
Swanton, VT 05488-0163
802-868-4781
missisquoi@fws.gov
http://missisquoi.fws.gov

City of Montpelier
Montpelier Park Commission
39 Main Street
Montpelier, VT 05602
802-223-7335
www.montpelier-vt.org/parks/

Moosalamoo Partnership
c/o Brandon Area Chamber of Commerce
P. O. Box 267
Brandon, VT 05733
802-247-6401
http://www.moosalamoo.com/

Mt. Independence, State Historic Site
Orwell, VT 05760
802-759-2412
http://www.historicvermont.org/mountindependence/

The Nature Conservancy—Vermont Chapter
27 State Street
Montpelier, VT 05602
802-229-4425
http://www.nature.org/wherewework/northamerica/states/vermont/

North Branch Nature Center
713 Elm Street, Route 12
Montpelier, VT 05602
802-229-6206
www.northbranchnaturecenter.org

Perkins Museum of Geology
University of Vermont
Colchester Avenue
Burlington, VT 05401
802-656-8694
http://www.uvm.edu/perkins/

Rock of Ages Corporation
558 Graniteville Road
Graniteville, VT 05654
877 225-7626
http://www.rockofages.com

Town of Shelburne
Parks & Recreation Dept.
P. O. Box 88
Shelburne, VT 05482
802-985-9551

Shelburne Farms
1611 Harbor Road
Shelburne, VT 05482
802-985-8686
www.shelburnefarms.org

Sterling Falls Gorge Natural Area Trust
250 Sterling Gorge Road
Stowe, VT 05672
802-253-9035
gander07@realtor.com

Stowe Mountain Resort
5781 Mountain Road (Rte. 108)
Stowe, VT 05672
802-253-3000
http://www.stowe.com/smr

University of Vermont
Environmental Program
155 South Prospect Street
Burlington, VT 05401
802-656-4055
http://www.uvm.edu/~envprog/

Vermont Agency of Natural Resources
Department of Forest, Parks, and Recreation
103 South Main Street, 10 South
Waterbury, VT 05671-0603
802-241-3655
http://www.state.vt.us./anr/fpr/parks

Vermont Department of Fish and Wildlife
111 West Street
Essex Junction, VT 05452
802-878-1564
800-640-3714
http://www.vtfishandwildlife.com/

Vermont Department of Fish and Wildlife
Nongame and Natural Heritage Program
103 South Main Street
Waterbury, VT 05672
802-241-3700

Vermont Division for Historic Preservation
National Life Building, 2nd floor
Montpelier, VT 05620-1201
802-828-3211
http://www.historicvermont.org/sites/

Vermont Folklife Center
88 Main Street
Middlebury, VT 05753
802-388-4964
http://www.vermontfolklifecenter.org/

Vermont Historical Society
Pavilion Building
109 State Street
Montpelier, VT 05602
802-828-2291
www.VermontHistory.org

Vermont Youth Conservation Corps
1949 East Main Street
Richmond, VT 05477
802-434-3969
http://www.vycc.org/

Town of Williston
Public Works Department
722 Williston Road
Williston, VT 05495
802-878-1239

City of Winooski
Department of Recreation
655-6410
www.onioncity.com

Winooski Valley Park District
Ethan Allen Homestead
Burlington, VT 05401
802-863-5744
www.wvpd.org

NEW YORK

Adirondack Nature Conservancy
& Adirondack Land Trust
P. O. Box 65
Keene Valley, NY 12943
518-576-2082
www.nature.org/wherewework/northamerica/states/newyork/

Ausable Chasm and Company
P. O. Box 390, Route 9
Ausable Chasm, NY 12911
1-800-537-1211
www.ausablechasm.com

BIBLIOGRAPHY

Bentley, W. A. and Humphreys, W. J. *Snow Crystals*. New York: Dover Publications, Inc., 1962.

Burns, G.P. and Otis, C.H. *The Handbook of Vermont Trees*. Rutland, Vermont: Charles E. Tuttle Company, Inc.

Cobb, Boughton. *A Field Guide to the Ferns*. Boston: Houghton Mifflin Co., 1975.

Day Hiker's Guide to Vermont, Third Edition. Montpelier, Vermont.: The Green Mountain Club, Inc. 1989.

DiCesare, Laurie. *A Guide to Colchester's Parks and Natural Areas*. Colchester, Vermont: Colchester Parks and Recreation Department and Paw Prints Press, Inc., 1993.

Dodge, Harry W., Jr. *The Geology of D.A.R. State Park, Mt. Philo State Forest Park, Sand Bar State Park*. Montpelier, Vermont: Department of Water Resources, 1969.

Exploring Lake Champlain and its Highlands. Burlington, Vermont: The Lake Champlain Committee, 1981.

Gange, Jared. *Hiker's Guide to the Mountains of Vermont*. Huntington, Vermont: Huntington Graphics, 1994.

Gibbons, Euell. *Stalking the Wild Asparagus*. New York: David McKay Company, Inc., 1972.

Higbee, William Wallace. *Around the Mountains*. Charlotte, Vermont: The Charlotte Historical Society, 1991.

Lawrence, Gale. *A Field Guide to the Familiar*. Englewood Cliffs, New Jersey: Prentice-Hall, Inc., 1984.

Lindemann, Bob, and Deaett, Mary, and The Green Mountain Club. *Fifty Hikes in Vermont.*, Fourth Edition. Woodstock, Vermont: Backcountry Publications, 1997.

Lingelbach, Jenepher. *Hands-On Nature*. Woodstock, Vermont: Vermont Institute of Natural Science, 1988.

Ludlum, David M. *The Vermont Weather Book*. Montpelier, Vermont: Vermont Historical Society, 1985.

Long Trail Guide, Twenty-fourth Edition. Waterbury Center, Vermont: The Green Mountain Club, Inc., 1996.

Louv, Richard. *Last Child in the Woods: Saving Our Children from Nature-Deficit Disorder*, Algonquin Books, 2005.

Miller, Dorcas. *Track Finder, A Guide to Mammal Tracks of Eastern North America*. Berkeley, California: Nature Study Guild, 1981.

Miller, Dorcas. Berry Finder, *A Guide to Native Plants with Fleshy Fruits*. Berkeley, California: Nature Study Guild, 1986.

Mikolas, Mark. *Nature Walks in Southern Vermont*. Boston: Appalachian Mountain Club Books, 1995.

Natural Communities of Vermont, Uplands and Wetlands. Montpelier, Vermont: Vermont Agency of Natural Resources, 1996.

Petrides, George A. *Field Guide to Trees and Shrubs*, 2d ed. Boston: Houghton Mifflin Company, 1972.

Stewart, David P. and MacClintock, Paul. *The Surficial Geology and Pleistocene History of Vermont*, Bulletin No. 31. Montpelier, Vermont: Department of Water Resources, 1969.

Stout, Marilyn. *Vermont Walks: Village and Countryside: Walking Tours of Forty-three Vermont Villages and Their Surroundings*. Montpelier, Vermont: Vermont Life, 1995.

Van Diver, Bradford B. *Roadside Geology of Vermont and New Hampshire*. Missoula, Montana: Mountain Press Publishing Company, 1987.

Vermont Atlas and Gazetteer, 9th ed.. Freeport, Maine: DeLorme, 1996.

Wessels, Tom. *Reading the Forested Landscape*. Woodstock, Vermont: The Countryman Press, 1997.

ALPHABETICAL LISTING OF AREAS

ABOUT THE AUTHOR:

 For much of her life Elizabeth Bassett has walked and hiked in Vermont, where her forebears settled in the 1770s. Elizabeth graduated from Wellesley College and earned a Master's Degree at Tufts University. A former banker and travel agent, Elizabeth moved to Charlotte with her husband John and two young children in 1985. It was with her family that she explored many of the walks in this book. Elizabeth has been a volunteer and board member for many community, educational, and civic organizations. Elizabeth is an avid cross-country skier, walker, biker, and hiker. She is a long-time columnist for *The Charlotte News* and contributes to other local and national publications.

· · · · · ·

Cover photo, by the author, at Shelburne Farms in Shelburne, Vermont, looking east over the Farm Barn toward Mt. Mansfield.